OFFICIAL REPORT

OF THE

TWENTY-SIXTH INTERNATIONAL

CHRISTIAN ENDEAVOR CONVENTION

HELD IN

FIESTA PARK, THE TEMPLE BEAUTIFUL AND IN MANY

CHURCHES

LOS ANGELES, CALIFORNIA, JULY 9 - 14, 1913.

First Fruits Press
Wilmore, Kentucky
c2015

First Fruits Press

The Academic Open Press of Asbury Theological Seminary

204 N. Lexington Ave., Wilmore, KY 40390

859-858-2236

first.fruits@asburyseminary.edu

asbury.to/firstfruits

LOS ANGELES CONVENTION COMMITTEE.

Mr. Leonard Merrill................................*Chairman*

Mr. Richard E. Small.......................*Vice Chairman*

Mr. J. O. Smith................................*Secretary*

Mr. J. P. Welles...............................*Treasurer*

Mr. A. M. McDermott.........*Chairman Entertainment Committee*

Mr. F. A. McBurney.........*Chairman Registration Committee*

Mr. James G. Warren.........*Chairman Reception Committee*

Mr. Harry H. Godber.............*Chairman Publicity Committee*

Mr. Paul Brown.....................*Chairman Music Committee*

Rev. Jesse P. McKnight.........*Chairman Pulpit-Supply Committee*

Mr. Fred P Rossiter.............*Chairman Committee on Ushers*

Mr. Harold Cross..........*Chairman Pages and Guides Committee*

Mr. Leon V. Shaw ....*Chairman Excursion Committee*

Mr. Bert Landers.................*Chairman Decorating Committee*

President John Willis Baer, LL.D.............*Advisory Member*

Mr. Arthur J. Gatter...........*Ex-Officio Member of Committee*

THE CONVENTION COMMITTEE

THE STORY OF THE
LOS ANGELES CONVENTION

THE OFFICIAL REPORT

OF

THE TWENTY-SIXTH
INTERNATIONAL . .

Christian Endeavor
Convention

HELD IN
FIESTA PARK, THE TEMPLE BEAUTIFUL
AND IN MANY CHURCHES

LOS ANGELES, CALIFORNIA, JULY 9-14, 1913

UNITED SOCIETY OF CHRISTIAN ENDEAVOR
BOSTON, MASS.

LINOTYPED AND PRINTED AT
THE PILGRIM PRESS
BOSTON, MASS.

CONTENTS.

ILLUSTRATIONS.

OFFICERS OF THE UNITED SOCIETY OF CHRISTIAN ENDEAVOR.

President:
Rev. FRANCIS E. CLARK, D.D., LL.D.

General Secretary:
Mr. WILLIAM SHAW.

Treasurer:
Mr. H. N. LATHROP.

Editorial Secretary:
Prof. AMOS R. WELLS.

Publication Manager:
Mr. A. J. SHARTLE.

Interstate Secretary:
Mr. KARL LEHMANN.

National Superintendent of Temperance and Christian Citizenship:
Mr. DANIEL A. POLING.

Superintendent of Builders' Union:
Rev. R. P. ANDERSON.

Auditor:
Mr. J. J. ARAKELYAN.

Office:
Tremont Temple, Boston, Mass., U. S. A.

DENOMINATIONAL TRUSTEES.

Rev. B. W. Arnett, D.D.	African Methodist Episcopal
Rev. Thomas Ashburn, D.D.	Cumberland Presbyterian
President John Willis Baer, LL.D.	Presbyterian
Rev. W. H. Barraclough, B.A.	Methodist Church of Canada
Rev. W. C. Bitting, D.D.	Second Baptist Church
Rev. J. Whitcomb Brougher, D.D.	Baptist
President C. I. Brown, D.D.	Church of God
Rev. W. L. Burdick, D.D.	Seventh Day Baptist
Rev. David James Burrell, D.D.	Reformed Church in America (Dutch)
Rev. Julian C. Caldwell, D.D.	African Methodist Episcopal
Hon. S. B. Capen, LL.D.	Congregational
Rev. G. C. Carpenter	Brethren
Rev. J. Wilbur Chapman, D.D.	Presbyterian
Rev. Francis E. Clark, D.D., LL.D.	Congregational
Mr. George W. Coleman, M.A.	Baptist
Rev. John E. Cox	General Baptist
Rev. W. J. Darby, D.D.	Presbyterian U. S. A.
Rev. Frank J. Day	Congregational of Canada

STATE TRUSTEES.

WORDS OF APPRECIATION.

To compile a report of a great International Convention of Christian Endeavor, especially one like the Los Angeles Convention, with its many simultaneous meetings, is not an easy task. More than one hundred meetings were scheduled, and in order to cover each meeting successfully it was necessary to enlist the co-operation of friends. The compiler of this Report, with a keen sense of appreciation for services well rendered, therefore wishes to heartily thank and thereby acknowledge the efficient services of Rev. R. P. Anderson, and the many leaders and reporters of meetings and conferences whose co-operation helped to make this Report possible.

We sincerely hope that the very helpful matter contained in this Report will prove the means whereby Endeavorers will do their best for Christian Endeavor and for the Church. With the hope for continued and increased efficiency, and with earnest prayer for the Master's blessing upon all that is done in His name, this Report of the proceedings of the Twenty-Sixth International Convention of Christian Endeavor is submitted.

A. J. SHARTLE,

Publication Manager
United Society of Christian Endeavor.

Boston, Mass., August 1, 1913.

A SMILING WELCOME AT THE STATION

CHAPTER I.

ON THE WAY

FOR one to cross the continent is always an interesting event. To many it was the opportunity of a lifetime. For all who were privileged to go it was a period of great expectation. Great, because of the many good things in store at the other end of the journey.

So, in order to have their expectations realized, and to add inspiration by their presence to the greatest of all great conventions, they came. Out from the great Northwest, the Middle West, the East, and the South. It was a happy, joyous, singing army of young people made up of many delegations. Some travelled by special train, others in special cars. Some preferred Pullmans, while others had a weakness for tourists. They came in groups of ten, twenty, fifty, and a hundred or more. A few travelled in companies of two like the disciples, then later formed a local union, but without exception they all were bound in the same direction—Los Angeles, and the Golden West.

New York, New Jersey, Pennsylvania, and Maryland, nearly two hundred strong, led by Mr. Gillespie and Dr. Chain, travelled all the way by special train. New England Endeavorers headed by Dr. Clark went on the Boston special. The Toronto special carried a splendid delegation of 136, led by Dr. Gilray. Chicago sent a big crowd by the Gates and Mee special, while Winnipeg and the Northwest added a large quota to the gathering hosts.

However, it remained for California, the Golden State, to exceed even its own fondest dreams from the standpoint of attendance. My, how they did come! San Francisco alone sent 750 down the coast on the New England steamship Yale to Los Angeles. Then, from every valley and hill, village, town, and city they came, smiling, happy, and hopeful until they numbered nearly 8,000 strong, possibly the greatest, livest, happiest delegation of live Christian Endeavor wires that ever came from one State to attend an International Christian Endeavor Convention.

What about the weather? Well, it was hot; but it takes more than mere weather to check the Christian Endeavor spirit and enthusiasm, especially when destined for a big convention.

Kansas City, Mo., on the glorious Fourth was the place where some of the special trains met for the first time en route to Los Angeles. To be sure, there were greetings. Yells, songs, and howdy's as we took possession of the Kansas City station, but then it was of short duration because we must be on our way.

We spent a safe and sane Fourth travelling through Kansas with its green and golden fields. Safe in the confines of an air-tight Pullman, and sane, because the only crackers we had during the day were Uneedas. However, we had a genuine Fourth of July celebration in the evening, and fireworks about ten o'clock. The expression "two in one" was literally exemplified by Mr. Sydney A. Clark, who was our orchestra of two pieces—voice and violin. Rev. R. P. Anderson read Lincoln's famous Gettysburg address. Dr. Clark recited Bret Harte's poem on John Burns, who wore a white hat, but never a white feather. President Chamberlin of the Massachusetts union recited a poem about a boy that came to grief through too familiar acquaintance with fire-crackers. Treasurer Lathrop gave one of Walt Mason's witty sketches. Miss Nichols, former president of the Massachusetts union, read a poem on the flag. Miss Antoinette P. Jones, related an incident about an Endeavorer in the Spanish War, and Mr. James Purinton of Beverly, Mass., recited a piece advocating a flowery Fourth—and then the ten o'clock display of fireworks.

Merrily we continued following the old Santa Fé trail across the barren plains of New Mexico towards our destination. How different from the days in the long ago! Then it required months of laborious travel, attended by great danger from all sides, and especially from hostile Indians in their effort to stem the tide of civilization on its march westward. Now it required but a few short days in comfortable Pullmans with every convenience, and with "Old Sol" as the only enemy threatening us. But, although Christian Endeavor may not be immune from the darts of "Old Sol's" smaller rival, who is always stalking abroad during Christian Endeavor Conventions, it is immune from anything "Old Sol" can deliver; otherwise there would be no Christian Endeavor Conventions held in July.

Our train is slowing up. Must be something ahead. Yes, there is! It's Albuquerque, New Mexico. One hour for dinner. Now for the attack on our hospitable host, then for a constitutional and a peek at the curios. Great place this—beautiful station and grounds. See those Navajo Indian squaws dressed in a riot of color, selling their wares! Particularly note that big one with a face like tan-bark balancing on her head an old dish-pan filled with apricots. She asked me twenty-five cents to take her picture, but later condescended to give me a bargain price. And that big "Injun" chief posing before a fountain that you may take his picture for ten cents. Vain creature! And that little Indian boy carrying his baby brother to a shady nook for a quiet rest! No hostility now, unless, as it appears to be,—to water. All aboard! Yes, we are coming!

Again we are speeding on over the hot sands and arid plains of New Mexico, with only a patch of sage-brush here and there to break the monotony of a long journey. As we cross the gullies and chasms made deep and treacherous by the periodical torrential rains, we are again forcibly reminded of those heroes of civilization who, many years ago, crossed these same dreary desert wastes in order to blaze the trail of civilization.

How our imagination began to work! We again saw the slow-moving immigrant train winding its way over the tortuous trail, tired, hungry, heart-sick, yet hopeful and undaunted by the seemingly insurmountable barriers that met them each step of the way to impede the steady progress of a people that would not be halted. But that is another story.

Here is Gallup, New Mexico, a typical frontier town where everything seems to centre near the railway station. It is Saturday evening of the day after the Fourth of July, and the buildings by their decorations still bear testimony to the celebration of the day before. Here Indians, who for a short time have forsaken their tepees on the plains for the more alluring and lively scenes in the town, may be found arrayed in all the glory of the red man's heart, making the celebration a three-day affair.

It was here during our evening meal that a stranger with anxious face entered with the question, "Are there any Christian Endeavorers from Massachusetts in this crowd?" Yes, indeed, most of them are. Then comes the introduction. He is the Rev. C. P. Emery, a Congregational minister at Gallup, formerly from Massachusetts. He wants to see somebody from way back home. He is the only Protestant minister in the town and the work is hard. So we take Mr. Emery to Dr. Clark and introduce him, and Mr. Emery, like the friends of old, hurries out for his family and brings them in because he has found some one from Massachusetts. There they are, a family group of four with happy, smiling, radiant faces. Somebody suggested three cheers and a tiger for the Emery family. Did we rise and give it? Well, do the birds sing? Dr. Clark then unfurled a beautiful Christian Endeavor banner woven in Navajo Indian style for Mr. Emery. Mr. Emery then spoke of the making of the banner, the work of his church, especially the work of his Endeavor societies, and the task of continuing the work under difficulty. But he was hopeful, courageous, and with the assurance of that faith which overcometh written on every line of his face. We left him, and Gallup. May God bless and prosper both.

The influx of special trains laden with delegates at the Grand Cañon, Arizona, was an inspiration. However, the greater inspiration came when the delegates got their first view of the Grand Cañon in all the grandeur of a beautiful sunrise. It was with reverence and wonder that we stood and marvelled at God's handiwork. It led us into the music-room of the hotel, where we held a fellowship service led by Dr. Clark. This service was attended by nearly four hundred Endeavorers and friends representing many States and several countries. Dr. Clark in his own inimitable, kindly way spoke of world-wide fellowship, especially in lands he recently visited. Rev. William Patterson, D.D., of Belfast, Ireland, brought a hearty greeting based on the wondrous beauty of surrounding nature to lift the soul nearer to God, and in so doing draw it nearer to its brother. Rev. Alexander Gilray, D.D., of Toronto, Christian Endeavor's grand leader of Canada, brought greetings from across the imaginary line. He related an incident that occurred at the last General Assembly of the Presbyterian Church in Canada. The moderator remarked, "Of all societies that we have tried, and we have tried many, we have come to see that Christian Endeavor is pre-eminently the most outstanding and best that we have ever known in the Presbyterian Church of Canada."

To many of the delegates and friends it was the first opportunity to meet and make the acquaintance of Rev. Henry Churchill King, D.D., President of Oberlin College, a splendid man, clean-cut, and just the kind of man one would wish to meet and hear. He was introduced by Dr. Clark. "In spite of wonderful advances in material science and inventions," he said, "we are nevertheless forced back to the thing for which Christian Endeavor fundamentally stands—religion in the life. Faith underlies all work that men undertake, and especially is this true in the moral world, where man fights not only his own battles, but the battles of his brothers. You are not going to pour out your life in a cause that is hopeless. You are fighting the battle of the universe, the winning battle of God."

With the shadows of the evening fast falling over the depths of the wonderful Cañon before us, we held a real old-fashioned Christian Endeavor prayer meeting on the veranda of the hotel, close to the very edge of the rim. President Chamberlin of the Massachusetts union presided. It was a wonderful meeting, and the inspiration coming from the many consecrated testimonies carried the hundreds in attendance to the very depths of a soul-searching attitude. Many a face was tear-stained and many a silent prayer ascended to the throne of grace in behalf of the convention, the delegates, the friends, and the sin-sick. Dr. Clark concluded this ever-memorable service by bringing in his arms a little Indian child from the Hopi house near by, and set her forth as a type of a race that needs our prayer and sympathy.

SAN BERNADINO RECEPTION COMMITTEE RECEIVING
NEW ENGLAND ENDEAVORERS

NEW ENGLAND DELEGATION
Reception and Service at the Redlands Station

It is our last day at the Grand Cañon, and it is a day of sightseeing. Just out beyond the piazza of the hotel there is a delegation of Endeavorers preparing to leave on burros, under the leadership of efficient guides for the very depths of the Cañon, seven miles beyond, to the shore of the Colorado River by way of Bright-Angel Trail. This trip, though hazardous, is alluring and fraught with excitement, admiration, and wonder, and will always remain a vivid memory of a day well spent.

Then there are others not caring to view the Cañon by the burro route, who take the very fascinating and more comfortable carriage-drive along the edge of the rim, while still others are pressing into service shank's mare.

Thus in diversified ways the day was made enjoyable and everybody satisfied, but one bright young man who, while standing on the rim and looking down into the Cañon asked, "Where is it, that once was where it now ought to be?" We'll leave it with you, dear reader, to answer.

We passed the "Needles." Was it hot? Well, it was, but not hot enough to penetrate our enthusiasm. To be sure, we got our first experience with the heat of the California desert, but then it was tolerable because there was nobody to ask us, "How do you like the climate?" So we rolled along in the bright sunshine of a cloudless sky toward the Mecca where its beauty and grandeur they say bankrupt the English language.

What a relief after crossing the hot, scorching sands of the desert to see now a little speck of real green here, and another there! Now a little more, then a few trees. Here an irrigation ditch skirted by a strip of green. Now, just see the little gardens and the shrubs. Note the cactus over yonder. Queer-looking things to a way down-East Yankee. And the palms,—beautiful! We must be getting close to a city. O! It's

SAN BERNARDINO

It was almost necessary to have shock-absorbers as we alighted and had our first taste of southern California hospitality. It was a royal reception prepared by the Endeavorers of San Bernardino. The white-clad young ladies and men literally covered us with flowers, and as to fruit, it was there in great quantities, and all free. We felt much like the little boy who visited his grandmother on Thanksgiving Day, and when he saw the table laden with good things beyond his capacity said, "O ma, I wish I was twins." With this feeling we left for

REDLANDS

Here we had a repetition of our San Bernardino experience. The station was beautifully decorated with streamers in purple and gold. An improvised speaker's stand was erected, and short addresses were made by Mr. Anderson, Mr. Lathrop, Mr. Shartle, and Dr. Clark. The Chamber of Commerce at Redlands was made our headquarters. Automobiles were provided by kind friends and the entire delegation had one of the most delightful drives through beautiful Redlands with its orange groves of wondrous beauty, magnificent Smiley Park, and incomparable suburbs. Surely, we wished to stay longer, but we must be on to

RIVERSIDE

With our pockets, our hands, our bags, and our hearts full, and no appetite, we landed in Riverside. The committee was there to greet us. There were flowers and fruit galore, not to mention the souvenirs. Oh! what a reception! We must be going. Mt. Rubidoux is our destination. Just a few quiet moments at the cross, then the sights of the city, a view of the country with its snow-clad mountains, and then to the Mission Inn. This is one of the most beautiful hostelries to be found anywhere. Unique, yes. Here we spent an evening that will always remain a red-letter night in the memory of those who enjoyed the matchless hospitality of "the master of the Inn," Mr. Miller, the owner.

Hospitality, like the fruits and flowers that grow in this wonderfully blessed country beyond the desert, is as big, as bountiful, and as beautiful as its product because its product is the best.

It was but a short ride from Riverside to the end of the first half of our journey. Our train is even now slowing up. We are entering the yards, and the city is in view. Yes, this is the Santa Fé station. It's Los Angeles! See those white-clad young people rushing towards our train. It's the reception committee. They are here! Welcome, Endeavorers, God bless you! No need to bother with your baggage. It's all provided for. Don't take a trolley-car. Here is a taxi, or that automobile is just the thing. And so we are off to our place of entertainment with nothing to do until to-morrow. We've crossed the continent. We came from the shores of the Atlantic to the beautiful blue Pacific. We are in the city of Los Angeles, where within a week the greatest of all great epoch-making conventions will be held. All honor to the matchless hospitality of the metropolis of the Golden West,—Los Angeles.

THE RECEPTION COMMITTEE AT THE SANTA FE STATION

CHAPTER II.
CORPORATION AND TRUSTEE MEETING
Hotel Alexandria
Corporation Meeting

THE first meeting of the United Society of Christian Endeavor (corporation) convened in the Hotel Alexandria on July 9, at 1.30 P. M. Dr. Clark presided, and the attendance of trustees, field secretaries, and officers was large. It was one of the largest gatherings of members of the United Society held for many years. It was one of the kind of meetings which clear the decks for the inspirational and educational work essential to successful conventions.

One of the delightful events of the opening of this meeting was an expression from Dr. Clark to the effect that he was two years younger than when we met at Atlantic City two years ago, and was therefore more willing to continue as president than at that time. "Of all the thirty-three years of Christian Endeavor work," said Dr. Clark to the trustees and field secretaries, "the last four have been the best. Christian Endeavor in the United States, Canada, and in all the rest of the world is now on a most substantial basis. Never was the organization so potent, so influential in its field, so alert to find the best things and the newest things and put them into practice for the propagation of this great work."

For the first time in twenty-one years the editorial secretary, Amos R. Wells, was unable to be present at the International Convention. The trustees sent him a telegram of greeting and good wishes.

Publication-Manager Shartle, Treasurer Lathrop, and Superintendent Anderson reported the work of their respective departments and the progress of the Building Fund. These reports were all very encouraging and received with unanimous approval. Field Secretary Lehmann's account of his work in the Southland and Canada stirred interest in the possibility of advance steps for Christian Endeavor there.

A letter from Rev. C. H. Hubbell, D.D., reported on rural Christian Endeavor, and the trustees voted that State conventions be requested to provide an opportunity on their programmes for the consideration of this topic.

There was a pleasant little series of ovations when Dr. Clark

presented several workers and visitors. First came Daniel
A. Poling, the new national superintendent of temperance and
citizenship, whose aim will be to co-ordinate the work of
temperance organizations and labor to make their efforts and
those of Christian Endeavor more effective. Mr. Poling was
hailed by President Clark as the "temperance peacemaker of all
the temperance forces in America." Mr. Poling said that there
was to be held at Columbus on November 14 of this year a
convention of representatives of all the temperance societies
and organizations in the United States. The convention will
be for the purpose of reaching a general and concerted plan
upon which all the societies may work toward a common end,
wherein the duplication of effort will be eliminated and a general head selected for the propagation of a more vigorous
warfare in which the apostles of prohibition present a solid
front. Letters were sent to 176 representatives asking them
to join in a national call for the Columbus convention, and
more than half that number already have signified their intention of taking part.

Then Rev. and Mrs. Edgar E. Strother, field secretaries for
China, were presented; Rev. T. Sawaya, from Japan, smiling
and happy; and Mr. P. N. Kahokuoluna and wife, from Hawaii.
These brought greetings from thousands of Endeavorers in
their respective countries.

Dr. Clark and the other officers of the United Society were
re-elected, together with the trustees, with the following additions and changes:

Rev. M. Rhodes, D.D., of St. Louis, was made honorary
trustee for the Lutheran Church. Rev. P. S. Henson, D.D.,
of Evanston, Ill., was also made an honorary trustee for the
Baptist Church. Both of these distinguished gentlemen have
served Christian Endeavor long and well, and will thus continue to be identified with the United Society throughout their
lives.

Rev. P. A. Heilman, D.D., of Baltimore, was elected a trustee to represent the Lutheran Church. Rev. A. L. Phillips,
D.D., superintendent of the Sunday-school and young people's
department of the Southern Presbyterian Church, was elected
trustee for that denomination. Rev. J. Whitcomb Brougher,
D.D., pastor of the Temple Baptist Church, Los Angeles, was
made a trustee for the Baptist Church.

The following officers of the United Society of Christian Endeavor were elected:

President, Rev. Francis E. Clark, D.D.; Vice-President, Rev.
Howard B. Grose; General Secretary, William Shaw; Treas-
urer, H. N. Lathrop; Publication-Manager, A. J. Shartle;
Auditor, J. J. Arakelyan; Editorial Secretary, Professor Amos
R. Wells; Clerk of Corporation, A. J. Shartle; Superintendent

of Builders' Union, Rev. R. P. Anderson; Interstate Field Secretary, Karl Lehmann; National Superintendent of Temperance and Christian Citizenship, Daniel A. Poling.

Trustees' Meeting

Perhaps one of the most significant letters ever read before the board of trustees was one from Mr. Charles G. Stewart, of Winnipeg, Man. Nearly all the work done for Christian Endeavor in undeveloped fields during the last few years has been due to the generosity of Mr. Stewart. He supports three field secretaries in Canada, and has given generous sums, not only for the work in Southern States, but also for work in Italy.

Mr. Stewart recognizes that what Christian Endeavor vitally needs is an adequate fund for its extension. *He suggests the raising of such a fund, and offers the trustees $5,000 for the purpose of financing a campaign to secure it.*

This offer delighted the trustees. Every speaker was enthusiastic and grateful. Dr. John Willis Baer, president of Occidental College, voiced the thought of many when he said, "All through the years we have been asking the young people to be loyal to the churches, and they have been loyal; now I am asking the church to be loyal to the young people." Every one believed that the time had come for Christian Endeavor boldly to ask for funds for its missionary work. A big programme will bring a royal response.

President Ira Landrith crystallized the sentiment of the meeting in a resolution to thank Mr. Stewart heartily for his offer, to accept it, and to refer the matter to the executive board with power to take whatever action may seem best.

The new trustees elected are:

Four-year term—Rev. J. Whitcomb Brougher, Baptist, Los Angeles; Rev. Julian C. Caldwell, African M. E., Nashville, Tenn.; Rev. W. J. Darby, Presbyterian, Evansville, Ind.; Rev. H. A. Denton, Disciples of Christ, Galesburg, Ill.; Bishop Samuel Fallows, Reformed Episcopal, Chicago; Rev. J. H. Garrison, Disciples of Christ, St. Louis, Mo.; Prof. James L. Howe, Southern Presbyterian, Lexington, Va.; President Ira Landrith, Presbyterian, Nashville, Tenn.; Rev. J. T. McCrory, United Presbyterian, Pittsburg, Penn.; Rev. Rufus W. Miller, Reformed Church in United States, Philadelphia; Rev John Balcom Shaw, Presbyterian, Los Angeles; William Shaw, Congregational, Boston; Rev. H. F Shupe, United Brethren, Dayton; Bishop Alexander Walters, A. M. E. Zion, New York; Rev. Albert W. Jefferson, Free Baptist, Portland, Me.

Honorary life members—Rev. P. S. Henson, Evanston, Ill.; Rev. M. Rhodes, St. Louis, Mo.

One-year term—Rev. P. A. Heilman, Lutheran, Baltimore; Rev. A. L. Phillips, Southern Presbyterian, Richmond, Va.

The following State presidents were elected State trustees:

Arizona, Arthur H. De Riemer, Phoenix; Kansas, Paul M. Williams, Hutchinson; New Mexico, Mrs. L. L. Shields, Jemez Springs; North Carolina, Rev. A. D. McClure, Wilmington; Ohio, Rev. John W. Day, Columbus; Oklahoma, H. F Henley, Muskogee; Tennessee, John M. Gore, Knoxville; Texas, Patrick Henry, Wichita Falls; Saskatchewan, H. C. Speller, Moosejaw.

The following committees were named and served throughout the Convention:

Business—William Shaw, Rev. Claude E. Hill, Rev. S. A. Martin.

Registration—F. A. McBurney, H. N. Lathrop, Rev. E. A. King.

Resolutions—Dr. Ira Landrith, Rev. D. A. Poling, Rev. J. T. McCrory.

Mr. and Mrs. P N. Kahokuoluna of Hawaii, reported that the work was progressing splendidly in the Hawaiian Islands, where there are 3,000 Christian Endeavorers. Mr. and Mrs. Edgar E. Strother of China, also reported a good growth in China, where they are at the head of the Christian Endeavor work.

CHAPTER III.

A MEMORABLE OPENING SESSION

FIESTA PARK was an Endeavor city. The auditorium was a vast tent seating ten thousand people, the serried platform, above which hung the letters of the word "Welcome" on gigantic oranges, being a great assembly-hall in itself. Looking down long avenues, beneath graceful clusters of tropical palm-leaves, one might imagine that one was in a virgin Californian forest.

The platform was decorated with a profusion of flowers—huge daisies, great bunches of irises, hydrangeas, and many other varieties.

Behind and entirely shut off from the auditorium were the State booths arranged in sweeping semicircles, gayly decorated with Christian Endeavor colors, pennants, monograms, and smiling faces. Hawaii's booth was festooned with yellow flowers woven into long chains. Winnipeg's section had a varied assortment of the products of the country, wheat, oats, alfalfa, hay, and so forth, not to mention piles of pamphlets telling the story of the Northwest. Around this semicircle all the local committees had their headquarters, and even the Chamber of Commerce had its section and display.

Ten trained nurses were in attendance, and three doctors, in case of accident or need. The Memorial Baptist Church near by opened a lunchroom with food guaranteed to be like that which "mother used to make." There was ice-water in abundance—in fact, the reception committee seemed to have provided for every possible contingency.

For instance, those pages! Young men and young women were stationed apparently everywhere, and their sole duty was to take care of the delegates. If one wished a service performed, or if one desired information, the thing to do was to call a page, and one was sure to find the help needed. Nothing had been forgotten. The arrangements were absolutely perfect, and the machinery worked like magic.

Even the reporters of the daily press had caught the happy spirit of the Convention. On the morning of the first day *The Tribune* brought out three snap-shots of General Secretary Shaw in action, and called him "The Roosevelt of Religion."

And now came the first public meeting of the Convention,

Wednesday evening, July 9. The platform was crowded with the Convention chorus, composed of nearly one thousand Endeavorers; and in front was a large and efficient orchestra. Every seat in the hall was filled; a great sea of eager, expectant faces gazed upward toward the speakers.

Percy S. Foster, of Washington, D. C., was the song-leader, and he lifted this great audience out of itself as he made the people sing some old, familiar hymns. Nothing was forced, and one felt that this meeting, the subject of unnumbered prayers, had the true Christian Endeavor ring.

"Praise God from whom all blessings flow" was the opening hymn of the Convention, followed by that hymn of the church militant, "All hail the power of Jesus' name." This was followed by the singing of "America." During the singing of the last verses the audience waved handkerchiefs and flags, and from every part of the auditorium flashed back and forth waving emblems. This was followed by the International Hymn, sung by the Endeavorers, and then again, binding as it were all the nations represented one verse of "Blest be the tie that binds," with the waving of flags and handkerchiefs, while 10,000 voices rang steady and true in the hymns of country and church.

Secretary Shaw said that he had no intention of introducing anybody, but he wanted to present the man "whose name and whose life and spirit are enshrined in the hearts of more young people, the world around, than any other man in the world," whereupon he presented Dr. Clark.

There was a great burst of applause, a waving of handkerchiefs and Dr. Clark smiled and introduced Rev. W. Leon Tucker, to lead the devotions.

The devotional service was beautifully conducted by Rev. W. Leon Tucker, D.D., of Los Angeles, whose forceful message was the new thought of the letter to the Ephesians, "that ye may be able," a happy motto for all to take.

Immediately following the devotions Mr. Leonard Merrill, chairman of the 1913 Committee, presented to Dr. Clark a gavel, one of the most remarkable and interesting ever presented at a Christian Endeavor Convention.

Little did the Franciscan padres dream, when they planted the tiny olive twigs sent from their own native Spain to the new land of the Californias, that a small piece of the first tree grown in California would provide the main portion for the gavel of the twenty-sixth International Convention of the Christian Endeavor Society, 144 years after the little twigs were planted at the first missionary effort in California, the San Diego mission.

Before an audience of nearly 10,000 people from all parts of the English-speaking world the gavel for the Convention of

AN ATTRACTIVE PAGE

ENTRANCE TO FIESTA PARK

1913 was presented to Dr. Francis Clark, to be placed alongside the other gavels of the twenty-five preceding Conventions.

The gavel was made even more interesting by the handle, which was carved from a small branch of the first navel orange tree planted in California, and the olive-orange gavel of California will go down to history as the most historic gavel yet presented to the society, uniting the romantic history of early California of Franciscan days with the later days of golden prosperity.

In his address of acceptance Dr. Clark spoke feelingly of the memories that would always surround the gavel and said that it was more typical of the Christian Endeavor movement than any gavel possessed by the society.

"When the little olive was planted, who would have supposed that it would have multiplied many millions?" asked Dr. Clark as he held aloft the shining piece of wood and continued, "And when that little orange slip was planted, who would have supposed that great golden groves of oranges would cover your great State? Just so was that first little slip planted in Portland, Me., multiplied to the 75,000 societies to-day. And just as the rain of God has nurtured your olives and your oranges, just so has the rain of God nurtured our little society. Never has a gavel given so symbolic a meaning to the movement as this California olive-orange wood gavel, and to succeeding generations of Endeavorers it will stand not only for the agricultural and the horticultural greatness of your State, but also for the spiritual growth to be found in California."

Mr. Leonard Merrill, chairman of the Convention committee, in his delightful way delivered his address of welcome to the delegates for the committee. It was characteristic of the man who for many years labored and prayed for the coming of the Convention to Los Angeles. He said:

ADDRESS OF WELCOME.

By Mr. Leonard Merrlll, Chairman of the 1913 Convention Committee.

It is a far cry from Boston, '95, to Los Angeles, 1913; and yet the Endeavorers of Los Angeles began preparations for this service of to-night as long ago as the fall of 1894, at which time the Los Angeles city union selected a committee, of which Rev. Bert Estes Howard was chairman, and I was honored with the position of secretary, for the purpose of making a campaign for securing the Convention for Los Angeles for 1897, which Convention many of us remember as having been held in San Francisco. A committee, composed of Rev. A. W. Rider, Herbert G. Wylie, and your speaker, going with a large delegation from Los Angeles and vicinity, represented the committee before a meeting of the officers and trustees of the United Society at Boston, and presented the invitation and claims of Los Angeles.

I remember that the Memorial Baptist society of this city had the largest representation, distance travelled considered, of all societies attending the Boston Convention. Two members of that society were on the committee just mentioned.

It is a matter of history of 1897 that the Convention held in San Francisco reached the high-water mark in attendance and interest for any Convention ever held west of New York. Eastern Endeavorers and friends received a typical Western welcome at the hands of the San Francisco young people, were entertained royally, and were privileged to attend one of the best Conventions Christian Endeavor has ever known.

Later, Los Angeles made another attempt to secure the International Convention; but the United Society trustees and officers decided that the Northwest was entitled to that Convention, which was held in Seattle in 1907.

Through all these years the young people of Los Angeles have looked forward to the day when they would be the hosts and provide the entertainment and machinery for a great Christian Endeavor International Convention. A little more than two years ago the third committee was selected by the Los Angeles city union, and after months of preparation a delegation left Los Angeles for Atlantic City, June 28, 1911. Your speaker had the honor of having served as chairman of that committee which succeeded in convincing the powers that be in Christian Endeavor that Los Angeles had now grown to be a big enough city, with sufficient capacity in the way of hotels and other places of public entertainment to take care of any number of people that should visit us two years from that time; and to our great satisfaction it was decided that Los Angeles would be the place for the 1913 Convention.

Thus it comes about that an ambition born in the hearts and hopes of the young people of Los Angeles is realized, and to-night we have but just begun the first session of a Convention that I hope will prove to be, if not the largest in attendance, the best in its ultimate results in development of spiritual power and efficiency amongst the young people of this country that we have ever held. To say that Los Angeles Endeavorers have been faithful in their efforts, self-sacrificing as to time and personal interest, with but one end in view, the advancement of God's kingdom in the world, is only stating the truth. For almost two years the 1913 Committee has been meeting regularly, their plans being developed from meeting to meeting, until a month ago, when it seemed to the chairman of the committee, as well as to the other members thereof, who are all of them chairmen of the several committees having the responsibility of this Convention, that those plans were complete. To-night we face the ultimate result of all of this work, time, and thought; and you, guests and citizens, may judge whether or not the work has been well done. Our chief satisfaction will be in the consciousness that the things that have been done meet with your approval, and that as our guests and friends you are satisfied with the preparations for your entertainment, and that the hospitality of the local organization has measured up to your expectations.

California has been noted for its open-hearted, I had almost said prodigal, if not lavish, entertainment when an opportunity offered at home or abroad. This applies not only to secular, but to religious, affairs.

The young people of our city are not one whit behind their elders when it comes to a question of hospitality, and from no class of people will any one ever receive a more whole-hearted greeting of welcome than from Christian Endeavorers.

We are especially happy on this occasion to extend this greeting to our fellow workers and Endeavor friends throughout the United States and Canada. We have looked forward to this evening for a long time. Our hearts are full of thanksgiving to Him who doeth all things well and bringeth to pass His plans in His own good time. We rejoice in believing that we are a part of this work of His great plan for the redemption of mankind.

To you, the officers and trustees of the United Society of Christian Endeavor, speakers upon this programme, leaders in schools of methods and other lines of definite Christian Endeavor work, to you the Endeavorers of the United States and Canada, we give our greeting, assuring you of our great pleasure in being thus permitted to entertain you. We give to you a typical Western, ay, more than that, a California, welcome, and trust that, when this Convention shall have closed, you with us will be able to say it has been a season of uplift and time of great profit, the crystallizing into a noble purpose for future realization the things that are worth while.

In the name of the Los Angeles city Christian Endeavor union, I bid you welcome, thrice welcome.

The welcome from the churches was given by the Rev. William Horace Day, D.D., of Los Angeles, who has the unique experience, not only of following his father in the ministry, but also of filling his father's pulpit.

ADDRESS OF WELCOME ON BEHALF OF THE CHURCHES OF LOS ANGELES.

By Rev. William Horace Day, D.D., Pastor of the First Congregational Church.

The churches of Los Angeles bid you welcome. You have come to a city typical of the Golden West, full of the love of pleasure and the worship of money.

> "Where the blindest bluffs hold good
> And the wildest tales come true,
> Where men bulk big and life runs large
> On the trail that's always new."

Emerson came to California, and found a few things up to the brag. A great many were not. God has lavished upon us glorious scenery, boundless resources, and men and women trained in the older communities who have brought with them a dauntless spirit. In our rare hours of insight we have yearned for spiritual and moral achievement worthy of His material gifts. We are like Lowell's "Western Goth," who needs to learn "that nothing pays like God." You come from older communities, where for decades the problems have been faced which begin to challenge us. We realize how much your presence may mean to our future. By your help we would gain a vision like Isaiah's, who saw the Lord high and lifted up; like him we wish to realize our need of the cleansing fire in order that we might accept our world-responsibility, and be ready for the same consecration, saying, "Here am I, Lord, send me." We clasp hands with you, and would learn of your experience how to meet our new occasions which teach us new duties, and so boldly launch our Mayflower on the tumultuous to-morrow's sea.

We welcome you, not alone for the holy vision of God your presence will help us to gain, but for that efficiency and social service we ought to reach as the result of the wise counsel you will bring to us from the rich experience in many other cities in which you have shared. Religious enthusiasm is a great thing, if it results in actual human service. The social life of our community is like a young but inexperienced swimmer, beset with many dangers from the crossing of conflicting currents. If the religious life of California is to become a constructive social force, it must needs learn from experience not her own.

Because of this Convention we ought to be wiser, as well as more joyous, Christians.

But most of all we welcome you for what you are, because we are happy to see you. The city is crowded with visitors; you may suffer some inconvenience. Would that the sincerity of our welcome might atone for any lack in the form of our hospitality.

Two Americans in Lower California sought shelter from a storm in the adobe cabin of a Mexican. With a courtesy which belongs to the Latin races, in which we Anglo-Saxons are too deficient, the Mexican bowed low, and, looking at his little house, said, "Poco house, mucha heart." In the same spirit we bid you welcome.

The citizens were happy in having the mayor of Los Angeles, Hon. H. H. Rose, present their greeting. He captured the audience at once with the warmth of his welcome.

"For all the people of the city, whom I have the pleasure to represent to-night, I wish to say that they extend to you the warmest welcome that the citizens of this great and glorious town can give to any people. You have done wonderful things and have taken great steps forward, and like a mighty river you must flow on. We have taken you into our hearts and we want you to enjoy every minute of your stay, and may God bless you all."

Dr. Clark in responding to these splendid, enthusiastic, and sincere greetings coming from the Convention committee, the churches, and the city said:

"I have been thinking just what it is that makes California so attractive; what is the lodestone that draws people from all parts of the world to California? It is not altogether your generosity, and that is one strong thing, but it is not only your generosity that makes us want to come back. It is something more—it is because of your great optimism, your onward look, always with something ahead toward which to look with an enthusiasm that cannot be extinguished by a freeze or the hot weather of the Needles, where it is 128 in the shade—it is your splendid enthusiasm that draws us here.

"We do not always have this spirit in all parts of our country. Sometimes our prayer meetings are spoiled by some one who is a pessimist and weeps and wails. But they do not do that in California—at least, if they do once, they never have the opportunity to again. Your splendid spirit of optimism fills us with the same spirit, and we will carry back with us something of this California spirit—the spirit of Jesus Christ, the great Optimist, the great hope of all the world."

The following letters were read at this time and were received enthusiastically by the audience. Dr. Clark read a letter from President Wilson:

"It would be a great pleasure to me if I could attend the International Christian Endeavor Convention at Los Angeles. Will you not convey to those assembled in that Convention my warmest greetings and my most sincere wishes for the happy success of their work?

"Cordially and sincerely yours,

"Woodrow Wilson."

Secretary Shaw followed with a letter from Secretary of State Bryan, regretting his inability to be present, on account of pressing affairs of state. "As you know," wrote Mr. Bryan, "I feel deeply interested in the Christian Endeavor movement, and appreciate its extended growth and great usefulness. It is one of our largest instrumentalities for Christian service, and I feel sure that its future labors will far surpass its present activities.

"W. J. Bryan."

The Christian Endeavor union of Hawaii sent its "Aloha Nui Loa," "Love very much," and the Endeavorers of Hungary also sent their greetings.

"I love you, California," with the special Christian Endeavor welcome chorus, was sung by the chorus under the leadership of L. F. Peckham. A short musical service was followed by a platform reception to Dr. Clark and the officers and receptions in the State headquarters, formally opening one of the most important conventions held by the society of Christian Endeavor.

CHAPTER IV.

THE QUIET HOUR

I F there was one concrete illustration of the sincerity and the deep spiritual devotion of the thousands attending the Convention, it was the great gathering of delegates each morning at the Sunrise Quiet Hour service, conducted by President Henry Churchill King of Oberlin College, Ohio, in Immanuel Presbyterian Church.

It revealed the real spirit of the Convention. These meetings were among the largest single gatherings of the entire Convention. The church was crowded each morning; and well it should be, because the discussion by Dr. King on some of life's fundamentals brought daily manna to the hungry and prepared each one for the work of the day.

President King's topics were "Facing the Facts of Life," "The Way into Life's Values," and "Reverence for Personality." His thought, which was simple yet profound, was strikingly fresh, and was enriched by illustrations from literature and the Bible. He touched the deepest springs of the heart, and liberated forces that will prove mighty factors in the spiritual life of those who were privileged to hear him. Dr. King's address follows:

THURSDAY MORNING.

1. *Facing The Facts of Life.*

1. Under every such series of addresses as this lie certain great assumptions.

(1) The supreme interests are those of character.
(2) Convictions and decisions are needed.
(3) To these time, thought, and attention are necessary.
(4) These are individual questions.

2. Every such series of addresses, therefore, must seek to produce convictions and decisions. These form the only justification for such addresses.

3. Are we really willing to face the facts of life—those great common facts that concern every man and are most important of all—or are we really ignoring them, as most seem inclined to do?

(1) The essence of unbelief lies in not treating the truth as true.
(2) This refusal really to face the facts, to treat them as really true, is cowardly, lazy, foolish.

(3) What are these great common facts, most important of all? Are we living our life on such a plan as to ensure that we are taking full account of these facts?

President John Willis Baer, LL.D.

President Ira Landrith, D.D.

Dr. John Balcom Shaw

Rev. William Patterson, D.D.

President Henry Churchill King

President Peery

a. The fact of our double nature, akin to the animal on the one side, akin to God on the other. Is the lower nature steadily losing its hold? is the higher nature steadily gaining?

b. The fact of the fateful gift of will that can choose with God or choose against God, and whose choices can be made by no other. Is the righteous choice gaining in steadiness, in breadth, and depth, and skill of application?

c. The fact of responsibility, that we are members one of another. No man can go up or down alone. We have no choice as to whether we shall influence others; we can only choose what kind of influence we shall have. Are we making it certain that that influence is increasingly for good?

d. The fact of our capacity for indefinite growth. Are we living as creatures simply of the day, or laying foundations that may make certain endless progress in knowledge, in power, in character?

e. The fact of sin, which our modern literature, as well as the ancient Jew, is forced to admit is an abiding fact and a growing fact, unless a man is steadfastly setting his face in the right direction. Are we making it sure that we are so living that sin is for us a steadily lessening fact?

f. The fact of death—the one certain event that awaits every man. Doubtless our generation is right in its insistence upon thinking upon living as the best possible preparation for dying; and yet it must be an unwise reaction that allows a man wholly to ignore this great and certain fact.

"I would hate that Death bandaged my eyes, and forbore,
And bade me creep past."

g. The fact of accountability, which remains though all pictorial ideas of a final judgment be set aside. "So then each one of us shall give account of himself to God."

h. The fact of the future life. There is much here that we cannot know; but, if there be a future life at all, there is one certain thing concerning it that we may know; every one of us must live with himself. Am I making it certain that this self, with which I am forever to live, is to be good company, rich and interesting, inspiring and noble?

i. The fact of the need of help for others. Are we living our lives on such a plan as to ensure that we are to have great convictions and hopes and aspirations, a great message of help that we may bring to others?

j. The fact of Christ, the greatest fact of all, that deepens every other. Setting aside every theological proposition, here at least is the best life that the earth has seen. Can any man pretend to be in dead earnest in the attainment of character, who is not putting himself steadily and intimately into touch with that life, to take on, as of second nature, Christ's thoughts and feelings and purposes?

FRIDAY MORNING.

2. The Way into Life's Values.

It is one of the chief ends of education to enable one to enter with conviction and appreciation into the great spheres of value; into æsthetic and intellectual and spiritual ideals; into the beautiful, the true, and the good; into music and literature and art; into the scientific, the historical, and the philosophic spirit; into the riches of friendship; into moral and religious ideals. Now it is particularly suggestive that it may be said that the way into all these values of life is essentially the same way. For to see that this is the case brings to one anew the sense of the singular unity and simplicity of life, and helps one to discern the great direction for significant living.

I. First of all, we are commonly introduced into all the great values of life through the witness of some other who has preceded us in appreciation of the value concerned.

One must live a very poverty-stricken life who should insist on discovering all values for himself. "Art is long, and time is fleeting"; and it is the very business of the teacher, the literary or art critic, the friend, the ethical or spiritual prophet, to help us to the vision of values that we should not discover for ourselves. It is not by accident, therefore, that Professor Bosworth should be able to say that the programme of Christianity is the conquest of the world by a campaign of testimony through empowered witnesses, or that in John's Gospel, side by side with the great words "light" and "life" and "love," there should stand the other word "witness." The natural way in which all values go forward is through honest testimony. Indeed, it may be said that there are only two supreme services that we can render another, the witness by life and the witness by word. For the highest service, therefore, there is needed above all the qualities of the effective witness, and these are deep personal conviction, unquestioned character and judgment, disinterested love, and power to put one's testimony home, to make real and rational and vital the value to which one witnesses.

II. In the second place, one is not prepared to come into any of the great values of life without utter honesty. In every case any element of pretence is a positive hindrance, whether in art, or music, or literature, or moral and religious achievement.

We are all tempted to take our values more or less second-hand, because we shrink from both the intellectual effort and the inner honesty required to get them first-hand. There must be no pretence either in the original experience or in our testimony to our experience, no careless handing on of what we have not ourselves verified.

III. But honesty is not inconsistent with modesty. It rather requires the open mind. Our own experience has not exhausted reality. And just as in the realms of music and art, so in the realms of morals and religion, we may hope for much more than we have yet achieved in the line of the experience of those who have given most time and thought to these realms. We need the testimony of these greater souls. Mental and spiritual fellowship is as indispensable as mental and spiritual independence.

IV. And the indispensable need of fellowship suggests, in the fourth place, the all-inclusive counsel that the one great way into all the values of life is: Stay persistently in the presence of the best in the sphere in which you seek achievement, with honest response. The rest will largely take care of itself. Hear persistently the best in music; see persistently the best in art; read persistently the best in literature; stay persistently in the presence of the best in character and spiritual vision, with honest response. This great law of association assures results that cannot possibly come in any other way. The best does not need defence. It needs only opportunity. Our great life-task, therefore, may be truly said to be to come into some rewarding fellowship with the great souls of human history, culminating in the matchless life of Jesus.

SATURDAY MORNING.

3. *Reverence for Personality.*

The supreme condition of fine personal relations, of character and influence and happiness, is reverence for personality. By reverence for personality is meant the sense of the priceless value and inviolable sacredness of every individual person; that a person, as Kant insisted, is an end in himself, and never under any circumstances to be mere means. As such, the principle involves both self-respect and respect for others.

I. Self-respect. Self-respect is neither self-conceit nor self-depreciation, but the recognition of one's self as a member of the whole, with his own individuality and insignificance, and, therefore, "called to an imperishable work in the world." Self-respect is necessary for character. The self-respect due to ourselves is the only measure we have for others or for the application of the golden rule. We have no right to "renounce our rights as living souls" to "exploiters of souls," however confident. Self-respect is also a basic condition of a permanent and valuable influence. We have only ourselves to give. If we do not value our individuality, but fall into imitation of others, we have practically no contribution to make. Such basic self-respect is essential also to happiness, for one needs the joy of knowing that he has a part—a real, a significant, a unique, a son's part—in life; a part to play that if he does not play simply will not be played. Individuality is the ultimate miracle of history.

II. Respect for Others. Respect for others involves, first of all, respect for the liberty of the other man. And such respect for the other's liberty is essential to character. One becomes a slave who treats another as a slave. And such respect for the liberty of the other's is equally essential to influence; for to win another to character one must enlist, not break, his will. The true father says not, "I will conquer that child, whatever it may cost him," but, "I will help that child to conquer himself, whatever it may cost me." And there must be some recognition of the liberty of the other man if one would make him even happy. He has a right to some sphere of action that can be called his own; the chance for decision and choice.

But respect for others involves also reverence for the sanctity of their inner persons. Such reverence for the inner personality of another is the finest flower of character. One falls inevitably below his best even in the closest relations, or with children, when he forgets that in the case of every human soul there is an inner sanctuary into which he may come only by permission. Like the Christ, he stands and knocks, but does not force the door. And the finest type of influence, too, is not possible to any man who has not this sense of the inviolable sacredness of the human personality. One cannot bring out in another this finest flower of character if he will not show it himself. And, if one would make another happy, he cannot be a benevolent tyrant, over-riding the finer spirits about him and insisting upon making others happy in his own way. Let one remember that pregnant sentence of Charlotte Yonge's: "It is a great thing to sacrifice, but it is a greater to consent not to sacrifice in one's own way."

It is in the Quiet Hour services like these, the moments of restful devotion in the early morning hours, that the quiet waters deep down in many a soul are stirred. There are mountain-top climaxes in many great meetings and experiences that are thrilling, but it is in the little quiet period of these blessed quiet devotions held before the hustle and rush of the day, when the spirit of the Master breathes softly over the meeting and hearts warm to the power of Him who leadeth us safely along life's highway, that man resolves to work, live, and pray to give the best that is in him.

CHAPTER V.

THE THEATRE BEAUTIFUL

Thursday Noon

WITH an audience that crowded the Theatre Beautiful to the doors the first of the four noonday meetings was opened by Rev. Francis E. Clark. The praise service was under the direction of Professor Percy S. Foster. Dr. Clark introduced the speakers, Dr. Ira Landrith, Presbyterian trustee and president of Ward-Belmont College. Dr. Landrith is one of the great men from the Southland. He is big of stature and big of spirit, vigorous, and as a speaker is a man "with a pinch." He is unsparing in his effort to crush the things that make not for sure righteousness. He believes in Christ, and in the efficacy of Christ's programme to save the world, and he has little patience with Christians who set anything before the Master of men. Mr. Landrith's address follows:

CHRISTIANITY'S SOLUTION OF CIVIC PROBLEMS.

Landrith Hot Shot.

Don't be a political laggard—go to the polls.

Every honest man should be active in politics.

The public weal and not private advantage must be considered.

Political parties have no time for aggressive advance; we are weary of broken platform pledges.

A consistent Christian has no place out of politics; a persistent looter has no business in politics.

The next generation will learn what should have been known ten generations ago, that public office is a public trust.

A good citizen ought to be so loyal to his party that he will abandon that party if it goes wrong.

CHRISTIANITY'S SOLUTION OF CIVIC PROBLEMS.

By President Ira Landrith, D.D., LL.D., Nashville, Tenn.

"Christianity's Solution of Civic Problems." Some of the problems which in his judgment Christianity could solve if it would are ballot-box corruption, the perjury of officials who wink at violated law, the bribery of voters, lawmakers, courts, and executions; the lobby that haunts with evil design the halls of Congress not only, but the city hall and the State capital as well—happily, and, it is to be hoped, permanently now, a scared and hunted lobby; graft in office, a crime of which public patronage is often the most dangerous element; demagoguery and sectionalism of the sort that keeps alive for partisan advantage the half-century-old prejudices

Rev. E. E. Strother

Mrs. E. E. Strother

Rev. J. T. McCrory, D.D.

Mrs. J. S. Norvell

Leonard Merrill

of an otherwise united and happy people; the licensing of evil; the segregation rather than the extermination of such iniquities as the saloon, gambling, and the social evil; too easy divorce; and the hundred other forces at work to crumble the foundations of the home; ultra-partisanship that sometimes makes even Christian voters forget their higher loyalty to the counsels of the Christ—in general, all public questions that are essentially moral, and most political issues are radically moral questions, from the uses of campaign funds to the adulteration of foods, from free trade to free whiskey.

Some of the speaker's opinions, reproduced in his own language, follow.

Because in a despotism Jesus Christ was not a suicidal anarchist, our friends, the enemy, would have us who profess to be Christians remain silent and non-combatant in a republic where every honest man ought to be active in politics and where every dishonest voter ought to be disfranchised.

Christian men in America could do what they would if they only would do what they could. If the so-called party-loyalty divorce court had not been so busy separating our politics from our religion, there would be few civic problems left to be solved. When we, who profess to vote as we pray, come to learn our civic duty on bended knees before the altar of God, and not before the shrine of our political parties, the public weal, and not private advantage, will become the chief concern of public officials.

A state that violates the Decalogue should receive an overdue house-cleaning by the citizens who respect the Sermon on the Mount. Vicious partnerships, whether civic or commercial, always hasten to disasters. Political parties with their ears to the ground have no time for aggressive advance, and we are growing weary of mere vote-catching party platforms that are built to be deserted after the election.

Christianity would soon solve the civic problems if many prominent Christians were not themselves such huge civic problems. Democracy presupposes the integrity of the electorate; and without such integrity republican government is a perpetual peril. Politically, as a rule, the upright are too indolent and the vicious too industrious. The consistent Christian has no right out of politics, and the persistent boodler has no right in politics. The man who buys is no better than the man who sells a vote. The man who stays away from the polls because he does not wish to lose the time, sells his ballot for the paltry price of a day's labor.

Political vice is a big braggart, but it cowers like a whipped cur before organized virtue. The trouble is that virtue won't always organize, a fact which would be more discouraging if it were not also true that vice cannot stay organized, because sooner or later the interests that are selfish fall afoul of each other.

Burke was right, however, in saying, "There never was long a corrupt government of a virtuous people," and in the main the American people are virtuous.

He is a politically blind man, afflicted also with the loss of memory, who does not know that Christianity is already solving multitudes of civic problems. The licensed liquor traffic has its back to the wall. Gambling is everywhere outlawed. Many a malefactor has gone lately from the palace to the prison, even United States Senators among them; and others are soon to start on the same melancholy journey. The lottery is dead. The food-adulterating assassin is getting his due. The plunderer of the public, from the wood-choppers in Uncle Sam's forest to the grafters who make laws in Uncle Sam's legislature, are being ruthlessly hunted down and punished. The public conscience is becoming so sensitive that it now recognizes a thief as a thief, whether he steals a ballot or a pullet, a franchise or a side of bacon, an office or an oyster.

There is hope that the generation we are now rearing will be able to be honest, however rich, and upright, however poor; for this rising generation has been told the truth, that there is no moral difference between political and personal corruption, between highway and trust robbery, between the sneak thief who steals your purse and the combination of tradesmen that dishonorably empties it. This next generation of voters will have learned, what ought to have been plain a dozen generations ago, that honesty is the best politics, that prejudice is neither kith nor kin of principle, that bribery is bribery, whether the price paid be a promise of cash in hand or of an office for your indigent brother-in-law, that public office is a public trust only when the trustworthy are elected, and that a good citizen ought to be so loyal to his political party that when that party goes wrong he will leave it till it gets right.

FRIDAY NOON

Every seat in the great Theatre Beautiful, with its tier upon tier of galleries, was occupied at Friday noon when Hon J. A. Macdonald, LL.D., editor of *The Globe*, Toronto, arose to deliver his address on "Christianity's Solution of the Problem of Capital and Labor."

Dr. Macdonald is one of the big-framed, hearty men that win by the greatness of their souls, men that radiate understanding and sympathy. He has risen from the ranks, but he has not forgotten the plain people from whom he has come; and, indeed, he is not apart from them, but one of them, a leader and a guide.

He is a born orator, a whirlwind that sweeps heart and mind along, clear in his reasoning and fervid in presentation of argument.

"Christianity," he said, "does not offer any dogmatic and final solution of any of our modern problems; but it does something far greater and better, it supplies principles that go to the root of our problems, and shows us how to apply these principles to trade, to commerce, to industry, and to social life."

"Christ," he continued, "faced industrial conditions with nothing but an idea wrapped up in His soul. If church-workers have nothing but an idea, they have all that Jesus had with which to revolutionize the world. What was His idea? It was the idea of a new social order. He called it the kingdom of God, a social order in which men should live happily and helpfully, an order in which there should be neither masters nor slaves.

"For two centuries the problems of industrial and social relations were settled in the active life of the church. The standard of life's greatness was not at that time patrician blood, or race, or position, or possessions, but service that sprang from love. This is the principle that solves all our problems."

Dr. Macdonald traced the sin of the ages, the apostasy of the church, to the domination of selfish ideals. This is the trouble in American life; all over the country there has arisen an industrial absolutism that is worse than the tyranny of the

Stuarts; and we need a John Knox, or a church of John Knoxes, who will stand for the rights of capital on the one hand and of labor on the other. The church must not be the ally of any party.

"The comfortable and well-to-do do not know the facts. The shining splendor of their own lives blinds them to the awful need of the poor. The church believes that emphasis should be put on the importance of the common man, and the church must fight to the last against all that denies this supreme importance. Christianity's solution of the great problems of to-day is *love*. Let love get into our corporations, and into our labor-unions, and into our hearts; and social problems will be no more."

Saturday Noon.

Winning Souls.

At the noon meetings in the Theatre Beautiful, always crowded, the singing by the male quartette was superb; but not only so; it was planned to lead up to the service to follow, and ministered mightily to the general effect.

On Saturday Dr. John Balcom Shaw was the speaker, and the theme was "Soul-Winning as a Daily Pursuit," a fundamental part of a Christian Endeavor, as Dr. Clark remarked in introducing the speaker.

From the first sentence a spell seemed to descend upon the audience, for Dr. Shaw spoke so manifestly out of experience that every heart was stirred.

"Many years ago," he said, "there was a church whose members entered into a solemn covenant to bring, if possible, one person into its membership at each communion; and, as this church held its communion every other month, I would call this bimonthly soul-winning.

"In America there is another church whose members seek to win one soul a week to Christ; this I call weekly soul-winning. But the ideal thing is neither bimonthly nor weekly, but daily, soul-winning, an unceasing, unflagging effort to lead men to Jesus Christ.

"I used to think, before I became a minister, that ministers made it their daily pursuit to lead their people to Christ. But alas! Some years ago at Northfield I was speaking on this topic, and I said, throwing out my hand, 'I suppose there are even ministers here in whose church there may be elders and members of the board of trustees to whom they have never spoken a personal word for Christ.'

"That afternoon on the train a young man laid his hand on my shoulder, and I recognized a young minister. 'Why are you leaving the conference so early?' I inquired. 'You sent me home. he said. 'How is that?' I asked. 'When you threw out your hand to-day,' he continued, 'you chanced to point at me; but your words were not chance words. They reached my heart. In my church there are five trustees to whom I have never spoken about Christ, and I am going back home resolved never to mount the pulpit steps again until I have spoken a personal word to them.'"

Dr. Shaw told how Dr. J. Wilbur Chapman tried one winter in his church to get the elders to help his Endeavorers to do personal evangelistic work. Dead silence fell upon them. Then one of them, a banker, spoke up, and said: "I have been silent, and the reason is a sense of inconsistency and contradiction. I have two boys at home. I have never spoken to them a personal word for Christ, and I cannot lead a movement for other men's sons when I have not begun in my own home. But I am going to begin to-night." That winter the boys were won for Jesus.

"The world is full of opportunities. At the New Year in Harrisburg I said to a porter in a hotel, 'I wish you a happy New Year, and I hope you have begun it by becoming a Christian.' 'I'm glad you said that,' he replied. 'I've been here for eighteen years, and nobody has ever spoken to me about my soul.'"

There are more people than we fancy that are waiting for our personal touch. Let us begin to pray for souls and to seek and make opportunities to reach them.

R. P. ANDERSON
SUPT. BUILDERS' UNION

H. N. LATHROP
TREASURER

A. J. SHARTLE
PUBLICATION MGR.

WM. SHAW
GENERAL SEC'Y.

REV. FRANCIS E. CLARK, D.D.
PRESIDENT

PROF. AMOS R. WELLS
EDITORIAL SEC'Y.

DANIEL A. POLING
NAT'L SUPT. TEMPERANCE AND CHRISTIAN CITIZENSHIP

KARL LEHMAN
INTERSTATE SEC'Y.

OFFICERS
—
UNITED SOCIETY
of
CHRISTIAN
ENDEAVOR

CHAPTER VI.
ADVANCE STEPS AND PRACTICAL EFFICIENCY.
Dr. Clark's New Campaign and Secretary Shaw's Lessons in Pictures.

EVERY road in Los Angeles seemed to lead to Fiesta Park on Thursday evening. Outside, a great crowd surged around the auditorium; inside, there was a scene of busy activity around the State booths and in the hall, where delegations were singing with all their hearts.

When registering, every one of the delegates received a copy of the new hymn-book, "Service Songs," compiled by General Secretary Shaw and John R. Clements. Some of the hymns are new, but Percy S. Foster, the chorus-leader, soon made the audience familiar with them. Indeed, one of the striking features of this Convention was the enthusiastic character of the singing.

President John Willis Baer was at his best in presiding. After prayer by Rev. W. T. Johnson, D.D., of Richmond, Va., President Baer presented Dr. Clark in what, after all, was the apostolic method—the method of the holy kiss. "What Dr. Clark seems to be to you," said Dr. Baer, "he *is*. If I could live until I became as old as Methuselah, I could not express sufficient gratitude for the help that he has been to me in my life." And then, while the Convention saluted in Chautauqua fashion, the two men, both of them leaders, embraced on the platform.

Dr. Clark outlined some of the campaigns undertaken by Endeavorers in past years, and delivered the following address:

ADVANCE STEPS IN INCREASE AND EFFICIENCY.
An Outline for a Great Yearly Forward Movement in Christian Endeavor.

Considering the average span of human life throughout the world, thirty-three years is reckoned as a generation of mankind. Thirty-three years ago, on the second of next February, the Christian Endeavor movement was born. It has, then, almost rounded out its first generation. It has seen children born, grow up through Junior and Intermediate and Young People's age to full manhood and womanhood, and take their places in all forms of activity and usefulness in church and community and State. It is well for us, as the second generation of Christian Endeavor work begins, to review briefly the past, and thank God for His abundant mercies.

Our First Generation.

It is difficult to get exact figures concerning an organization that has reached every quarter of the globe, whose members speak a hundred different languages, and whose statistics, if given this month, may be far below the mark next month; but it is safe to say that the one society of February 2, 1881, has multiplied one hundred thousand times, and the original fifty members have grown to five millions. In this enumeration I am counting those societies which have substantially the Christian Endeavor principles and methods, the great majority of which have the Christian Endeavor name and fellowship. If we reckoned all those organizations that confessedly have drawn their inspiration from Christian Endeavor, though adopting different methods and principles, the reckoning would be much larger than one hundred thousand societies and five million members.

The average generation of mankind throughout the world is reckoned at three and thirty years; but the average generation of *active* Endeavorers is much less than this, probably not more than six years, though many, I am glad to say, give to the cause many more years of active service. Undoubtedly, at a low estimate, fifteen millions of young people in these nearly thirty-three years have passed through the open door of Christian Endeavor.

Christian Endeavor Millionaires.

In these days we are inclined to reckon not in units or hundreds, but in millions. The millionaires occupy much space in our newspapers and in our national thought. Why should not Christian Endeavor reckon itself among the millionaires? not in dollars,—alas, no! our friends have combined to keep the United Society and the World's Union poor, relying upon Providence, according to the old story of the minister and his parishioners, to keep us humble,—but there are other sorts besides the dollar millionaires.

At least ten million former members are now active and useful in church-work to a degree far in excess of what would have been their activity without their Christian Endeavor training. There have been at least four million associate members brought to Christ and into church-membership, in part through the influence of the society. At least twenty millions of dollars have been given to local church, missionary, and charitable objects by Endeavorers. More than fifty millions of young people's meetings have been held, with an aggregate attendance of at least one billion five hundred millions. At least one hundred thousand union meetings and conventions representing all evangelical denominations have also been held, with an aggregate attendance of fifty millions, giving a tremendous impetus toward interdenominational fellowship. These figures, enormous as they are, astounding as they may seem to some, have the power and eloquence of an understatement.

But who can reckon in millions or billions the amount of Christly activity in prisons and hospitals, on ships, among the poor, in fresh-air camps, for Sabbath-observance, municipal reform, civic betterment, temperance, social purity, for evangelism, Bible-study, mission-study, systematic giving, and for international peace and arbitration? Who can weigh, measure, or tabulate the religious influence and impulse of these generations of Christian Endeavorers? I have rehearsed them that we may record our gratitude to God, and that we may begin our next generation— get a "running start," as it were, toward our second three and thirty years with new courage, with new purposes, with higher aims for a larger and more substantial advance in all noble endeavors.

Results in Europe and the Orient.

During the past two years I have carried out a plan, which I had long cherished and prepared for, of visiting all the countries of Europe and the nearer East, doing what little I could to strengthen their Endeavor societies and to bring to them the realization and joy of our world-wide fellowship.

With this purpose in mind I have, since last we met in an International Convention, visited Germany, Holland, Norway, Sweden, Denmark, Finland, Russia, Austria, Hungary, France, Switzerland, Italy, Greece, Macedonia, Turkey, Syria, and Egypt; and in almost all these countries I have found at least the beginnings of a vigorous Christian Endeavor movement, and in many of them an aggressive and well-developed national organization.

The news that comes to us from the great lands of the Orient,—India, Burma, China, and Japan,—and even from the little islands of the sea, is even more encouraging and hopeful, and tells us how exactly the simple, sturdy principles of Christian Endeavor are fitted, so far as we can see, to the needs of every race and language and tribe and kindred on the face of the earth.

An event of national importance of the past year is the revivification of our temperance and good-citizenship department, under the leadership of our beloved co-laborer, Daniel A. Poling, on the broad, co-operative, non-partisan basis for which Christian Endeavor has always stood, an effort from which we may hope for so much for the purification of the dark and noisome cesspools of the nation.

Two Great Advance Steps.

But especially have the past four years been marked by two great advance steps in Christian Endeavor circles, the Increase Campaign and the Efficiency Campaign. The one has added thousands of societies to our ranks; the other has increased the working efficiency of thousands of our societies.

The evident blessing of God upon these efforts points the way to the future. It is His guide-post telling us what to do in the days to come,—namely, to continue, to intensify, to make permanent these efforts. Let them be no longer mere campaigns for a year or two years, but integral parts of our movement which shall gather strength and power as every year goes by.

You have often asked me for a watchword for the years to come. Let us take the motto which Providence seems to have thrust upon us: *"Increase and Efficiency."* Four years ago *"Increase"* was our motto, and ten thousand societies were added to our ranks in two years. Two years ago *"Efficiency"* was the word, and marvellous advances in efficiency have been made by a multitude of societies. For the years to come let us combine the two words which have been so greatly blessed in our work, and take for our motto, *"Increase and Efficiency,"* or, to paraphrase Daniel Webster's immortal words, "Increase and Efficiency, now and forever, one and inseparable."

Our Watchword.

This motto I believe we can make an accomplished fact by keeping *Increase and Efficiency* steadily in view in our work throughout the year, *and by having once a year, the country over, a great round-up of our activities, counting up our gains with gratitude to God, if we have made them, deploring our losses, if such we find, and seeking to enlarge and strengthen with His help, all our work.*

What week in all the year is so appropriate for this task as that in which Christian Endeavor Day falls? It is the high tide of the church year. It is the week of happy memories and large anticipations. It is the week that celebrates our birth as an organization. It is the week which will always have a special significance for Christian Endeavorers.

If during that week we are willing to deny ourselves some ordinary luxury, or even something that has come to seem a necessity, it will emphasize its character as a week of holy, strenuous, joyous endeavor. We can at least, by planning in advance, give extra time and effort, a form of self-denial as acceptable to God as a money gift if we have little of the latter to give. But let us combine gifts of time and money and effort, and have in the early days of February every year a great

Increase and Efficiency Work.

the continuation of our year of Increase and Efficiency.

This, then, is the definite proposal which I trust will meet with your ready and enthusiastic response:

> *That we henceforth make the week in which occurs the second of February, our Christian Endeavor anniversary, an INCREASE AND EFFICIENCY WEEK, when we shall take stock of our activities, see whether we are in any good measure living up to our ideals, and go forward in the Master's name to new and larger endeavors.*

Let me outline a programme for the week, in which you may at least find some practical suggestions, suggestions which are always subject, of course, as is everything in Christian Endeavor, to the approval of your church and pastor and your own conviction of what the Master would have you do.

A Programme for the Week.

Beginning the Sunday before the second of February, let us make that and the following six days days of glad and grateful giving of time and strength and money with some definite end in view, taking for our motto and our warrant our Lord's own words, "He that would come after me, let him deny himself and take up his cross and follow me." Let us make of this Sunday also a Decision Day, an ingathering-day, when, in our society and in the Sunday school, if possible, the net shall be drawn, and decisions for the Master earnestly invited.

If every evening of the week should be devoted to religious work, it could not, for one week in the year, be called religious dissipation, a kind of dissipation of which some people are so needlessly afraid. One evening might well be devoted by each committee and by the whole society to discovering its rating in efficiency by the Efficiency Chart, and to prayerful plans for its betterment.

For a Great Ingathering.

Another day should be an ingathering-day, devoted to a canvass of the Sunday school, church, and community for Active, Associate, and Honorary members, making sure that no former Active member, who lives a worthy life, is left out of the Honorary list, and that every young person in the community who ought to be an Endeavorer is approached with an earnest invitation.

Another evening might be profitably given to a meeting of the local union, where the themes discussed would promote the highest and largest purposes of the week.

Another might well be devoted to a getting-together social, when we shall remember not only our immediate companions, but our great Christian Endeavor fellowship in all the world, and have their work and fellowship vividly brought before us.

In this "Increase and Efficiency Week" it is expected that Junior and Intermediate societies will share, as well as the Young People's societies, and that their superintendents, co-operating with the older society, will take such reckoning of the past and such forward steps for the future as will mark a distinct and definite advance for the year to come.

On the evening of the midweek prayer meeting let us cheer, possibly surprise, our pastors with the largest and most responsive attendance of Endeavorers they have ever seen, occupying the front seats, an earnest of a year of faithful church-attendance.

The Climax of the Week.

Then when the following Sunday comes, *let us make it the high day · of all our Christian Endeavor year, the glad day to recount God's mercies and to gather the results of our "Increase and Efficiency Week" and year.* Perhaps our pastors, in many cases, will preach on this day a sermon of encouragement to the Endeavorers, but, in any event, in our regular or special meeting for that day we may receive from such a service, the culmination of such an anniversary week as I have outlined, an inspiration which will illumine the whole horizon of the year to come, and an impetus which will send us further along the road of Increase and Efficiency than we ever went before.

These are suggestions approved, I hope and pray, by the Holy Spirit of Wisdom for a long yearly advance step by all Endeavorers who will heartily adopt them. They involve some self-denial, some self-inspection, some real service, and a definite, resolute purpose to know just where we stand, and to go forward in the name of the Lord.

Thus Christian Endeavor Week will be each year the climax of a year of better work than the last, because it will be a definite seven days when we shall plan for an advance all along the line; when, humbled by our short-comings, but inspired by our opportunities and strengthened by self-denial, we shall, trusting only in the Lord Jesus Christ, go forward joyously to new victories in His name.

O what might not such a week mean· for the church, for our country, for the world, if heartily entered into by the millions of Endeavorers! It would mean multitudes born into the kingdom of God. It would mean hundreds of thousands of additional dollars in Christ's treasury. It would mean wise plans, prayerfully conceived and carefully carried out. It would mean new life in old activities. It would mean new activities inspired by new enthusiasms. It would mean self-examination, mortification possibly, as we courageously faced our failures, but it would mean sure future success, born of humility and of a larger vision. It would mean not only new spiritual vigor for our societies, but also for each Endeavorer who gave his money, time, and strength in any unusual measure, for it would place him in the goodly company of God's heroes, in whose heart of hearts has always been loving self-sacifice. It would transform his weights into wings. It would put a new song in his mouth. He would run and not be weary; he would walk and not faint.

Who will join me in this "forward march"? I have too often tested your courage, your faith, your high purpose, your determined zeal, fellow Endeavorers, to doubt it now.

"Lead on, O King eternal!
  We follow, not with fears;
For gladness breaks like morning
  Where'er Thy face appears.
Thy cross is lifted o'er us;
  We journey in Thy light;
The crown awaits the conquest.
  Lead on, O God of might!"

Treasurer Lathrop's address reminded us of the tremendous power of the consecrated dollar with the consecrated soul to spend it; for, after all, what the church needs is money *plus* men, with the emphasis on the *men*.

TIME, TITHES, AND TREASURE.

The Report of Hiram N. Lathrop, Treasurer of the United Society of Christian Endeavor.

To be an Endeavorer is to be a "world power." We read and talk about "the great powers," but you ought to know that the greatest power in the world is a consecrated dollar, with a consecrated soul to spend it.

There never was a time when your money, spent for yourself either for luxuries or necessities, purchased so little as now. There never was a time when your money *plus yourself* counted for so much in God's service as now. It is equally true of the humblest Junior's dime or the wealthiest philanthropist's million.

The arithmetic of heaven cannot be calculated by any earthly rule of three. It isn't necessary for us to understand how the Lord Almighty uses the multiplication table. It is only necessary for us to comply with the simple conditions, according to our ability, in *tithes* and *time*, and the result is as sure as God is sure.

Notice the two things, "tithes" and "time." There is many a man who has sinned by writing a large check, when God called louder for his time than for his money.

If God is pleased with Christian Endeavor through these thirty-two years, it is in no small degree because the key-note was personal service, a giving of ourselves in time. Judged by world standards, your leaders, Dr. Clark, Mr. Shaw, Prof. Wells, and others are sacrificing time every day of their lives in Christian Endeavor that might give them fourfold if used for producing the utmost in material revenue. From these same leaders $23,400 has already come for the Christian Endeavor Building, and there is at least $5,000 more to come.

But it is no sacrifice to do the things you love, and every leader and true-hearted Endeavorer *loves the cause.* Why shouldn't we love it? If any movement on earth was ever blessed by God, it would seem to be the Society of Christian Endeavor, with its millions of earnest, consecrated young people.

The tools used by these young people are furnished by the Publishing Department, with its large stock of Endeavor literature and supplies carried in both Boston and Chicago.

The business of our Publishing Department for the year ending May 31, 1913, was $65,164.14, an increase of $10,000 since the Atlantic City Convention. The total receipts for the last two years are $132,216.00, of which $17,825, or nearly 14 per cent of the gross receipts, was contributed to the Missionary Department. That's better than the scriptural tithe, better than most of us do for missions; and all honor to the man, Mr. Shartle, who has made such a glorious record.

The total assets of your society, the United Society of Christian Endeavor (Corporation) are now as follows:—

Publishing Department net assets .... $ 30,965.73
Real Estate in Boston, land and buildings, for International
 Christian Endeavor Headquarters 116,625.52
Cash in banks 4,597.68

$152,188.93

That's our best report, but we can and should do better. The Publishing Department needs $10,000 additional capital to do its best and most efficient work, and I am not a bit afraid to trust Mr. Shartle with it. Are you?

The Building Fund needs $28,000 more than is now pledged or paid, if we are to keep faith with you and not create a mortgage. Twenty-eight thousand dollars would come right out of your pockets so easily if you didn't hold on so tightly.

Do you know that the day we move into our International Headquarters $5,000 annual rent stops, and *that* $5,000 will then be used for spreading the gospel of Christian Endeavor?

Help us get that $28,000 before we leave Los Angeles!

In presenting General Secretary Shaw as the last speaker Dr. Baer said that he had conferred upon him the title of M. S.—Master of the Situation. Mr. Shaw replied in his inimitable way:

"I don't know what you're going to have, but I'm going to have a good time. I'm going to have the lights turned down, and if you're sleepy and want to go to bed you can just slip out quietly and I won't mind. You've been having a good time with all these noted speakers, and I know that a secretary's report is as dry as the sawdust under your feet. I know all about them; I've been making them and hearing them too long. I'm not sleepy. I'm not going to bed—I'm going to stay right here and have a good time."

Secretary Shaw's report was fittingly called a "Demonstration of Practical Efficiency." It was a stereopticon lecture with nearly one hundred pictures showing Christian Endeavor scenes from almost every country in the world. It revealed to many interesting phases of Christian Endeavor activity, prison work, hospital work, fresh-air work, athletics, socials, and so forth, picture after picture calling forth ringing applause.

A DEMONSTRATION OF CHRISTIAN ENDEAVOR EFFICIENCY:

Biennial Report of William Shaw, General Secretary of the United Society of Christian Endeavor.

I know of no more appropriate words with which to begin my report of the past two years of service by our Societies of Christian Endeavor than those of our Master, spoken three days before His crucifixion, and recorded in the twenty-fifth chapter of the Gospel according to St. Matthew, when He said, "Come, ye blessed of my Father, inherit the kingdom prepared for you from the foundation of the world; for I was a hungred, and ye gave me meat; I was thirsty, and ye gave me drink; I was a stranger, and ye took me in; naked, and ye clothed me; I was sick, and ye visited me; I was in prison, and ye came unto me."

And, when they disclaimed any knowledge of having ministered to Him, He said, "Inasmuch as ye have done it unto one of the least of these my brethren, ye have done it unto me." And these further words, spoken the day of His ascension and recorded in the twenty-eighth chapter: "Go ye therefore, and teach all nations."

With the clear and definite suggestions of the Efficiency Campaign proposed by Dr. Clark at the Atlantic City Convention to serve as a guide, the societies have had two years of splendid, fruitful service. This, it seems to me, can be best expressed in terms of concrete examples that can stand as types of similar service rendered by a multitude of Endeavorers.

Our Primary Purpose.

It should never be forgotten that the primary purpose of Christian Endeavor is to train the young people for the service of Christ through His church. The record of societies that have completed twenty-five years of history abundantly proves that the Society, wherever it has had intelligent, sympathetic leadership, has fulfilled its mission.

A typical case is that of the Fourth Congregational Society of Christian Endeavor of Hartford, Conn., which has recently celebrated its twenty-fifth anniversary. The total membership for the twenty-five years was about three hundred and sixty, the male members having a majority of two. Out of this company of trained young people have gone a dozen or more ministers, missionaries, Young Men's Christian Association secretaries, and other professional workers; also five of the eight deacons, all but one of the officers of the Sunday school, and eighty per cent of the teachers. Here was an organization that had never numbered ten per cent of the church or Sunday-school membership, but which had furnished from sixty to ninety-nine per cent of the volunteer leaders and workers in that church, and had contributed a host of helpers to other religious enterprises.

The following list shows something of the character and variety of work done by societies of Christian Endeavor. If time and space permitted, it could be multiplied indefinitely. Here is enough, however, to show clearly the spirit and purpose of the movement.

Some Sample Lines of Service.

Increased the attendance and participation in the midweek church prayer meeting.

Are encouraging the young people to unite with the church.

Changing doubtful young people into earnest Christian workers.

Conduct cottage prayer meetings.

Hold open-air meetings in the summer.

Conduct hospital services two Sundays each month.

Took charge of church prayer meetings while the church was without a pastor.

Providing weekly calendars for the church.

Maintain a Sunday-school teachers' training-class.

Have a Christian Endeavor class in Sunday school, from which substitute teachers are taken.

Put new electric lights into the church building.

Have a class for training personal workers.

Bought a new piano.

Furnished the chapel with pulpit and hymn-books.

Maintain strong missionary interest.

Support their own missionary.

Have special Bible-study classes.

Conduct mission-study classes.

Have ten-minute supplemental study of the denominational history, in connection with the meeting.

Conduct services at a jail.

Organized a social-service committee to co-operate with the Associated Charities.

Co-operated in no-license campaign.

Had liquor advertisements removed from bill-boards.

Got all the members to sign a temperance pledge.

Had a street-railway company discontinue liquor advertisements on trolley transfers.

Agitated for better observance of the Sabbath.

Closed the post-office on Sunday.

Are looking out for foreigners in suburbs.

Have classes in winter to teach foreigners our language.

Decorate the church every Sunday.

Helping the pastor to solve the Sunday-evening problem.

Send fruit and flowers to sick and shut-ins.

Formed a literary circle.

Provide wholesome socials and entertainments for the young people.

Conduct singing-class.

Organized a Christian Endeavor chorus for society and church services.

Have a baseball club.

Have a committee on athletics.

Conduct meetings in the city mission.

Widening Activities.

But the activities of Christian Endeavor do not end with the local church and community. Mission-board leaders testify that a very large percentage of candidates for missionary service say that the determining factor in the choice of their life-work was their missionary service in the Young People's society. This is true also of Young Men's Christian Association and Young Women's Christian Association secretaries and social workers.

When you put a boy or girl at work on the missionary committee of your society, you never know where that experience may lead. A company of redeemed black people from the fever jungles of Africa may rise up in the day of judgment and say, "I was hungry for the bread of life, and ye fed me." Or it may be a group from the sun-baked plains of India who will say, "I was thirsty for the water of life, and ye gave me to drink." Or it may be a boy or girl from the slums of our great cities who will say, "Ye ministered unto me."

In the midst of the insistent voices that challenge the church to social service it should be remembered that it is for just such service that Christian Endeavor through all the years (and never more so than now) has been training the young people. But it has always begun with the challenge of personal surrender and loyalty to Jesus Christ. Social service is not a substitute for salvation. The being precedes the doing. The spiritual dynamic is essential to permanent reformation.

A convincing testimony to the value of Christian Endeavor training is that given by Mr. Fred B. Smith, leader of the Men and Religion Movement, who said that, while the Society of Christian Endeavor could not join the Men and Religion Campaign officially, because its work was not exclusively for men and boys, yet it must be represented and its work presented at the closing meeting in New York *because* he had found by personal experience in the campaign that so large a proportion of the workers in the different cities had been trained in Christian Endeavor. He gives this personal testimony: "The very first Christian work I ever did in my life was in the Christian Endeavor Society." Similar statements have also been made by such conspicuous leaders in Christian activities as the late John B. Sleman, of the Laymen's Missionary Movement: Mr. M. A. Hudson, founder of the Baraca Class; Mr. Andrew Stevenson, a Brotherhood pioneer; and many others. "By their fruits ye shall know them."

But how about the hungry and thirsty, the stranger, the naked, the sick, and those our brothers in bonds? Would that I could describe in some adequate way the splendid service that Christian Endeavor has rendered along these lines.

Fresh-Air Hospital Work.

The fresh-air homes of the Brooklyn, Baltimore, and New Jersey Endeavorers, where thousands of little children and tired mothers from the tenement-house districts of the large cities find renewed health of the body and soul, speak in language that the most ignorant understand of Him who came "not to be ministered unto, but to minister." The special remembrance at Christmas-time and the follow-up work during the winter enable the workers to keep in touch with the summer visitors and help them in many ways.

The "Country Day," when the societies in the country churches receive a crowd of children from the city mission, and give them a day of wonder and delight, is another form of fresh-air work in which many societies can engage.

The blessed ministry to the sick in hospitals, such as is carried on by the Chicago Endeavorers in the Cook County Hospital, by the California Endeavorers in many of the county hospitals, and by workers in other places, has brought healing to the souls as well as to the bodies of a multitude of stricken ones.

Some idea of the extent and importance of this work can be gained from the report of six months' service in the Cook County Hospital, Chicago, Ill.

Total attendance at meetings	3,427
Requests for prayer	1,267
Conversions	216
Portions of Scripture given away	740
Letters and postal cards written	244
Bouquets distributed	36,400

A kindred work to this is that of visiting the almshouses, old folks' homes, and similar institutions, where religious services are held. Gifts of candy, fruit, jellies, etc., are taken to the inmates with loving greetings that mean more to them than material gifts.

Prison and Floating Work

The prison work in twenty-three of our State prisons and penitentiaries has brought liberty to a multitude of men and women who had gone there hopeless and discouraged. Prison wardens speak in highest praise of the helpful influence of the society work upon the men.

The Floating work for seamen, carried on in the ports of the Atlantic and Pacific coasts and the Great Lakes, has been a blessing to this great host of neglected men. The Chicago workers are able to visit about ninety boats a year. Meetings are also held on the piers. Sunday song-services and monthly entertainments are given at the Marine Hospital.

A report of three months' work by the California Endeavorers shows good work being done at Eureka, San Francisco, Oakland, Vallejo, San Pedro, and San Diego. More than three hundred meetings were held in the Seamen's Homes and on board ship, with an attendance of more than six thousand. Socials and entertainments were also provided. Comfort-bags, Bibles, and literature were distributed in large quantities. Many conversions were reported.

With the Army.

The successful Christian Endeavor society at Fort Snelling, Minn., with its membership of fifty-seven soldier boys, shows what might be done in most of our army posts. Six denominations are represented in the membership. Live prayer meetings are maintained. A bicycle club to visit the parks and lakes in the vicinity, and touring parties to visit the manufacturing and other establishments of the Twin Cities, are helpful social features. The society is a member of the St. Paul union, and the members in dress uniform attend the rallies and socials, where they receive a royal welcome. One of the members is now in a missionary training-school, preparing for missionary service. The success attending the work is largely due to the enthusiastic leadership of Chaplain S. C. Ramsden.

Other Lines of Effort.

Christian Endeavor has led in placing emphasis upon the obligation resting upon Christians to apply their religion to the improvement of civic conditions. The recent appointment by the executive committee of the United Society of Christian Endeavor of Daniel A. Poling as national superintendent of temperance and Christian citizenship is a long step forward, and will mean increased efficiency in this department.

The missionary activities of our societies have steadily increased, as shown by the multiplication of mission-study classes, the increased emphasis upon the spread of missionary information, and the enlargement of missionary contributors.

The Tenth Legion, an enrolment of those who give at least a tenth of their income for the spread of the Kingdom, now numbers 29,645. There has been a steady increase in the ranks of the Comrades of the Quiet Hour, who now number 72,970.

Christian Endeavor Experts.

It is a pleasure to report here in California that the first Christian Endeavor Expert to receive his degree was Mr. LaRue C. Watson, of Visalia, Cal., and that the total number of registered Experts is 1,089, while hundreds more are pursuing the course of study.

Efficient Societies.

The first society to qualify as a one-hundred-per-cent society in the Efficiency Campaign was the Cumberland Presbyterian society of Knoxville, Tenn., whose pastor is Rev. Thomas Ashburn, D.D., a member of our board of trustees. The second was the First Presbyterian society of Cañon City, Col., and the third was the Congregational society of Newfane, Vt.

More than three thousand societies are now conducting their work along the definite and practical lines outlined on the Efficiency Chart, and Australia has also started the campaign. The results have been surprisingly successful. Starting with a rating of twenty-five per cent or even less, they have speedily climbed to fifty or more, showing an immediate gain of one hundred or more per cent in efficiency. The last twenty-five per cent is of course the hardest to gain, but that only adds to the interest and zest of the undertaking.

At first, societies were afraid of it, it seemed so big an undertaking; but, when they realized that all they had to do was to begin just where they were, and do just one thing at a time, they saw how practical and sensible the plan was, and entered heartily into it.

While the Efficiency Campaign was at first planned for two years, it has so demonstrated its helpfulness that it is now incorporated into the regular working-plans of our movement. If your society is not one of the thousands that are reaching for the one hundred per cent, begin now.

The more than seventy-five thousand societies and nearly four million members were never doing better work.

Juniors and Intermediates.

No department of Christian Endeavor has in it greater possibilities than our Junior work. Here, under intelligent leadership, is our chance to lay the foundations for the future church-membership that shall be more efficient than the present or past membership has been.

Here is an organization that can provide for the spiritual, mental, and physical activities of the wide-awake boys and girls. It can combine the work of the missionary band, the Temperance Legion, the Band of Mercy, the pastor's class, and the social and athletic clubs in one organization, with the Junior meeting as its centre, and its ultimate circumference the mature service as members of the church.

Through graduation into the membership of the Intermediate or Young People's society it provides for the continuous training of the boys and girls along the lines of normal church service. It ought to command a larger share of the time and interest of the pastors and older Endeavorers.

The Intermediate society is the youngest branch of our movement and the smallest in point of numbers. No department, however, is of greater importance. It takes the young people at the most critical period of their lives, but at the most hopeful also. More persons definitely surrender to the leadership of Jesus Christ during the years covered by the Intermediate society than during all the rest. It is the time of decision.

Christian Endeavor Unions.

Our Christian Endeavor unions, State, district, county, and city, are steadily developing in efficiency and usefulness. Through their influence all the societies are being lifted to the level of the best. Their meetings and conferences are genuine educational institutions for practical Christian service, and through their committees and varied lines of work they have applied the most approved laboratory methods of training for service.

They are laymen's seminaries for the training of volunteer, unpaid workers in the service of the churches. Their value and importance are not yet fully appreciated by the majority of our pastors, or these would take a larger personal interest, and give more generous and outspoken co-operation and approval of the work.

In Foreign Lands.

One of the most inspiring features of our work is the progress of the movement in mission lands. As a training-school for the native converts it is of peculiar value. It appeals to them, and wins a response that no other organization has been able to secure. As an evangelistic agency it is unexcelled.

Bishop Whitehead of India has emphasized in a recent article the great contribution Christian Endeavor has made to the work there by its emphasis upon the training and development of the individual members, the working *with*, instead of *for*, others. "It teaches us to take for our model, not the potter moulding the clay, but the sower sowing the seed."

May this be our ideal as we enter upon two more years of endeavor "for Christ and the church"; and may the harvest, under the blessing of the Spirit, be at least one-hundred-fold.

While a Hawaiian group was on the screen, five Hawaiian Endeavorers sang a native song with guitar accompaniment. Like Mr. Shaw's sparkling illustrated address, this sweet music came as a happy surprise, and was thoroughly enjoyed by the great audience.

THE USHERS

CHAPTER VII.

THE FELLOWSHIP OF THE CHURCHES.

Friday Afternoon, July 11, Auditorium Endeavor.

Auditorium Endeavor, the palm garden of the Convention, even though in California, was not the coolest place to hold the fellowship meeting. However, the auditorium was well filled on Friday afternoon to listen to the splendid addresses on the fellowship of the churches.

Dr. Landrith was the first speaker, and thrilled the audience with his masterful address on "How Christian Endeavor has Promoted Fellowship." He paid a glowing tribute to Christian Endeavor as the divinely appointed instrument for bringing in the kingdom of brotherly love. His address in full follows:

HOW CHRISTIAN ENDEAVOR HAS PROMOTED FELLOWSHIP.

By Rev. Ira Landrith, D.D., LL.D., Nashville, Tenn.

Dr. Landrith paid grateful tribute to Christian Endeavor as the divinely appointed instrumentality for bringing in the kingdom of brotherly love. Among other things he said: When we have grown far enough away from the beginning of Christian Endeavor to trust our perspectives, we shall give it first place among the agencies that created and nurtured a hundred wholesome forms of fellowship. Who knoweth but that it came to the kingdom for just this, that the prejudice born of ignorance might be kept away from the hearts of the youth of yesterday that are statesmen, educators, and the church-leaders of to-day?

Intersectional fellowship had enjoyed few opportunities before Christian Endeavor began to hold, North and South and East and West, great conventions to which came by thousands the representatives of every section. In closer association our imaginary differences have disappeared, and political dividing lines have faded in the direct sunlight of brotherly love and mutual acquaintanceship.

As races habitually at enmity similar blessing has come to us from the generous hand of Christian Endeavor. We have learned that it is unfraternal and unfair to judge a race by its poorest rather than its best representatives; that the Golden Rule has an inter-racial as well as an individual application; and that though there is no Christian demand for the universal application of the rules of interracial social equality, when such rules are neither applied or observed among uncolored Caucasians. We have merely learned the Master's will that Christian men ought to give every worthy man a Christian man's chance.

But Christian Endeavor would deserve the immortality that seems to be ensured if it had promoted no other than international fellowship. Accepted as from God, Christian Endeavor has entered the heart of nearly every nation of the earth; and every such heart has warmed toward all the others. Information is the prolific mother of those heavenly twins, Interest and Sympathy; and in our conventions, in the literature of Christian Endeavor, and in a hundred other ways this movement has opened an entrance for international education, world-vision.

There is not time to speak of the benefits of fellowship which Christian Endeavor has bestowed upon our local churches through the association, in worship and service of their own young people. Even such association, under church supervision and Christian care, did not exist before Christian Endeavor set them together in local societies.

But, Dr. Clark, the society which our Father honored you with the privilege of founding, deserves the beatitude of the peacemaker for its pioneer work for interdenominational fellowship, once the mere hope and dream of a devout Portland prophet, but now the all but universally accepted spirit of Christendom. Many agencies have helped in this; many daughters have done well; but Christian Endeavor, it is not invidious, to speak the truth, thou excellest them all. Christian Endeavor proclaimed and practised this doctrine of fraternity when it was not only not popular, but actually hazardous; but the time has come when no sectarian has the temerity to insult public opinion and Christian intelligence by preaching that gospel of despair, "The only way to heaven is through my church." We work for the union ultimately, the communion and co-operation immediately, of all of the churches of Jesus Christ.

An unusual period on this programme was a solo entitled "Hold Thou My Hand," by America's Indian tenor, Mr. Elmer N. Lafonso, of Chico, California. He captivated the audience by the sweetness of his beautiful tenor voice.

"The Scandal of Sectarianism" was the theme of Rev. Dr. Charles W. Recard's address. Dr. Recard is one of a group of eloquent young men in the United Brethren Church. He poured fine scorn upon the struggles of sects that have claimed ownership of the blessings of salvation, and described the part that Christian Endeavor has in putting the verbal weapons of sectarianism into the museum of to-morrow.

THE SCANDAL OF SECTARIANISM.
By Rev. Charles W. Recard, D.D., Canton, Ohio.

This assembly proves that the prayer of Jesus for a united church is being answered. How his great heart must rejoice over this fine sample of the union of all believers! Christian Endeavor is a pioneer. She has cut her way through a vast section of the dense jungle of sectarianism and made possible this good fellowship of believers from many camps. When the implements of the bad old days of the battles of religious sects are stored in the museums of to-morrow, the inscription over all will read, "Made useless and unnecessary by the victories of Christian Endeavor."

The scandal of sectarianism has a hoary and heartless history. It seems to have taken germinal form on the day of our Lord's crucifixion. While the world's saving blood was flowing warm from Calvary, at the foot of the instrument of death men cast dice for the spoils of murder. Those dice spots symbolize the age-long scandal. Soldiers of the cross of Christ have continued to gamble for the seamless robe. Words of Holy Writ have served as dice for the determination of right to the robe of righteousness until hundreds of sects have declared ownership. This devilish skill in verbal legerdemain is largely responsible for the cruel contentions of Christendom.

It is supreme bigotry, folly, and nonsense for any body of believers to be claiming the exclusive ownership of the covering for sin. The Golden

Fleece of the precious Lamb of God is not won by barter, debate, nor the black art of textual gambling. It belongs to us all. It is ample in large-ness to cover a race of sinners, and sufficiently flexible in warp and woof to give comeliness and comfort to the temperamental peculiarities of all believers. I am willing to be dubbed any kind of a heretic for the posi-tion taken here. A jubilee is on in my soul when I reflect that every poor prodigal from God who nestles by faith underneath this garment of grace is at home and safe forevermore. I dare go farther and declare that even to touch the hem of this garment gives healing and saving to the un-soundest of earth's defectives:

This conception does no violence to correct ideals of the church of Christ in her militant organization. It simply asserts that all churches may have a place beneath the ample folds of the seamless robe. Location of particular regiments of the army of God should be strategic. My par-ticular camping-ground to-day may be logically correct with reference to the general engagement of to-morrow, but no pretext for declaring that my regiment is deserting the great army of God. The outworks of the kingdom belong to him as well as the inner citadel.

Jesus laid the foundations of "the church" and not of "a church." A church may be built upon this true foundation. The church is the king-dom of God in all its wealth and reach and power wherever truth abounds. All truth is of the Kingdom, whether it be found in mighty fulness in the heart of a saint or in meagre measure in the breast of an infidel.

Why, then, this clash of creeds and unholy quest for divine sanction of our bigotry and base exclusiveness? Does it not come of our failure to fellowship fully with the great Head of the church? We lust after some old landmarks of creed or theology more than we pant after the Good Shepherd.

Old landmarks may be a curse rather than a blessing. Some people are afraid of anything religious that is less than a century old. Old wells are considered the best. If men cannot drink from those their fathers digged, they refuse to drink at all. God help us to be brave enough to drill new wells down through the hard beaten surface of modern materialized life and bring forth the artesian currents of divine refreshment. Some people cannot worship joyfully unless they go back to an old Bethel at which great-grandfather Jacob got a blessing. God help us to erect new Bethels along the rocky road of the modern pilgrim.

We do not impoverish the church by shedding it of some old relics and traditional lumber any more than the great oak destroys its vitality by shedding last year's leaves. As long as we do not give up the Christ, the living sap, there is little danger. What other men thought of Christ and how they worshipped him may have some value to us as history of the pathway along which the army of God has travelled, but is of no essential value as a programme for the movements of the army to-day. Moulds of doctrine and forms of ecclesiasticism suited to the needs of other days may be a positive handicap now. Some antiquities for which churchmen suffered death rather than surrender them we despise as mere bones of contention. We should be laughed out of court if we even hinted that these old bones should live. The key-note of the gospel should not be changed. Jesus Christ, the same yesterday and to-day and forever, must never fall out of our ministry. A revised theology may be timely, but a revised Christ is powerless to save. A mass of trappings designed by men must be torn away and the living Christ re-incarnated in human person-alities.

There is a sort of ghastly consistency in the way in which we cling to some old mummies of orthodoxy. We pelt one another with hard words when our particular mummy is despised or ignored. We have subtle pleas-ure in snubbing one another. We talk to God in a common language; but, when we talk to one another, we begin to dispute and dissent. We sing the same songs, and breathe out the same prayers, and profess the warmest intimacy with the same Christ, then draw chalk lines, and fling out the slogan of battle. Against this whole business of bigoted, close-fisted, heartless unchristlikeness let Christian Endeavor launch a mighty protest of fire.

Because Christianity is so large, men may have so many different opinions of it. Two persons see a text from different angles. This should not bring a breach between the individuals, but mark the greatness of the text. We should rejoice that there are so many ways of representing our Christ. There is more truth in His life than can ever be crowded into definition. Let us have nothing to do with an alleged truth that only a priest or a preacher can explain.

Uniformity is not essential to unity. Nature and grace enter radical protest here. We have no right to try to force uniformity and baptize it with the sacred name "union." What are the wild waves saying? They declare that they move in harmony with the mighty astronomic forces, pulsing, throbbing, thundering on the shore; yet all belong to the same sea. Christian union is not formal, but spiritual, not founded upon human notions of Christ, but found in personal, intimate fellowship with Him. The united church is a royal democracy, a rapturous brotherhood. The cure of disunion is not in the destruction of sects but in the abolition of sectarianism.

There is only one Percy Foster, and it required only the inimitable Foster to bring that magnificent chorus of beautiful voices to the front at the close of Rev. Dr. Recard's address to sing as only Californians can.

"The Power and Possibilities of a United Church" was indeed an inspiring topic in the hands of Rev. Frank M. Goodchild D.D., pastor of the Central Baptist Church, New York City.

THE POWER AND THE POSSIBILITIES OF A UNITED CHURCH.

By Rev. Frank M. Goodchild, D.D., Pastor of the Central Baptist Church, New York.

Augustine, the greatest of the early Christian Fathers, once said that there were three things he was sorry he had not seen—Christ in the flesh, Paul in the pulpit, and Rome in her glory. To these three we may add a fourth thing that we are greatly eager to see; and that is a perfectly united Christian church; a world-wide church which shall include in its membership all those who love the Lord in sincerity and truth; a church in which all the members, forgetting their differences and laying aside their prejudices, shall stand shoulder to shoulder, having but one purpose—obedience to the Saviour, and moved by but one desire—to bring honor to his dear name.

Augustine was so anxious to have the first of his wishes, the wish to see Christ, gratified, that, when he was commenting on the text, "Thou canst not see my face; for there shall no man see me and live," he promptly wrote down this earnest petition, "Then, Lord, let me die that I may see thy face."

The Lord Jesus was so anxious to see a perfectly united church that he spent some of his last breath on earth in praying for it. Many a care distracted his mind on that last night of his life. Many a woe pressed heavily on his heart. And yet, when he lifted up his soul in one long, last prayer to the Father, this is the petition that came repeatedly to his lips: "May they [the disciples] be one, even as we are one." He was not thinking only of his immediate followers who stood about him in that upper room. He looked down into the future, and saw Christendom divided and Christians at war with one another. He said, "Neither pray I for these alone, but for them also which shall believe on me through their word, that they all may be one." It is fair to say that this great meeting today, in which we are thinking and praying about the much-divided Christian church, had a place in the Saviour's prayer on that sad night so long ago.

The prayer of the Saviour is as yet unanswered. The unity he longed to see in his people is as yet unattained. The perfectly united church is as yet only an ideal to be striven towards. The apostolic church just after Christ's ascension came near to realizing the divine ideal; but in a little while this distraction and that came in, and, instead of the great multitude's being of one heart and one soul, they had as many minds as there were thinkers, and as many sets as there were leaders. And in our day these unhappy divisions have been so multiplied as to have become positively ludicrous. The old minister of the Free Kirk who prayed that we might all be baptized in the spirit of disruption has had his prayer fully answered. And there are men who in spite of the Saviour's prayer justify these divisions and look askance at the man who speaks out against them.

Not long ago, when I said to a friend of mine that I was coming here to speak on the power of a united church, he smilingly cautioned me against the utterance of any heresy. But I am quite willing to run the risk. A man who is frowned upon on account of his advocacy of church union, has a fine defence to hide behind in the Saviour's prayer for the unity of his people.

There are those, to be sure, who contend that he did not mean organic unity, to which I reply that the Saviour himself answered that objection when he prayed that his people might be "perfect in one." When the denominations realize what the Saviour's prayer means, they will be so absolutely united that you will not be able to find any trace of a dividing line between them. I take my stand on the Saviour's prayer. You may quote me as strongly as you please. I long for church union. I am not afraid to say that I do. I pray for it daily, and I lead my people in praying for it whenever we come together. I will go as far as Jesus Christ did in favor of the unity of Christian people. I will go as far as Paul did. The great apostle was horrified when divisions seemed imminent in his day. He classed divisions with drunkenness and fornication. The Christian preacher to-day should have the same horror of schism in the body of Christ that Paul had, and he should inspire that feeling in his people.

There are several advantages that the Saviour says will come to the united church. He says that, when the church is united, it will be invested with glory. "The glory which thou gavest me I have given them, that they may be one even as we are one," are the Lord's words. There can be no doubt that in these days the church's glory is dimmed, and you can trace it all back to the divisions among us as the cause. Whether we feel the shame of our divisions or not, our enemies exult in them. O that we might have the glory that the Saviour said belongs to the united church, and that we might go about our work with the sweet consciousness of his approval!

The union of the churches will bring a sense of completeness which we now lack. The denominations are called sects; and, though we dislike it, the name is a just one, for no one of these bodies is the whole church. Christ said that we could be made perfect only as we are "one." "I in them and thou in me, that they may be made perfect in one." Even those that delight in denominationalism admit that each denomination emphasizes some special truth. Why not have but one church giving to each truth its appropriate amount of emphasis? Our hymnals are made up of hymns written by men of every Christian complexion, and we sing them all in blissful unconsciousness of their being anything but Christian. So the ideal church will be made up of the contributions of all Christian sects, and will have a charm and an efficiency that no sect could have.

And only as the church is united can we win the world for Jesus Christ. The denominationalist maintains that the division of the church into rival denominations has stimulated Christian effort. But I cannot be moved from the belief that what our Lord prayed against cannot be permanently profitable to the church. Whatever men may say about it, there can be no doubt that Christ said that the unity of the church would make the world believe on him. In business, men have learned that competition is not the life of trade, but is often the death of trade and the ruin of the tradesman. It is better to stand in with your business rival than to stand out against him. And it is saner for the churches of Jesus Christ to stand together than to pull apart. A divided church never can win the world for Christ. When the churches everywhere can gather with one accord in one place as we are gathered here to-day, and lift up their voices unanimously to God, there is sure to be some result. The place where they meet will be shaken, grace will be shed upon all, great voices will be heard, great sights will be seen, and such power will come out of our unity in Christ that newly saved ones by thousands will be added to the church.

A service new at our Conventions was introduced by Rev. Lapsley A. McAfee, D.D., of Berkeley Cal., a decision-service, in which the leader gathered up the principal ideas of the addresses, and put them in the form of questions to which the audience responded. "How many, believing that it will please Christ, are willing to pledge themselves to pray and work for the unity of the church of Christ?" he asked.

A sea of hands was raised in response, and Dr. McAfee followed with a quiet, earnest prayer for strength for all to carry out this purpose.

And so with the question of absolute surrender to Jesus, that He may be Master and Lord, that He may lead all the way. Then a solemn call to associate Endeavorers or non-Christians, and a call to doubters that wished prayer for help. The hush of heaven, the very peace of God, was upon the gathering, and hearts were moved to decision to live always, only, for Jesus. Then the great host of Endeavorers pledged themselves anew to be true to Christ, to His church, and to live in happier and kinder relations with one another.

THE JUNIOR RALLY AT THE LOS ANGELES CONVENTION

CHAPTER VIII.

THE JUNIOR AND INTERMEDIATE RALLY

The Story of the Wounded Angel

Saturday afternoon, July 12, Auditorium Endeavor.

A hot afternoon. Beautiful palm garden, seating thousands. Big platform containing large cross in centre. Hundreds of boys and girls—Junior rally—Auditorium Endeavor.

To the strains of that soul-stirring hymn "Crown Him with many crowns" a great throng of the little men and women of sunkissed California marched into Auditorium Endeavor and down the aisles between clusters of ferns and groups of flags of all nations up to the platform. Each Junior carried a small bouquet of California daisies, and wore a garland or small crown of the same beautiful flowers. It was a sight that will long linger as a pleasant memory of an unusual event. As the little men and women mounted the platform, they took off their flowery crowns, and handed them to one of several angels, —white-clad young women,—who piled the garlands at the foot of the cross in token of the time when we shall lay our crowns at His feet.

About two hundred Juniors took part in the exercise. One could not listen unmoved to the sound of their childish voices singing "Crown Him Lord of all."

The exercise was divided into three parts: preparation, including the Bible, prayer, and the Holy Spirit; coronation; and consecration.

It was a song service—songs and recitation of Scripture verses by the Juniors themselves, simple, direct, and exceedingly touching.

Mrs. Fred P. Rossiter and Miss Dorothy Dukes sang a delightful duet, "Come unto Me." Then Dr. Clark spoke to the Juniors about the angel that there is in every boy and girl.

"Not long ago," he said, "I was in Finland, in the city of Tammerfors, where in a beautiful church I saw a peculiar and striking picture on the church wall. The picture presented two boys, and between them they were carrying a kind of litter, two poles on which was placed a little platform, and on the platform an angel.

"And as I looked, I noticed that the angel was wounded. From her side the blood was trickling down. What did this mean? I think it meant that every Junior is carrying an angel within him; but, sad to say, some Juniors hurt the good angel within, so that they are carrying a wounded angel. Bad words, disobedience, ugliness, indifference to good things, wound the angel, and sometimes even kill her. I hope none of us will do that."

Then to stirring song the children marched down the aisle, throwing their daisies among the audience as they passed.

A flower shower is always characteristic of California, and who that was in attendance at this beautiful Junior scene will ever forget the shower of daisies?

THE INTERMEDIATE RALLY

Saturday Afternoon, July 12, Immanuel Presbyterian Church

Intermediate rallies at International Conventions are a fixture. Among the many first things at the Los Angeles Convention the Intermediate rally will stand as one of the most inspiring and significant.

The great auditorium of the Immanuel Presbyterian Church was well filled with an enthusiastic crowd of young people full of vim and vigor. Life in all its hopefulness and freshness was represented there.

It was a genuine Intermediate programme, with just a bit of balance from big-hearted Dr. John Balcom Shaw, who spoke on "Life as an Investment."

Mr. Sydney A. Clark, Mr. Harry Hill, Miss Hazel P. Smith, and Mr. Charles Trout gave capital talks on the Intermediate in relation to his school life, his associates, his amusements, and his life-plans.

Miss Alma Robinson spoke from a superintendent's standpoint. Ten one-minute testimonies regarding the value of the Intermediate society followed her address.

Miss Lillian Waghorn, Califorina's superintendent, gave a cordial welcome, read a greeting from Australia, and called attention to an Australian flag that accompanied the greeting. Miss Anita Lake conducted an uplifting devotional service. General Secretary Shaw presided, and declared that the Intermediate rally at our great Conventions has come to stay.

Christian · Endeavor · Efficiency
STANDARDS

1. Christian Endeavor Training 9

2. Executive Committee 4

3. Prayer-Meeting Committee 4

4. Lookout Committee 4

5. Missionary Committee 4

6. Information Committee 2

7. Flower Committee 2

8. Good-Literature Committee 2

9. Sunday-school Committee 2

10. Temperance or Citizenship Committee 2

11. Junior Committee 2

12. Public Prayer 5

13. Original Testimony 5

14. Consecration Meeting 4

15. Leaders 3

16. Singing 3

17. Society Finances 3

18. Giving 4

19. Business Meetings 3

20. Socials 3

21. Evangelism 4

22. Study Course 3

23. Private Devotions 5

24. Honorary Members 2

25. Associate Members 4

26. Church Services 6

27. Aiding the Pastor 3

28. The Union 4

Work of the Society

19 Standards	Charge of The President		76 Per Cent
	19. Business Meetings	3	
	28. The Union	4	

Charge of Executive Committee		Charge of Prayer-Meeting Committee	
1. Christian Endeavor Training	9	13. Original Testimony	5
2. Executive Committee	4	14. Consecration Meeting	4
27. Aiding the Pastor	3	23. Private Devotions	5
22. Study Course	3	15. Leaders	3
17. Society Finances	3	12. Public Prayer	5

Charge of Lookout Committee		Charge of Social Committee	
25. Associate Members	3	20. Socials	3
26. Church Services	6	24. Honorary Members	2
21. Evangelism	4	? ? ?	

Summary

President - - - 7

Executive Committee	22	Information Committee	2
Prayer-Meeting Committee	26	Flower Committee	2
Lookout Committee	17	Junior Committee	2
Social Committee	5	Sunday-School Committee	2
Missionary Committee	8	Good-Literature Committee	2
Music Committee	3	Temperance or Citizenship Committee	2

Total - - - 100 per cent

Charge of Missionary Committee		Charge of Music Committee	
18. Giving	4	16. Singing	3

Work of the Committees

4. Lookout Committee	4	3. Prayer-Meeting Committee	4
5. Missionary Committee	4	11. Junior Committee	2
6. Information Committee	2	9. Sunday-School Committee	2
7. Flower Committee	2	8. Good-Literature Committee	2

9 Standards	10. Temperance or Citizenship Committee 2	24 Per Cent

CHAPTER IX.

CHRISTIAN ENDEAVOR EFFICIENCY

First Methodist Episcopal Church

MR KARL LEHMANN, Interstate Field Secretary of the United
Society of Christian Endeavor, Leader.

THIS series of three conferences conducted by Field
Secretary Lehmann, on "The Practical and Most
Efficient Side of Christian Endeavor," was largely attended and of great interest and attraction to the delegates. There was sufficient opportunity for note-books
and pencils because of the many bright, helpful, and efficient
methods and plans introduced during the rapid-fire discussion.

First Conference. In this first conference the Efficiency Campaign Chart was introduced and thoroughly explained. It has
been said that the Efficiency Campaign is the finest, biggest, and
best campaign any religious movement has ever had outlined
for it. Among the many testimonies coming from the workers
present at the meeting, and among the many things said were,
"The Efficiency Campaign has done more than any other thing
to make our society a success." One delegate said that, if he
had any criticism to make on the campaign, it would be simply
this, that a campaign of such proportions and so helpful to societies should have been given to the societies years ago.

Christian Endeavor training was thoroughly discussed; the
leaflets were described; and the qualifications necessary to become an expert Endeavorer were explained, The conference
next emphasized the importance and value of the executive
committee, and laid great stress upon holding regular executive-
committee meetings. Business-meeting plans were given with
good success. Society finances received much attention, and
especially the need of a budget for every society as a means of
helping to handle the finances more intelligently. It was
further suggested that a finance committee should be created in
order to secure from each Endeavorer a subscription, payable
monthly, to the work of the society and to missions.

A large number of Endeavorers from many States and Provinces in Canada participated in this discussion. After the discussion Rev. Harrie R. Chamberlin, president of the Massachusetts Christian Endeavor Union, gave the closing address. His

subject was, "Christian Endeavor Vision." Among other things
he said:

"The first and great counsel about the Efficiency Campaign
is to begin it. Get the chart. Its very presence in the society
room will suggest and inspire its use. Its definite presentation
of just the things that will better the society will stimulate the
members to do those things.

"The best result of the efficiency enterprise is the sure projec-
tion of its spirit over into all the church life. Efficient Christian
Endeavor trains the younger church-leaders to expect the
church to be a clearing-house of many and diverse Christian
activities, to be finding new places for service, and to be enlisting the whole membership in action.

"The experience of efficient Christian Endeavor unions leads
toward the co-operation of churches, and points to Christian
union as the inevitable goal. Dr. John R. Mott has been demonstrating that foreign missions can succeed only through
team-work. The same is true of city missions in America.
Efficient Christian Endeavor urges that an efficient Christian
church must be one.

"Christian Endeavor efficiency spreads also into the community Christian enterprise, the service of the kingdom of God.
Local unions may give themselves to definite forms of social
service, as has our Brockton union in Massachusetts. I regard
this as one of the most hopeful new developments in our State
work. The same Christian Endeavor spirit also inspires the
life-work of our best Christian Endeavor graduates, men of
original genius, like George W. Coleman, ex-president of the
Massachusetts union, founder of the Ford Hall meetings, and
the man who as president of the Advertising Clubs of America
has more than any other put high moral purpose into that great
business organization.

"In a word, Christian Endeavor efficiency reaches outward,
embracing in its ideal the whole world for the kingdom of
Christ on earth."

Second Conference. In the second conference the first topic
discussed related to the two-per-cent sections of the Efficiency
Campaign as outlined on the Efficiency Chart. Among the
suggestions made that would be helpful was the introduction
of an information committee consisting of three members, to
read *The Christian Endeavor World* and denominational papers,
and to have five minutes at the opening of each Christian Endeavor prayer meeting to report the progress of Christian
Endeavor and missionary work. Also it was suggested that
this committee be held responsible for the securing and keeping
of the society bulletin-board.

The flower committee's work was discussed, and emphasis
was laid upon the need of securing flowers to be used in deco-

rating the church and prayer-meeting room, these to be used afterward in cheering the sick, the shut-ins, and others that need their cheer, the committee to keep a list of the birthdays of members and others who should be honored by the society.

The good-literature committee in helping to attain the standards counting two per cent is to secure subscriptions to the Christian Endeavor and denominational papers, to gather other papers and magazines, and send them to prisons, hospitals, lumber-camps, poor families, orphanages, and old ladies' homes. The good-literature committee, wherever possible, should also keep a Christian Endeavor literature-rack in every depot in America, well supplied with bright, fresh, up-to-date literature, tracts, etc.

The work of the Sunday-school committee was also discussed, and it was suggested that it might be well to try to lay special emphasis on an endeavor to increase the enrolment and attendance of Sunday-schools. The value of a Christian Endeavor teachers' training-class with three to twenty Endeavorers as members, to study the Sunday-school lesson one week in advance, in order to be ready to substitute, was also thoroughly discussed and approved.

The temperance and Christian-citizenship committee work was thoroughly discussed. It was stated from the floor that this committee should always be known as the temperance and Christian-citizenship committee instead of simply naming it the good-citizenship committee. A reporter for each Christian-citizenship committee was further suggested, in the belief that a worker of this kind on each committee, having opportunity to make a report of five minutes in each Endeavor prayer meeting on the bills pending in State, Provincial, and national legislatures, would be of great help to the committee.

The work of the Junior committee and the honorary members was thoroughly discussed. It was said that in order to make Junior work more effective the Junior committee should assist the Junior superintendent, and that, if there is no Junior society to keep in touch with, then the "big brother and sister" movement should be introduced to help these younger members along in their religious life.

The average life of a boys' club, it was said, is only about eight months. If the results of this work are to be considered, the club must be associated with the church through its Sunday school or Junior Christian Endeavor work. The weakness of the modern and popular boys' club is that usually it eliminates the religious element. Better not have a boys' club at all if Jesus is not to be magnified in it.

The honorary membership in the society was the last thing discussed, and its importance was urged by Dr. Clarence H.

Chain, of Philadelphia, superintendent of Junior work in the Pennsylvania Christian Endeavor Union.

The closing address of this conference was made by Mr. A. J. Shartle, publication-manager of the United Society of Christian Endeavor, Boston, Mass. It was a clever presentation of a most interesting theme entitled "Our Christian Endeavor Arsenal." He made some happy comparisons between the army arsenal and our Christian Endeavor arsenal, and presented a magnificent analysis of the Efficiency Chart, which is here illustrated. Mr. Shartle's address follows:

OUR CHRISTIAN ENDEAVOR ARSENAL.

By A. J. Shartle, Publication-Manager, United Society of Christian Endeavor, Boston, Mass.

When I was informed of my assignment to speak on this subject, I began to think how I could intelligently apply a public establishment for keeping or making arms and munitions of war to our Christian Endeavor army and arsenals so as to meet the greatest need in Christian Endeavor to-day.

While I was thinking about this, it occurred to me that I once heard a man say that he disliked to hear addresses, especially in religious meetings, when couched in terms of war. I remember that he disapproved because of the possibility of infusing too much of the martial spirit into the minds and hearts of the flower of American manhood and womanhood.

I was therefore undecided whether to accept this man's version and ask for a new topic, or to accept the assignment and prove that in order to attain the object for which we are organized it is essential that we have not only an army, but also an arsenal filled with ammunition which, when placed at the disposal of the army, will raise both the standard of efficiency and that sanctioned, righteous, martial spirit so greatly needed in the work of the church.

So I applied the safe old rule never to accept as final the opinion of any man upon a subject of importance before I knew that he knew his subject sufficiently well to express an opinion. Then I began to analyze this man's work, his worth to the church, and his position in life. I found in the final analysis that this man belonged to that class of church-workers frequently compared with the second verse of the twenty-third Psalm, where it reads, "He maketh me to lie down in green pastures."

He was like the Irishman who, when he joined the army and was assigned to his company, was put in the front ranks, only to be in the way. So they put him in the rear ranks the next day. Then they lost him. He lacked that persistent, aggressive, intelligent, Christian martial spirit which impels men to go forward in the face of apparently insurmountable barriers, and do things. He lacked the faith, the fire, the push, the preparation, and prayer so essential to the success of the worker for God. He failed to realize that men, whether in the army of God or that of our country, must not only be alive, but also awake and alert. He was filled with the partial instead of the martial spirit, and his partiality sought refuge in "can't" rather than "can." So he was canned.

Since I am to talk about armies and their arsenals, and now that you know my position on this subject, I wonder how many here present have ever taken time to compare the several armies maintained by various countries with our Christian Endeavor army, the arsenals these governments employ to meet their need, with the Christian Endeavor arsenals employed to meet our need. If you did, have you noticed the striking similarity between both armies and arsenals in their organization, and then the great difference in their purpose and effort to conquer?

The one is organized, trained, and maintained to annihilate the enemy, and at all times, when called upon, to uphold the honor and dignity of the nation.

Christian Endeavor is organized, trained, and maintained to annihilate the ever-present enemy, and to uphold the work of the church by rendering more efficient service.

One will house its members in barracks, where under the direction of efficiency experts recruits are instructed and drilled in the tactics of the army.

Christian Endeavor will house its members in the church, where under the direction of efficiency experts in the society members are taught and trained how to become more useful in the service of God.

One is formed in companies of sixty, with captain and lieutenants.

Christian Endeavor is found in societies of sixty, with president and officers.

The one takes ten companies, and forms a regiment.

Christian Endeavor takes ten societies, and forms a union.

In one it requires many regiments to make a brigade.

In Christian Endeavor every State or Province has a brigade.

The one uses smokeless powder to discharge its missives of death.

Christian Endeavor employs smokeless Endeavorers to discharge its mission of hope.

One uses big guns that are fired to destroy.

Christian Endeavor employs big guns that are fired to save.

The one has arsenals that are filled with ammunition and supplies.

So has Christian Endeavor.

One places its arsenal at the disposal of the army.

So does Christian Endeavor.

The one has arsenals that sometimes explode.

Not so in Christian Endeavor.

The Christian Endeavor arsenal, which is nothing other than the publishing department of the United Society, was established in the city of Boston twenty-five years ago. It was established with a twofold purpose. First, for the general diffusion of knowledge pertaining to the Christian Endeavor movement, through its literature and supplies. Second, for the purpose of making the work of the United Society self-sustaining by using the profits from the sale of Christian Endeavor ammunition.

That the publishing department met the purpose for which it was organized you already know, but in view of the fact that the personnel of Christian Endeavor changes about every six years it may be surprising for you to know that one of the greatest needs in Christian Endeavor to-day is not more money, not more new methods or plans, but rather more knowledge of the things pertaining to Christian Endeavor, especially its literature and supplies, where to get them, their purpose, and their need.

This monumental ignorance on the part of thousands of our present-day Endeavorers is due to the fact that there are too few readers of *The Christian Endeavor World* and that we should have more subscribers. Also, that the older Endeavorers, in passing from the activities of the society to the honorary list have in a measure failed to inform and instruct the Endeavorers of the present day how and where to secure the proper authorized helps and supplies which they from time to time may need.

It is almost heart-rending to meet with Christian Endeavor officers so sincere, yet so densely ignorant and helpless as to the work of their office that they can scarcely be moved unless they are put on roller skates. On the other hand, there are thousands of up-to-date officers so active and well informed that there is no chance for skates. The solution of this problem is "The Officers' Handbook" found on the shelves of our Christian Endeavor arsenal, and sold at thirty-five cents.

I wish it were possible for me to make the point of contact with the many helpless prayer-meeting committees that I might say to them, "Get the book called 'Prayer Meeting Methods,' and be alive." Or to the many lookout committees who are neither looking out or into their society, I would say "Have you ever tried 'On the Lookout'? It will keep you awake, and improve your work."

Some social committees cover a multitude of sins in their failure to provide socials that will entertain. But the biggest sinner on the committee is the chairman, who instead of smiling comes to the social with a face as long as an early-morning breakfast. If I were to appoint a social committee to-day, I would use the most social woman here present to lead the committee. It would be a committee of five with two absent, and in the hands of the remaining three I would place a copy of "Social to Save," "Eighty Pleasant Evenings," and "Social Evenings," the three greatest books on socials in our arsenal.

Many helps might be mentioned that would be a source of information, inspiration, and power to the missionary, Junior, information, Sunday-school, and the host of other committees enlisted in Christian Endeavor; but suffice it to say that one of the most timely books appearing at a moment when thousands of superintendents were at a loss to know what next to do is the new "Intermediate Manual," by Rev. R. P. Anderson, asociate editor of *The Christian Endeavor World,* and that all of the the books here mentioned and hundreds more, covering every phase of Christian Endeavor work, and all the supplies necessary, from pins to wall-pledges, are now on sale at the United Society's official booth in Auditorium Endeavor.

Two years ago, during the great Convention of Christian Endeavor held at Atlantic City, Dr. Clark gave to us as the work for at least the next two years the Efficiency Campaign for societies and unions.

From the very beginning of what has thus far proved to be the greatest work ever introduced by the United Society this campaign was an unbounded success. During these two years thousands of societies have been strengthened. Ten thousand copies of the book "Expert Endeavor" are now being studied by as many Endeavorers, while more than one million Efficiency leaflets are in the hands of societies, from which 1,070 members have thus far graduated as Expert Endeavorers.

Great as this work has been during the past two years and now that it is to be continued indefinitely, there are still many societies that have not introduced it, because they either fail to understand it or consider their society too large or too small to begin.

Let me say that the work of Efficiency will fit any society, regardless of size. The only thing to know is how to begin, what to do, where to get supplies, when to report.

If you should visit our Christian Endeavor arsenal in Boston, you would find rows of small shelves and large projectiles loaded with Efficiency matter ready to be fired at the first command. We are equipped to serve every branch of the Christian Endeavor army at short notice.

The cost of having us serve you is insignificant when compared with the results. If you are alive to your opportunity, and no doubt you are, you will, if you are ready to introduce Efficiency, want to know what the initial cost represents. If your society is a society of fifty members, having eight officers and ten committees with four members on each committee, the initial expense represents the cost of eight officers' leaflets, four by ten, or forty, committee leaflets, plus three of each of the general leaflets for every member in the society, making a total of 198 leaflets, at a cost of one cent each, or $1.98. Add to this $1.00 for the complete Efficiency Wall

Chart, and 50 cents for a copy of "Expert Endeavor"; and you will have the complete outfit for $3.48.

With the expense for Efficiency helps and supplies so insignificant, no society need hesitate to enter this campaign. Efficiency is here to stay because it is needed and covers every phase of the Endeavor work with conveniences, with suggestions, with a practical helpfulness you will want to introduce in your society.

This fact alone should be an incentive to thousands of Endeavorers throughout the country to start things along the lines of Efficiency, because many societies no doubt need to be encouraged to develop both the practical and the spiritual side of Christian Endeavor.

There may be some here who will say: "Our society is too small. We cannot do it." There is no society so small in numbers that it cannot do some of the things suggested in this campaign. No one need introduce all these standards at once. This campaign of Efficiency is not inflexible; but rather it is flexible, and can be adjusted to cover your need, so long as the need is not provided for in the plan.

The plan of how to work the Efficiency Campaign is very comprehensive, and there is nothing that will help the Endeavor society contemplating entering this campaign so much as the leaflet entitled "Standards of Efficiency." This outlines the Efficiency Campaign from beginning to end; but, if there should be some one here to-day who still hesitates to enter the campaign because the society is small in numbers, there need be no hesitancy, in view of the fact that there is nothing to prevent any society from taking up as many standards as the membership will permit, and bringing these standards up to 100 per cent in Efficiency, and holding them for three consecutive months, and then crediting the society on the Efficiency Chart, and dropping them. Other standards can be taken up likewise until finally a small society can attain 100 per cent in Efficiency, although not in one year, but possibly in two years. Even though you should fail to reach the 100 per cent, the fact that you have been striving and making earnest endeavor will reveal its effect in the strength and efficiency of the society.

The society that is ready to introduce the campaign of Efficiency should first of all take an inventory of what has been done in the past and what is being done at present, credit itself for work done, and then take up the most important standards that have not been considered, and introduce them by having each member of the society fully understand what is expected of him.

One of the first things to be considered is "Christian Endeavor Training," Standard No. 1. You will note that it is possible to attain 9 per cent for the fulfilment of this standard alone. While this may seem confused to some who have not considered it thoroughly, yet as a sample I might say that, should your society of twenty-seven members introduce the campaign, then just as soon as three members of this society, or one-ninth of the total membership, have passed the examination on the leaflet pertaining to the work of their offices and the three general leaflets, you are at liberty to credit yourself with 1 per cent, and then just as soon as six members have passed the examination, you credit yourself with 2 per cent, and so on until the entire society has passed the examination on the leaflets pertaining to their work, and you finally reach the 9 per cent. This is simply an illustration to show you how easy it is to accomplish what seems to some Endeavorers a difficult problem.

When we introduced the Efficiency Wall Chart and presented it for the first time to some of the religious leaders of the country, the consensus of opinion was that the chart would prove to be the best thing ever introduced by the United Society of Christian Endeavor. It is very comprehensive. The standards appear in their legitimate order, and any society placing a chart of this kind in its prayer-meeting room and following the plan as outlined will not only be a better society spiritually, but a more efficient society, because it is better prepared to meet the larger work of the church. While it is true that some Endeavorers have said the chart was not sufficiently plain to make it interesting to the average Endeavorer, yet we believe that by giving it careful study before proceeding in the work they will find it very easy to follow.

In order to make it as easy as possible for any society to understand the Efficiency Chart and the entire campaign, I have made an analysis of the chart, and would call your attention to the illustration which you have in hand and also the chart here on the platform. You will find that in the final analysis of the Efficiency Chart one of the stock complaints coming from some societies is that the work cannot be accomplished by a small society, because they do not have a sufficient number of committees. This complaint is entirely unfounded, because you will note that out of the twenty-eight standards, nineteen standards pertain to the work of the society as a society, and that these nineteen standards comprise 76 per cent of the possible 100 per cent to be attained. In order to illustrate, you will find that 7 per cent of the work is in direct charge of the president. This 7 per cent relates to Standard No. 19, "Business Meetings," and Standard No. 28, "The Union." Then we have 22 per cent in charge of the executive committee, which is made up as follows: Standard No. 1, "Christian Endeavor Training," 9 per cent; No. 2, "Executive Committee," 4 per cent; No. 27, "Aiding the Pastor," 3 per cent; No. 22, "Study Course," 3 per cent; No. 17, "Society Finances," 3 per cent, making a total of 22 per cent of the possible 100 per cent, which is work in charge of the executive committee, but to be done by the society as a whole.

In this further work of the society in their attainment of the 76 per cent the prayer-meeting committee will have charge of Standard No. 13, "Original Testimony"; No. 14. "Consecration Meeting"; No. 23, "Private Devotions"; No. 15, "Leaders"; and No. 12, "Public Prayer." The lookout committee will have charge of Standard No. 25, "Associate Members"; No. 26, "Church Services"; No. 21, "Evangelism"; and the social committee will have charge of Standard No. 20, "Socials"; and No. 24, "Honorary Members." The missionary committee will have charge of the Standard No. 18, "Giving," and the music committee of Standard No. 16, "Singing." This is the complete outline of nineteen standards, representing 76 per cent to be attained directly in charge of the committees here mentioned; but the work is distinctly that of the society, and not of the committees.

We now come to the work of the committees; and you will find that the work for, of, and by committees only is Standard No. 4, lookout committee, 4 per cent; No. 5, missionary committee, 4 per cent; No. 6, information committee, 2 per cent; No. 7, flower committee, 2 per cent; No. 3, prayer-meeting committee, 4 per cent; No. 11, Junior committee, 2 per cent; No. 9, Sunday-school committee, 2 per cent; No. 8, good-literature committee, 2 per cent; No. 10, temperance or citizenship committee, 2 per cent; making a total of nine standards as the work of the committees, with a total of 24 per cent of the possible 100 per cent to be attained. This makes it very evident that the largest part of the work rests upon the society as a society, and not upon the committees. You will therefore note that it is possible not only for a large society, but also for a small society, to accomplish the things here outlined.

I would, however, remind you, whether you have already introduced this campaign or not, that the society who would travel the highway to Christian Endeavor success, especially in this campaign of Efficiency, will find it macadamized with consecration, with sacrifice, with service, with plans, with prayer, grit, and sand; and that no society can expect to accomplish this great work for the Master without applying five of the big things in Christian Endeavor that begin with the letter P. They are Preparation, Plans, Push, Power, and Prayer. There cannot be thorough preparation for any department of this work unless there are efficient plans, and there cannot be efficient plans unless there is thorough preparation, and I pity the society or union who will enter this campaign and endeavor to push it without that power which can be gained only by persistent prayer.

During the Civil War one of the generals, rushing up to an officer in command of a regiment, said to him "Colonel, will you take that fort on the end hill?" and the colonel said, "I will try." The general again repeated, "Will you take that fort?" and the reply was, "I will do my best." When for the third time the question was asked, "Will you take that fort?" the colonel's reply came, "I will"; and he did. I am now asking you, "Will you introduce the Efficiency Campaign in your society when you reach your home if you have not already done so?" and the only answer I expect from you is, "I will."

It was General Phil Sheridan who in one of his battles, when he saw victory was coming his way, in his dashing fashion rode up in front of his army and shouted, "Let everybody go in, bands of music, infantry, cavalry, everybody"; and we to-day say to you, "Let everybody enter into this great campaign of Efficiency—Junior societies, Young People's societies, Senior societies, Mothers' societies, Floating societies, unions, everybody." And in the language of our sainted Frances E. Willard we would say that by and through Christ's dear grace there shall come out of this great campaign a better and more spiritual home and a redeemed republic in Christ's dear name.

Can you, therefore, remain content with the work you have been doing, or with the one or two committee ideas, when you can now secure in order to help you the brains and experience of experts? Can you afford to wonder and blunder and worry and work over problems that have been solved long ago, when you can buy their proved solutions in leaflet and book form at a cost that will prove the best investment you have ever made?

Just think what all this means to the ambitious Endeavorer or society. It means that now and for the first time you have at your disposal the crystallized experience of world-wide Endeavor. It means that what every Christian Endeavorer used to have to find out for himself he can now find out through the Efficiency Campaign literature. It means that with a minimum of effort and expense you can now eliminate from the work of your society the uncertainties, the guesswork, and the things that are neither applicable nor practicable.

Do you realize how great a help this will be to societies that have been struggling with problems in the past that seemed impossible to solve? Many societies in their attempt to find a way unaided have failed, due to the fact that the proper helps perhaps were lacking, and willing workers remained untrained.

You have my message. It is now up to you to act. You belong to the greatest organization of young people ever enlisted under the banner of Christ. You have splendid opportunities for advancement. We have the greatest army of young people known anywhere, now numbering 3,500,000. You have at your disposal an arsenal that is filled with things that make for a higher standard of efficiency in Christian Endeavor and the larger work of the church.

This arsenal is maintained for your benefit, and is the only financial support of the United Society of Christian Endeavor. Should you by withdrawing your patronage make it possible that there would be no arsenal of this kind, then there could be no United Society of Christian Endeavor; but, as you leave this convention and go to your homes, there to meet the stern realities of life, especially those of you who are out on the firing line of Christian Endeavor, rest assured that there never was a time in the history of this great world-wide movement when there was such a deep undercurrent of religious effort by Christian Endeavorers everywhere as there is to-day. Christian Endeavor lives; Christian Endeavor moves; and it is great to belong to this movement; and to-day, after more than thirty-two years of practical experience in church-work, Christian Endeavor is making its presence felt everywhere. From the intelligent American citizen with the Christian Endeavor pin on the lapel of his coat to the dark-brown African Zulu, with scarcely enough clothing on his body to put on a pin without drawing blood, there is a mighty host of Endeavorers going forward, vitalizing, energizing, Christianizing, evangelizing, all nations of the earth regardless of color or tongue, longitude or latitude.

Yes, Christian Endeavor lives. You are a part of it. Will you do your best, and work and live for it?

Third Conference. The final conference on efficiency related to the missionary work of the society, and brought out many very helpful suggestions of practical value. The lookout committee, through which seventeen per cent may be earned in the Efficiency Campaign, was first discussed. It was said that we must remember it is more important that we win ten or even five young people to Jesus Christ and into the membership of the society, and hold them, than to get one hundred or fifty through contests, schemes, etc. Personal work is the only successful way to get new members. Evangelism must have a greater emphasis in all our work.

The prayer-meeting committee can earn twenty-seven per cent of the one hundred per cent in this campaign, first, by keeping the prayer meeting strong and vital. A real prayer meeting of six earnest souls is worth while. There is power in prayer. Prayer meetings should be planned, and the young people should be taught to pray. Use the "big brother and big sister" idea in developing beginners in the matter of prayer-meeting participation.

The Quiet Hour offers wonderful opportunities for real personal spiritual growth.

The campaign as applied to Junior societies was explained and urged.

The closing address to this conference was given by Rev. W. A. Jones, D.D., of Pittsburg, Penn., president of the Pennsylvania Christian Endeavor Union. It was a strong plea to Christian Endeavorers to take up and push hard this great Efficiency Campaign. Dr. Jones's address follows:

We are now at the close of a series of most remarkable conferences on the Christian Endeavor Efficiency plans, remarkable not only from the material presented by our leader, but also from the large and increasing attendance and interest each day.

The churches in which these conferences have been held have been crowded, and the interest manifested by the hundreds who took part indicates the hold Efficiency has taken upon Endeavorers everywhere.

Your speaker sustains no special reputation as an expert on this subject, but, having been an active member of the same Christian Endeavor society for twenty-four years, and in that time never being absent from a meeting without an excuse he could conscientiously give his Master, and having in the membership of that society twenty-four expert Endeavorers, he may be able to say something of practical help to the Endeavorers here from all parts of the world, anxious to promote the great cause of Christian Endeavor through these Efficiency plans.

We can testify to-day with hundreds of other pastors that where these plans, or any portion of them, have been worked by a society with the end in view of keeping their spirit and purpose—the training of the youth for permanent service for Christ and the church, there have come to both the Endeavorer and the church new interest and a new zeal for the cause of Christ.

Some of our pastors have complained in years past that our organization has not been efficient. We admit that we have wasted time and energy and opportunity, but not more so than the average church organization. I am a pastor, knowing the burdens of the ministry, and would not criticise; but my experience has led me to the conviction, and I speak it out boldly, that, if more of our pastors would give the young people's organization their hearty and sympathetic support, their burdens would be fewer, and their church-work would be more easily performed. Personally I have tested it, and know whereof I speak. Christian Endeavor points proudly to a record of efficiency in service which has attracted the attention and commanded the admiration of the Christian world.

Mr. Lehmann has put the emphasis in the right place. The Efficiency plans will not work unless we work them to the glory of God through the development and strengthening of character in training for service. The purpose is not to lift the mercury by pasting on a few stars. These things follow when careful, skilful, consecrated workers lead us slowly step by step from one degree of Efficiency to another in the various activities and departments of Christian Endeavor work.

We know a society that reached a high per cent by a sort of mechanical movement, only to fall back in a few weeks to a condition almost disastrous. And we know a society which by careful study, consecrated leadership, and determined effort has trained its members into an efficient organization of helpful workers upon which the pastor and the church can lean permanently.

May the blessing of God continue to rest on these plans, and may our young people increase more and more in the service of their Master till the results of their enthusiasm and devotion shall attract the world, even as it was attracted by the devotion of the early disciples when men said, "These men have been with Jesus."

CHAPTER X.

DENOMINATIONAL RALLIES.

O NE of the special features at all International Christian Endeavor Conventions is the denominational rallies. These denominational rallies are always a delight to the delegates, and have been very largely attended in the past; but hardly ever have there been such overflow gatherings as those at Los Angeles. The meetings were held in the afternoon Thursday, July 10, and the streets leading to the twoscore churches where the various groups were together were filled with bands of young people clad in garments as bright as California's golden sunshine. By the hour appointed the churches were all packed to the doors, and in many cases hundreds had to stand. The denominational feature at this particular Convention will always remain as a pleasant memory in the minds of those who attended these wonderful gatherings.

Baptist Rally—First Baptist Church.

At the Baptist rally Pastor C. M. Carter of the First Baptist Church, Los Angeles, called the meeting to order, spoke a few words of welcome, and introduced the presiding officer, Dr. Samuel Zane Batten, of Philadelphia, who delivered a thoughtful and rousing talk on "The Young People's Movement." Field Editor Arthur Leonard Wardsworth, of South Pasadena, was elected secretary. Pastor L. T. Barkman of the Bethel Church led the song service. Percy S. Foster of Washington, D. C., brought a very happy message, and led the audience in singing "Blest be the tie that binds," and accompanied his daughter in singing a beautiful song entitled "The Name of Jesus." Rev. W. T. Johnson, D.D., of the First African Baptist Church, Richmond, Va., spoke on "The Christian's Horizon." Rev. George E. Burlingame, of the First Baptist Church, San Francisco, delivered an address on "The Life of Service"; and Rev. Frank M. Goodchild, of the Central Baptist Church, New York City, delivered an address on "The Changed Attitude of the Churches Toward the Young People."

Allen Endeavor and Varick League Rally—African Methodist Episcopal Church.

The rally of the Allen Christian Endeavor Leagues and Varick Christian Endeavor societies was held in the First African

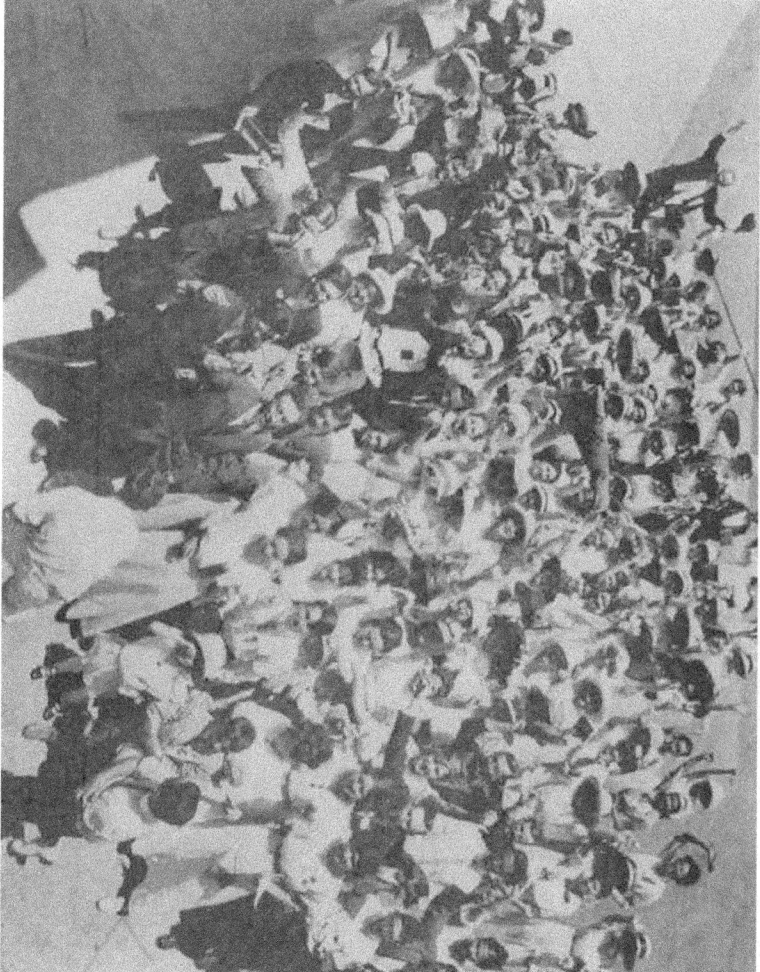

A. C. E. RAH RAH CROWD

Methodist Episcopal Church, and was led by Bishop Alexander Walters. The church was beautifully decorated; the music was splendid; and the spirit of gratitude to God for all blessings animated every heart. Other features of this denominational and young people's meeting were a strong feeling of enthusiasm for Christian Endeavor, the spirit of brotherly love, loyalty to the church, gratitude to the Giver of all good things—Christian Endeavor one of the greatest.

Splendid addresses were delivered by Rev. Julian C. Caldwell, D.D., and Bishop Walters. An address of welcome was delivered by the pastor of the church, Rev. J. Jesse Peck, D.D., and Rev. Mr. Kinchion. There were a number of white Christian Endeavor friends present, who were cordially received and enjoyed the meeting.

In behalf of the thousands of colored Endeavorers in the South who could not attend the Convention, especially coming from so great a distance, Miss Grace A. Townsend, secretary of the Florida Christian Endeavor Union, brought greetings.

General Secretary Julian C. Caldwell read statistics showing the rapid growth of colored Endeavorers in his and other denominations. There was great rejoicing over the good news that Christian Endeavor seemed to be a blessed and vital power in the hearts of those present.

Greetings were brought by Mr. Leonard Merrill, chairman of the Los Angeles Convention Committee; Mr. H. N. Lathrop, treasurer of the United Society of Christian Endeavor, Boston; Mrs. Lucy I. Dinsmore, of Maine; Mr. Walter L. Jaeger, of Colorado; Rev. H. H. Rottmann, of Oregon; Mr. E. P. Gates, of Illinois; and Rev. Harrie R. Chamberlin, of Massachusetts. Greetings were sent to the Baptist Young People's Union of America, then in session in Brooklyn, N. Y.

The registration of delegates at the rally represented twenty States, also delegates from Nova Scotia, New Brunswick, and British Columbia.

Brethren Rally—First Brethren Church.

It was the unanimous opinion of the young people of the Brethren Church that this particular denominational rally was the best held in many years at an International Convention of Christian Endeavor. The First Brethren Church was filled with interested, enthusiastic Endeavorers, and the splendid programme prepared in advance was rendered to the satisfaction and delight of everybody present.

Rev. J. A. Garber, the national president, sent a message outlining for the coming year plans for advance in Junior and Intermediate work, missions, tithing, temperance, and citizenship; and the meeting unanimously approved the plan.

Rev. G. C. Carpenter, the national secretary, presided. Among the speakers were Dr. C. A. Bane, Rev. T. H. Broad, Rev. Mark Early, Rev. A. V. Kimmel, and Rev. L. S. Bauman. Mission work that the Christian Endeavor societies are doing among the mountain people of Kentucky received special attention. The local Endeavorers furnished the dinner to all delegates present at the close of the service, and this was followed by a pleasant social hour.

Congregational Rally—First Congregational Church.

It seemed to be the opinion of all present at the Congregational rally that this particular rally was not only one of the best of their denomination, but the best ever held at an International Christian Endeavor Convention. Rev. Charles M. Sheldon, D.D., author of "In His Steps," presided; and the programme was filled with short, pointed addresses, all seeking to stimulate the best that Congregationalism contains. President Henry Churchill King, of Oberlin, spoke on "Training Congregational Leaders"; and Rev. George F. Kenngott, Ph.D., who had just come from Massachusetts to make his home in Los Angeles, gave the address of welcome. Rev. A. B. Patten, of Sacramento, spoke on "Our Response to the Challenge of Present-Day Conditions," and Rev. J. P. Huget, of Detroit, Mich., on "Our Missionary Responsibility."

Christian Endeavor presidents and secretaries representing the States of Iowa, Ohio, Washington, California, and Wisconsin, and Japan packed great inspiration into a five-minute allowance of time. Dr. Clark and his youngest son, Sydney A. Clark, concluded the programme. Dr. Clark told the story of Congregationalism in many lands, and his son Sydney spoke on "The Importance of Junior Christian Endeavor." Splendid music was rendered by the Hawaiian delegates. Rev. William Horace Day, D.D., the pastor of the church, offered the closing prayer and benediction.

The great church was filled to the doors, and the rally was marked by the strong spirit of Christian unity and enthusiasm.

The Canadian Presbyterian Rally—Plymouth Congregational Church.

The Canadian Presbyterian young people and their friends held a splendid rally in Plymouth Congregational Church, presided over by Rev. S. A. Martin, of Winnipeg. After the devotional service the roll was called, and responses were received from Prince Edward Island, Nova Scotia, New Brunswick, Quebec, Ontario, and Manitoba. Mr. Martin spoke briefly on "The Condition of the Young People's Societies in the Dominion." He strongly urged a consecrated effort on all sides to develop the work of Christian Endeavor among the young people.

Miss E. Hall, of Montreal, gave a splendid report of her recent campaign, which was very encouraging. Rev. William Patterson, D.D., of Belfast, Ireland, gave an inspiring address on "Christian Endeavor in Canada." He spoke of his first society, which very shortly after its organization was the largest in the world, having more than six hundred members. He also drew attention to the number of Canadian people who had gone to mission fields through the influence of Christian Endeavor.

Hon. J. A. Macdonald, editor of the Toronto *Globe,* in speaking of the foreign element that is pouring into our country every day, pointed out that the only way in which this problem can be properly met would be to have every pastor, every elder, every member of the church, and every member of the young people's society trained and ready for service. He said: "The greatness of life is a service to others. We must give ourselves for service, and go back to our society inspired to serve. Put this work of service with the work we have to do, and it will be the secret of our success."

Mrs. J. A. Macdonald in a short address dwelt particularly on the work of the Women's Home Missionary Society among the children in the Tuelon Mission School. This splendid rally closed with the hymn "Blest be the tie that binds."

Christian (Disciples of Christ) Rally—First Christian Church.

The rally of the Disciples of Christ was held in the First Christian Church, Rev. Claude E. Hill, D.D., national superintendent of young people's work, presiding. Both the church auditorium and the Sunday-school room were filled to overflowing. Stirring talks were made by Rev. H. C. Kendrick and Rev. S. J. Buckner. Rev. P. J. Rice, D.D., of El Paso, Tex., addressed the gathering on "First Principles of Christian Endeavor," dwelling on three fundamentals—the pledge, the prayer meeting, and committee work. He said the three principles which centre in these three particulars are loyalty, expression, and training.

Rev. Russell H. Thrapp, pastor of the church, described an ideal Christian Endeavorer, using Paul as an example. Pledges were taken to help the work of Christian Endeavor extension among the Disciples.

The rally was perhaps the largest in point of numbers that the Disciples have had for many years, and the spirit of interest and enthusiasm was very gratifying.

During the rally it was announced that a very considerable

majority of the Los Angeles local officers and Convention chairmen were members of the local Christian church, and a number of them were introduced and brought greetings.

Friends' Rally—Friends' Meeting-House.

The Friends' rally was very largely attended, and was of the enthusiastic kind. Mr. Ashton Otis presided; and the Rev. Wallace E. Gill, resident pastor, conducted the singing. The theme of the rally was, "As ye have received Christ Jesus, the Lord, so walk ye in him." Delegates were present from Indiana, Iowa, Kansas, California, New York, Nebraska, Oregon, and Ohio. Invitations were extended from Pasadena and Whittier to the delegates to visit these places.

Rev. Robert E. Pretlow, of Seattle, Wash., spoke on "Young Friends and Christian Endeavor." He showed how beneficial the Christian Endeavor movement has been to the Friends in their work.

A beautiful solo was rendered by Clifford Smith, entitled, "He Careth for Me."

Thomas Neulin, president of Whittier College, made a telling speech on "The Church and Social Problems." He said: "The Christian church came not to be ministered unto, but to minister. The church must concern itself with economic problems. Does the church care for the housing and the homes of the laborers and workers of the country? The workers and the children must be thought of. Recreations and means of pleasure must be provided for the boys and girls. The whole problem calls for the union of all our forces to go forward and adapt our methods to the needs of the times. Never was there a better opportunity than to-day in California.

Several returned missionaries were present. They all were Endeavorers. Testimonies were given by Miss May White, a missionary from Jamaica, Miss Edna Chilson, from East Africa, Miss Esther Smith, from Guatemala. Mrs. Ashton Otis sang "Who Will Go and Tell Them the Story?" Mr. Thomas Elliot from the Young Men's Christian Association of Hongkong, China, developed in an interesting way the subject of "Christian Service. Whom do we serve? What are the essential qualifications?"

Lutheran Rally—First English Lutheran Church.

A practical feature of the large Lutheran rally was an offering taken to help to buy an automobile for a missionary physician in India. President R. B. Peery, Ph.D., president of the Lutheran Christian Endeavor Union, presided over this enthusiastic rally. Besides strong, spiritual addresses there was a helpful discussion on the topic, "What Lutheran Young People

Can Do for the Kingdom." It was the unanimous sentiment of all present that the time has come for an advance movement among the young people in the church, and that the young people are the ones to make it. The tendency of the Lutheran Church to stand aloof from such interdenominational religious work was deplored, and the need of an active participation in it was urged upon all. The splendid opportunities offered the old mother church of the Reformation in the great State of California were brought out and impressed upon the audience, and the need of more aggressive work there was emphasized.

One of the delightful features of the rally was the presence of Dr. Nelander, president of the Swedish Lutheran League of California. In a most pleasing manner he brought the hearty greeting of that body, which is a distinctive young people's society of the Lutheran Church.

The meeting was productive, not only of mutual acquaintance and good fellowship, but also of greater devotion to the cause of Christ and Christian Endeavor.

Methodist Rally—First Methodist Episcopal Church.

The Methodist rally resembled in some respects an old-fashioned love-feast with hand-shaking and good fellowship. Mr. H. Gordon Lilley, president of the Manitoba Christian Endeavor Union, led the meeting. The audience was composed of Methodists from every point in Canada, England, Mexico, and the United States. Mr. Lilly introduced Rev. C. T. Scott, of Victoria, B. C., who gave a stirring address on "The Needs of the Present Day," speaking of the proposed union of the three great Protestant churches of Canada, and the part that the young people's movement had in furthering this project. Rev. Mr. Scott deprecated the trend of the time toward entertainments and pleasure of the light kind, holding out to the young people the higher ideal of work for Christ and the church.

Mr. W. J. Shortt, president of the British Columbia Christian Endeavor Union, spoke on "Christian Endeavor as a Means of Building Character and Advancing Civilization." The feeling of the delegates present seemed to be for the extension of Christian fellowship, and the meeting was thrown open for testimonies and suggestions as to what might be done to secure more co-operation with the other denominations. Many responded. All expressed the desire to have all Methodist young people's societies in the Christian Endeavor fellowship.

In drawing the net the leader of the meeting suggested that all arm themselves with the knowledge of the true principles of Christian Endeavor and go forth prepared to speak of its objects and possibilities.

Seventh-Day Baptist Rally—Seventh-Day Baptist Church.

A very profitable and enjoyable rally was held in the Seventh-Day Baptist Church. The delegates present were chiefly from young people's societies in Southern California. The Rev. William L. Burdick, of Alfred, N. Y., led the meeting. A short devotional service was held, after which Mrs. G. E. Osborn presented a fine paper on "The Spirit of Christian Endeavor." Rev. G. W. Hills urged the Christian Endeavorers to consecrate their lives to the service of Christ. Rev. Mr. Burdick in his address set forth the value of Christian Endeavor and the good that should be sought in all subsequent conventions, and considered some phases of the work of the kingdom of Christ that particularly concern the Seventh-Day Baptists.

After the addresses there was an open parliament in which questions were asked and impromptu addresses given. The rally closed with a feeling that it was good to have been there.

Southern Presbyterian Rally—Central Presbyterian Church.

The Southern Presbyterians had two rallies; first, one of their own; and then, immediately following their own, a joint rally with the United Presbyterians, with which church the Southern Presbyterians are now considering union. In this second rally they were warmly received.

At the first rally Rev. G. W. Benn, former Christian Endeavor president for Texas, gave an inspiring account of what Christian Endeavor is accomplishing in the churches. Among other things Rev. Mr. Benn said that Christian Endeavor is making rapid progress in the Southern Presbyterian Church in the Southwest, giving examples of the fine work being done by societies in some of the largest congregations of the denomination in Texas, which have come into the Christian Endeavor fellowship within the last year or two. The Efficiency Campaign has proved especially helpful.

Dr. A. L. Phillips, secretary of young people's work in the Southern Presbyterian Church, followed with a very helpful address. He called attention to the fact that Christian Endeavor had received the official sanction of the Assembly of the church, and suggested that societies should well be called "Westminster Leagues of Christian Endeavor."

The closing address was by Mr. E. M. Stewart, of Welsh, La., who spoke particularly of the need of evangelistic home-mission work in his State and of the fine service that Christian Endeavor renders in this respect.

After these addresses the meeting adjourned to the United Presbyterian rally to meet with the representatives of that church. They met with a very cordial reception. The same speakers were called upon to express themselves there, and did so in words of brotherly fellowship. The brethren responded in a very delightful manner, and messages brought were thoroughly enjoyed.

Reformed Churches Rally.

The rally of the young people of the Reformed Church in the United States and the Reformed Church in America was a well-attended gathering of young people coming together for mutual benefit, for the renewing of old acquaintanceships, the making of new friends, and to cement further that bond of Christian fellowship and mutual helpfulness that exists between the young people of the two branches of the Reformed Church. Delegates were present from Ohio, Indiana, Maryland, New Jersey, New York, Pennsylvania, Massachusetts, and California. The meeting was held under the dual leadership of Rev. Joseph T. Hogan, of New Brunswick, N. J., and Mr. A. J. Shartle, of Boston, Mass.

After a very helpful and spirited song service, which was followed by consecration and prayer, short, inspiring addresses were delivered by Rev. D. E. Tobias, West Salem, O.; Rev. J. W. Barber, Lindsay, O.; Rev. E. E. Young, Wooster, O.; Rev. J. T. Hogan, New Brunswick, N. J.; Rev. A. P. Steinebrey, Los Angeles, Cal.; and Mr. A. J. Shartle, Boston, Mass., on the subject of "Church Extension, Church Loyalty, and Society Affiliation."

The open meeting, with its free discussion from the floor, in which a number participated, was both helpful and inspiring. It was unanimously agreed to suggest through the proper representatives to the respective synods the need for more aggressive departmental young people's work and the affiliation of more young people's societies with Christian Endeavor as a means of increasing the standard of efficiency in the larger work of the church.

At the close of the rally there was held an informal reception such as can be held only by those who are young in years and spirit, three thousand miles from home, and members of one big Reformed family.

The Presbyterian Rally.

More than 1,800 Presbyterian Endeavorers filled the church to overflowing. Dr. Lapsley A. McAfee, pastoral counsellor of the California Christian Endeavor Union, presided. No fewer than six State presidents who are Presbyterians brought greetings. Dr. John Willis Baer, president of Occidental College, made an eloquent plea for loyalty to the cross, the blood of Christ, and the Bible, while Rev. John Balcom Shaw, D.D., who is soon to take the pastorate of a Los Angeles church, pleaded for more enthusiastic soul-winning. Field Secretary Lehmann spoke on loyalty to denominational work, and Dr. Ira Landrith gave a clarion-call for service to Christ.

The Mennonite Rally.

The Menonnite rally was held in the mission on San Fernando Street. The hall was crowded with delegates and visitors, most of them from California, but representing many States where they had their former homes.

A fine talk was made by Rev. H. J. Krehbiel, of Reedley, Cal., on "Opportunities"; and Rev. E. F. Grubb read a paper sent by Rev. N. B. Grubb, of Philadelphia, one of the United Society's trustees, on "Why the Church Should Welcome Christian Endeavor into Its Midst." Rev. J. C. Mehl told about the preliminary steps toward the founding of the mission in Los Angeles, and the general theme of other speakers was the thought of closer fellowship one with another.

The United Evangelical Rally.

The United Evangelical rally was significant because of the fact that a resolution presented by Dr. Charles C. Poling, of Portland, Or., declaring for the organic union of the Evangelical Association and the United Evangelical churches, was enthusiastically carried. Rev. Charles Stauffacher and Rev. Stanley B. Vandersall, manager of *The Ohio Endeavorer*, were the speakers. Superintendent Daniel A. Poling led the rally, which was followed by a half-hour of delightful fellowship.

The United Presbyterian Rally.

The United Presbyterian rally was held in the First United Presbyterian Church, and was a great success.

Every congregation of Los Angeles Presbytery was represented, and seven States, as far east as Pennsylvania and West Virginia, answered the roll-call. Both the Reformed and the Southern Presbyterian churches were also represented. Brief and stirring addresses were made. Supper was served to about three hundred persons, and a delightful social time was enjoyed.

STATE HEADQUARTERS, FIESTA PARK

A CANADIAN GROUP, PART OF A DELEGATION OF 200
By the kindness of the Los Angeles "Examiner"

CHAPTER XI.

FRESH-AIR AND HOSPITAL CONFERENCE, FIRST UNITED BRETHREN CHURCH.

THE hospital conference was held as scheduled, with Miss Clara P. Hassler, California State superintendent, in charge. No representatives of this work outside the State of California were present. The first hour of the conference was given over to the reports of the county and district superintendents of California, who brought greetings from their respective counties and told of work being done by their unions.

At half past ten o'clock the conference adjourned to the main auditorium of the church, where the chief addresses of the conference were given. In introducing the first speaker Miss Hassler explained that the work of the Los Angeles County Hospital committee is very definitely organized, and suggested the theme of the speaker's remarks, Hospital Organization.

Mrs. E. R. Hudson, superintendent of hospital work for Los Angeles County and city unions, made the first address, in the course of which she gave a brief outline of the organization of the work there, as follows:

The work done is confined entirely to the county hospital, demanding the entire attention of the workers. There are three distinct departments of the hospital work, the evangelistic or chapel work, the library work, and the benevolent work, under the direct supervision of the superintendent. The entire work is under the supervision of a board of directors, consisting of the pastoral counsellors of the city and county unions, the presidents of the county and city unions, two members at large from the county, and three from the city.

The superintendent is in touch with the work done in all three departments, and is to a great degree responsible for it. She gains the co-operation and interest of the different societies through a hospital committee composed of the chairmen of those committees in the individual societies, and by furnishing speakers at rallies, conventions, and other meetings of that character. Slides are used so that the lectures given are made intensely interesting and instructive in the matter of hospital service.

Some of the results of the unceasing and prayerful efforts

of the workers have been seen in the last two years in the form
of a splendid $12,000 Christian Endeavor Memorial Chapel,
dedicated a year ago, and the new library building, now in
construction.

The benevolent work is under the direct supervision of the
superintendent, and is varied to meet the individual needs of
different cases. Contributions to this work are entirely voluntary, and come in from individuals interested in it, Christian
Endeavor societies and unions, and other organizations.
However, the supply is never so large as the demand. At
Christmas time and New Year's there are always large donations of food, clothing, and other things, which are given out
at once whenever the need seems greatest. There is very little
miscellaneous distribution, as in nearly every case personal
investigation precedes the gift, which is made in as personal
way as is possible.

Following this Mrs. Gardner told about the library.

The library department has grown steadily since its initial
appearance five years ago in one end of a hall, until now there
is in construction a fine library building, the lower floor of
which will be used for entertainments, etc., and the second
floor for reading-rooms, while the rest of the building will be
devoted to the nurses' dormitory. Both this and the chapel
are due to the instrumentality of Christian Endeavor. The
library is stocked with carefully selected books, some of which
are donations from individuals or societies, while others are
obtained from the public library after being discarded there,
mended by two or three workers who give one day a week to
this business, and put into circulation at the hospital library. A
paid librarian has charge of the work. Branch libraries are
established in the tubercular ward, the surgical, contagious,
children's, and lepers' wards.

The evangelistic work is by far the most extensive work
done in the hospital, and the burden of it will be realized in
some degree when it is known that literally thousands of people
pass through the hospital every year, and efforts are put forth
to reach every one of them to bring them into personal relationship with Christ. Regular chapel services of song, testimony,
and short talks are held every Sunday afternoon, and are in
charge of the different Christian Endeavor societies. Song
services are held in front of the tubercular ward also, and personal workers go among the patients that are confined to their
beds. Wednesday evenings Bible classes are conducted by
trained workers, and Thursday night is prayer-meeting night.
A large part of the chaplain's work consists in giving advice,
help, and encouragement to scores of people through correspondence after they leave the hospital, and the larger part of
the day is spent in going about through the wards, talking

personally to the patients there, and seeking before all else to win them for Jesus Christ. A Chinese pastor visits the hospital regularly, as do also a Christian Jewess, a German, a Mexican, and workers of other nationalities, who are wonderfully successful in soul-winning because of their ability to speak to men in their own language, thus appealing in a way such as no one of another nationality is able to do. Scores of souls are won in this way, and in almost every case it is found that those who accept Christ in the hospital leave it to win others.

The Fresh-Air Movement.

Mr. Payne, of Brooklyn, N. Y., addressed the conference on the subject of the Fresh-Air movement in that city, telling briefly of the need and method of the work done.

The demand for this work lies in the fact that so many children are housed in congested tenement-houses, where unsanitary conditions make healthy bodies, clean minds, and happy hearts impossible. The need for a place where children could be taken for a few weeks during the heat of the summer months inspired the Endeavorers of Brooklyn several years ago to buy a large place on Long Island, where comfortable quarters for housing thirty or forty children at a time are now established. The land and improvements are now valued at about six thousand dollars, and belong to the Endeavorers of Brooklyn, who have paid for it to within a few hundred dollars. That these outings given to the children are conducive not merely to sound minds and bodies, but to an awakening of interest in Jesus Christ, is proved by the many instances of children's returning home and leading their parents into the church.

The financial end of this work is handled in practically the same way as the hospital work of California, all contributions being voluntary, while lectures are given to awaken interest in the camp and its purpose, this being furthered by occasional trips on the part of different Endeavorers for week-ends and holidays.

Mr. Payne's address closed the conference.

(It will be found in the "Chapter of Addresses.")

THE CHRISTIAN-CITIZENSHIP CONFERENCES.

First United Presbyterian Church.

Daniel A. Poling, National Superintendent of Temperance and Christian Citizenship of the United Society of Christian Endeavor, Leader.

The first Christian citizenship conference of the Convention was largely attended on Friday morning, July 11, the auditorium of the First United Presbyterian Church being filled. Under the head of "Community Evils" the discussions were most interesting and widely representative of the practical activities of Christian Endeavor in municipal and general reforms. Among those who spoke were Dr. Samuel Zane Batten, of Philadelphia, secretary of the department of Social Service and Brotherhood for the American Baptist Publication Society; Dr. George F. Burlingame, of San Francisco; Dr. D. M. Gardner, legislative superintendent of the Anti-Saloon League; and President Fisher, of the Colorado Christian Endeavor Union.

Civic indifference was unanimously named as the supreme difficulty in the way of civic, industrial, and political reform. Rev. G. W. Benn, president of the Texas Christian Endeavor Union, delivered the closing address. He sounded the note of high spiritual motive, and placed emphasis on the recognition of Jesus Christ as the pre-eminent leader in all reform.

The closing Christian-citizenship conference, on Saturday morning, was epoch-marking in that it enthusiastically approved the proposed programme of the new department of temperance and Christian citizenship. Resolutions were passed commending the legislature and the governor of California on the passage of the "red-light" abatement and injunction bill, and expressing confidence in the defeat of the corrupt interests of the State in their effort to defeat the measure by a referendum vote.

Among those who participated in the discussion were Dr. Charles C. Poling, of Portland, Or.; President Benn, of Texas; Rev. Mr. Beeman, of Indiana; and Dr. Batten, of Philadelphia.

The climax of the conference was reached in the address of Rev. P. J. Rice, of El Paso, Tex., who spoke eloquently on the "Requisites for the New Christian-Citizenship Leadership." These requisites he named as follows: First, an absolutely clean life; second, an intelligent grasp of the whole situation; third, a thoroughly aroused interest; fourth, a militant challenge; fifth, the spiritual objective. The policy for the next two years, which was presented by the national superintendent, and which received the unanimous approval of those present, is as follows:

"In harmony with the Atlantic City resolution of two years ago, 'A Saloonless Nation by 1920, the three-hundredth year from the landing of the Pilgrims at Plymouth,' and as the next step toward that great consummation, we declare for national prohibition, an amendment to the Constitution of the United States.

"Because out of past bitter defeats we have come to realize the vital mistake of intrusting good laws to unfriendly and uncommitted administration we declare for the election to office everywhere in the nation of political candidates and administrations outspokenly committed to the enforcement of existing laws and to the destruction of the liquor traffic, we unite for the ushering in of the day when by all political parties the liquor problem shall be recognized as, and so declared, the supreme and immediately vital issue before the American people.

A United Temperance Movement.

"With enthusiasm we indorse the movement for a national convention of all the temperance forces of the country, to be held in Columbus, O., November 14, this year. To the council of one hundred temperance leaders soon to make public the call for this epoch-marking convention we pledge our hearty support and unswerving co-operation. We are profoundly convinced that the hour has arrived when, without prejudice to, or interference with, the fundamental principles and policies of any particular temperance organization, all temperance organizations should unite upon a comprehensive, nation-wide programme of education and extermination.

Good-Citizenship Day.

"We reaffirm our indorsement of Good-Citizenship Day, the Sunday immediately preceding the Fourth of July. We call upon our young people to make this day truly a national institution. Let it command pulpit, prayer meeting, press, patriotic and fraternal organizations, until the united voice of a free people shall lift to high heaven a tocsin for peace, brotherhood, Christian citizenship, and freedom from rum. We request the department of temperance and Christian citizenship to prepare a suitable programme for the use of Christian Endeavor societies on Good-Citizenship Day, and to suggest such plans for the observance of the day as will make it an occasion of uplift and practical inspiration.

Policy and Programme of the New Department of Temperance and Christian Citizenship.

"We recommend the following as the policy and programme of the new department of temperance and Christian citizenship, and call upon all local societies and unions to actively co-operate for its universal adoption.

"1. The preparation of a series of twelve leaflets on the nature of alcohol, and the relation of the liquor traffic to industrial, social, and political conditions, for the use of Christian Endeavor societies and unions. These leaflets, with suggestions for their use, to be prepared by the editorial secretary and the temperance superintendent of the United Society of Christian Endeavor.

"2. Publicity and Education Campaign; the distribution of temperance literature; the placing of temperance posters in public places; the attractive presentation everywhere of the known facts concerning alcohol and the organized liquor traffic, along the lines laid down from time to time by the temperance and Christian-citizenship department; the holding of temperance mass-meetings in the great centres of population, addressed by the recognized Christian-citizenship leaders of the nation; the instruction of the young people in the principles and obligations of Christian citizenship; the creation of libraries of social service and political reform.

"3. The co-operation and active participation in local, State, and national campaigns for temperance and prohibition with all other organizations uniting in a common forward movement.

"4. The institution of campaigns against desecration of the Lord's Day, law-violation, and for public progress and civic betterment such as the organization in cities of flower-culture clubs for beautifying waste places, the financing of summer outings for poor children, the institution of campaigns for tuberculosis hospitals and against spitting in public places; anti-cigarette propaganda; movements against prize-fighting and for the elimination of Sunday racing; campaigns for the strict enforcement of Sunday and other liquor laws; investigation of civic and community conditions, with a study of the prescribed duties of all public officials and the carrying out in many instances of city and rural surveys; the rendering of assistance to social-settlement centres; hearty co-operation in the national movement for one day of rest in seven for all workers.

"5. A nation-wide pledge-signing crusade.

"6. The observance of Good-Citizenship Day.

"7. Active participation in campaigns recommended to the united temperance forces of the nation by the national convention to be held in Columbus, O., November 14, 1913.

"8. A hearty and unswerving effort to secure the participation of all young people's societies of the nation in these or similar efforts.

"9. Pre-eminent emphasis on national prohibition and an amendment to the Constitution of the United States.

"10. The enthronement in the minds and hearts of the Christian Endeavorers of America of the highest spiritual objective for all temperance and Christian-citizenship activities, 'that in all things he might have the pre-eminence.'"

THE WORKERS IN CONFERENCE
A SERIES OF INSTRUCTIVE CONFERENCES

The practical side of Christian Endeavor was never more fully and more vividly presented in conference than at Los Angeles. At no time in the past did Christian Endeavorers maintain their interest in the things pertaining to the work of Endeavor more than during the daily two hours' period.

Each conference was of the greatest help to the seekers after knowledge that promotes efficiency. Again and again the rapid-fire questions and answers presented opportunities for the discussion of problems that were of vital interest to the delegates present.

While the remarkable inspirational addresses were of the greatest importance and helpfulness, it was those never-to-be-forgotten conferences where the real heart of things was touched.

Reports from these conferences follow.

THE JUNIOR EFFICIENCY PLANS
First Christian Church, July 10-12

Rev. George F. Kenngott, Ph.D., Los Angeles, Cal., Leader.

These conferences were held in the First Christian Church, Eleventh and Hope Streets, on Thursday, Friday, and Saturday mornings under the efficient leadership of Rev. George F Kenngott, Ph.D., superintendent of the Congregational Church-Extension Society of Los Angeles, for twenty years pastor of the First Trinitarian Congregational Church of Lowell, Mass., and for many years superintendent of the Massachusetts Junior and Intermediate Christian Endeavor societies. There was a large and varied Junior Endeavor exhibit consisting of models illustrating Bible objects, materials used in the manual methods of Junior societies, charts, maps, papers, and a large library on Christian nurture and the psychology of religious pedagogy. This interesting and instructive exhibit attracted many teachers and Junior superintendents.

Miss Mabel M. Culter, Junior superintendent of the California Union, conducted the brief devotional service at the beginning of each conference. The leader gave an address each morning on "The Why and How of Junior Endeavor," which was followed by a lively discussion and conference on the various points in the Junior Endeavor Efficiency Chart.

The presentation of the subject by the Rev. Mr. Kenngott and the discussion which followed demonstrated the fact that the reasons for the organization and vigorous support of the Junior Endeavor society were found in the insufficient Christian nurture in many homes, in the inadequacy of any home to train the children without association with other children, in the fact that the public school does not give distinctively Christian training, and in the inability of the church and Sunday-school through the regular services to give the largest and fullest opportunity for the freest expression of the religious impressions received at home and school, in church and Sunday-school.

The Junior Endeavor society, flexible and adaptable, lends itself readily by its meetings on week-days after school to the parochial-school idea, and may become the pastor's training-class at certain seasons of the year. The Junior Endeavor society is the practical application to modern life of Horace Bushnell's "Christian Nurture." It is essential to the life of the church and the growth of the Young People's society.

It is designed especially for boys and girls from eight to twelve years of age, when there is slow physical growth, with good health and bodily vigor. During this period the receptive power of memory is great, and the Bible passages, hymns, and poems may be committed to memory with profit. The sense of reality and certainty is strong; the historic sense is being developed; and the outlines of Bible history and geography may be learned. The characteristic emotional life is that of instinctive feelings, with imitation and curiosity strong; and the egoistic emotions reveal themselves in emulation and acquisitiveness. The play instinct is strong and keen, and should be gladly recognized in Christian nurture. The spontaneous interests are those of adult life and utilitarian ends. Companionship is essential. Self-interest is the central fact, but conscience is present. The child will pass in this period from a self-centred existence to life centred in another, even Christ. Memory work, such as the outlines of Bible-study and stories from mission fields, is in order.

Through the pledge, the meetings, and committee work, the Junior Endeavor society conforms to the laws of the psychology of childhood. Indeed, Dr. F. E. Clark was the early practical exponent of these laws as applied to the religious life of the child. His "Children and the Church" is an epoch-making little book. And if to any pastors and teachers the Junior Endeavor society seems to violate these laws of psychology, it is either because they do not understand the society, its "why and how," its purposes and methods, or else they have not read the psychology of religious pedagogy correctly. The child learns by doing; there should be no impression without expression. The Junior society requires various methods of expression, by words as well as by prayer, reading, and testimony, by acts as well as by committee work and manual methods.

As to method, the preposition "with" should be emphasized in the phrase "Work *with* God and the child." "Wouldst thou teach the child, observe him; he will teach you what to do." The children should be studied, as well as the Book, to discover their endowments, physical defects, developing periods, spontaneous interests, differences in temperament, and mental processes. The child is a person, with wonderful powers of mind, such as the sense of ownership, justice, fear, anger, love, the will, confidence, emulation, memory, suggestion, imitation, imagination. His confidence must be won; his taste for music and art must be trained; he can be taught through the instinct for play.

"The child's mind ripens and expands to abstract truth only by and through the concrete," said Froebel. He learns by the example set before him; therefore the teacher or Junior superintendent must be that which he would have the child become. "What you are speaks so loud, I cannot hear what you say."

There must be the adaptation of the truth to the age and experience of the child; there must be co-operation, gaining and keeping attention through interest. Malachi, the prophet, early recognized this principle when he used for the terms "teacher" and "scholar" words which mean "the one that awakes" and "the one that responds." We shall proceed from the known to the unknown, using easy words and apt illustrations. We must not scatter our fire, but have one central spiritual truth. While there must be order and orderly service, we must change our plans and methods often, and fix knowledge by review. Remembering the children's interest in stories, we shall use the best stories to inculcate spiritual truth.

Then "Forward, the Juniors," was the watchword of all the addresses and discussions, including the stirring address of Mr. D. A. Poling, field secretary of the Ohio union, the new national superintendent for the department of Temperance and Good Citizenship of the United Society of Christian Endeavor; the sympathetic and practical address of Mr. Sydney A. Clark of Boston, an ex-Junior, with all the enthusiasm of a well-trained Junior for Christian Endeavor in general and Junior work in particular; and the fine address of Rev. T. Sawaya, field secretary of Japan. When the leader joined the stars and stripes with the flag of Japan, and the banner of the cross above both, the great audience of Junior superintendents arose with fine enthusiasm and gave their hearty greetings to Mr. Sawaya.

MISSIONS.

First Baptist Church, July 10-12.

Rev. A. L. Phillips, D.D., Richmond Va., Superintendent of the Sunday-School and Young People's Work of the Southern Presbyterian Church, Leader.

Three sessions of the missionary institute were held. Thirty-five chairmen of missionary committees were present, with as many more members of committees. The programme was followed closely, and developed in rich and varied details. Questions and answers with testimonies and illustrations, songs and prayers, were features.

The work of the missionary committee was considered from three viewpoints; the personal, meetings, and the yearly programme. It was suggested that for the best results the committee should consist of three or five members, profoundly interested, skilled, enthusiastic, enterprising, and prayerful. It was further suggested that the life of the committee should be long enough to ensure the carrying out of a definite policy through the year.

A programme of work carefully planned for the whole year, including definite arrangements for *study* of Bible teaching, missions, races, countries, great religions. Old and New Testament biography, was considered essential. Also great emphasis was laid upon systematic, individual, and proportionate giving. Another helpful thing discussed was a missionary budget for the society, prepared by the committee after conference with the pastor and president, the amount of the budget to be secured by a canvass of all the members of the society for definite pledges.

The spiritual character of the missionary meeting was strongly emphasized under the two heads, the topic and the programme. The topics are of the utmost importance. Those given in the Prayer-Meeting Topics and Daily Readings were suggested. Great emphasis was given to the necessity for thorough preparation, with these suggestions worked out fully: first, get it up; second, study it through; third, divide it around; fourth, pray it in; fifth, work it out. It was clearly brought out that every programme should provide for at least six things—first, Bible reading, brief and pointed; second, songs, old and new; third, prayer, brief, definite, prepared; fourth, an offering, unhurried, reverent joyful; fifth, testimony, bright, emphatic; sixth, activity, very brief but snappy reports concerning some phase of the society's own missionary activity. The programme should have very definite aims.

About eight weeks for mission study was suggested as a period for best results. The members of the class should be hand-picked with reference to leadership and life-work. The course should deal with the home and foreign fields in just proportion. The method of study should be by text-books, with accessories such as maps, charts, pictures, curios, etc. Special subjects of research should be assigned to members of the class. The purposes of this study are three: the awakening of missionary interest, the approval of the missionary cause, and especially to secure co-operation with God's plans for the whole world.

During the institute hours Mrs. E. E. Strother, Christian Endeavor field secretary for China, made a strong plea for that mighty republic, laying special emphasis on the present crisis there. Rev. Robert E. Pretlow, pastor of the Memorial Friends' Church, Seattle, Wash., spoke on "America as a Field for Heroic Endeavor." Three addresses were delivered during the conference periods: "Religious Work among the Japanese of the Pacific Coast," by Professor H. H. Guy, with the introduction of the Japanese secretary of the Board of Co-operative Missions; "The Mormon Menace," by Mrs. W. P. White, representing the International Council for Patriotic Service, New York; "The American Indian of To-day," by Mr. and Mrs. F. G. Collett, field secretaries of the Indian Board of Co-operation, San Francisco.

CONFERENCES FOR PASTORS AND CHURCH-WORKERS.

First Congregational Church.

REV. CHARLES M. SHELDON, D.D., TOPEKA, KANSAS, LEADER.

These conferences were three in number, on Thursday, Friday, and Saturday mornings.

The outline covered topics suggested by problems in the church, the home, the school, the press, and the state. The general plan of each conference covered the answers to questions submitted by members of the conference, and first answered by Mr. Sheldon, then submitted to the members in general for brief answer and discussion. The range of the conference practically covered the extent of all human conduct in each of the five fields mentioned.

Under the head of "The Church," questions were answered concerning the old and the new forces that work for power. The old and established forces for power in the church were mentioned as preaching and worship, the use of the Bible as the greatest text-book in the world, missions, all kinds of social service, and the presentation of Jesus to men as the world's greatest hope.

New forces mentioned were the use of religious drama, a larger use of young life in the church, and teaching additional to the Sunday-school curriculum, the use of midweek services for religious education, the establishment of a Christian daily paper and a monthly magazine covering the world and printed by all the denominations, and the federation of Christendom.

Questions discussed about the home covered the ground of teaching about sex; amusements; the authority of parents; the time for play by children with their parents; religious training; family worship; problems of companionship, friendship, and courtship; also questions relating to divorce and marriage, closing with practical suggestions for making the home life more powerful.

Under the head of "The School" questions were asked and answered concerning the Bible in education, the influence of the fraternity life in the university on democracy, the results of a true education, reasons why students are choosing certain pursuits, why education is costing more now than it did fifty years ago, the need of Christian teachers in the State universities.

Under the head of "The Press" questions were asked and answered about the failure of established dailies to help in great questions like temperance, on account of fear of losing advertising. The need of a Christian daily was discussed from many points. The advantage of a universal monthly magazine, which would give news of the Kingdom, was also discussed at length.

Under the head of "The State" questions were asked and answered concerning Christian business methods, the relation of the church to the state, the problems of city life, the proper superintendence of great institutions like penitentiaries, the practical Christian management of great business organizations, and the failure of non-Christian business to demonstrate the practical side of making a living in absolutely clean and honest ways.

The summing up of the conference included an outline of the programme of the gospel, and its application to every phase of human energy.

The conferences were attended by pastors of all denominations, Sunday-school teachers, members of the Christian Endeavor societies, business men, and school-teachers. The deepest interest was shown in the discussion of the profoundest topics. The following questions, taken from a list of several hundred submitted, will indicate something of the ground covered.

1. Would the Christian daily you talk about pay financially if objectionable advertisements were eliminated?

Answer. Yes.

(The general answer given to the question was given either by Mr. Sheldon, or was the general consensus of answers given by members of the conference.)

2. What would be the politics of a Christian daily?

Answer. Independent.

3. Do you think the home is better or worse than it was years ago?

Answer. Better, because the world is better.

4. Do you favor physical examination before granting marriage licenses?

Answer. Yes.

Does this not destroy the romance of love-marriage?

Answer. No; the young people will take care of that.

5. Should a child be allowed to decide whether he will go to Sunday-school or church?

Answer. No.

6. How may a home be maintained by a family who have to live in a hotel?

Answer. A real home cannot practically be maintained in a hotel, but the family life can be maintained by devout Christian people.

7. Is the small Christian college holding its own with the large universities?

Answer. Yes, on the whole.

8. Why do not the great dailies help the churches fight the saloon?

Answer. For fear of losing advertising matter.

9. Is a Christian daily owned and controlled by the churches possible and practical?

Answer. Yes.

10. What is the most hopeful note in the church life of to-day?

Answer. The movement towards federation.

11. How can church people improve the theatre when non-Christian men are in charge of this business?

Answer. They can censor bad plays by leaving the house, but the real improvement of theatres must come from Christian management.

12. Are there real American homes in the United States?

Answer. A great many.

13. What of fraternities in the colleges and universities? are they necessary or useful?

Answer. If the fraternities in the universities tend to destroy social democracy or a sense of the brotherhood, they are a blunder, and do more harm than good.

14. What is the best thing about our public schools?

Answer. Democracy; the public schools are the greatest mixers we have for our boys and girls.

15. Why does education cost so much, and is the product any better than it was years ago?

Answer. It costs more because everything does; the product is not necessarily any better than it was, but with increased appliances in education there should be larger results from an educated person's life.

16. What is some of the objection connected with the use of the religious drama by the church?

Answer. Making it entertainment merely, or using it for the purpose of making money.

17. If, as you say, the new policeman must be a college-trained man, where will you get such people for seventy-five dollars a month?

Answer. Get them from the ranks of the Christian Endeavor young people, who are willing to serve anywhere in missionary service.

18. What is the first step towards federating three different churches in one small town, which is big enough to support only one?

Answer. The first step is getting the ministers to come together to talk it over. If they are not Christian enough to do that, it is hard to see what the first step can be. The people in the churches are ready for federation; the church boards and officials are the forces that object, if any.

19. Can we hope to have the Bible in our public schools?

Answer. Yes; and, if at the present time we cannot teach it there, no State law can take it out of the home.

20. Is it possible for large Christian business to be carried on under the present financial methods?

Answer. No; the methods must be radically changed before what is known as real Christian business can be carried on.

These questions are fair samples of the hundreds submitted and discussed. In the nature of the case, the answers were brief and in no sense exhaustive in the way of treatment; the time did not permit.

It was evident that the people who composed the conference were in earnest, as they remained at each conference for the full two hours, and groups met afterward for further discussion of questions in which individuals were interested.

The ground covered by the institute was probably too large for the most effective treatment; two, or at the most three, of these great subjects would have been ample for the three days' time. A programme covering as much ground as this could be more wisely handled in a week than in three days.

The matters that seemed to create the greatest interest, and around which centred the widest discussion, were: the Christian daily paper; the question of marriage, sex, etc.; the federation of the churches; the question of amusements and religious drama; and questions relating to the use of more power in Sunday-school work and with young people.

INTERMEDIATE EFFICIENCY PLANS.

Immanuel Presbyterian Church, July 10-12.

PAUL C. BROWN, FIELD SECRETARY OF CALIFORNIA UNION, LEADER.

Under the very tactful and efficient leadership of Mr. Brown the Intermediate Efficiency Conference was made very helpful to those in attendance during the three days' sessions.

The first hour was given to the Efficiency Campaign and to questions and answers. It was developed in the conference that the Efficiency Campaign is applicable to the work of Intermediate societies. It was demonstrated that a society of eighteen or twenty can easily carry forward the work of this campaign, but it was very wisely suggested that not all of the kinds of work should be started at once. Socials should be kept in the hands of consecrated boys and girls. It was a very spirited conference, giving very helpful suggestions under wise leadership.

Mr. G. Evert Baker, president of the Oregon Union, closed this conference with an exhortation to continue the campaign for the Christian life means doing things, and we must learn to do them well. Among other things Mr. Baker said; "Do not close the Efficiency Campaign, for it opens a new door. The spiritual life is active, and is doing things. Too many older people may stand in the way of the younger Endeavorers, and will not permit them to do the things that ought to be done. The greatest blessing is to take charge of this life and become an Intermediate leader. Throw out your 'life-line' into the life of one who is about to pass from the Junior life into the Intermediate life and be a great spiritual blessing. Live the life-line life, so that they may know you are a Christian."

The second meeting was made a testimony meeting, and the Intermediates and workers told what the Efficiency Campaign had done for them, revealing to one her spiritual poverty; to another, how time must be given to worth-while work; to a third, how conversions in a society may be brought about by fuller consecration of the members. As an illustration, one delegate testified that Intermediate Endeavor work revealed to her that she could not lead another to Christ until she lived closer to Him herself. Another was impressed with the way in which the Intermediates were spending their time and were willing to take more time for service for the Master. It was inspiring to note here the testimony coming from an outsider, who stated that he was impressed very much by the Intermediates clinging so closely together and to the heart of the Convention. One county superintendent testified that one society in his county always had at least one member join the church at every communion service, while another delegate from Los Angeles told of the evangelistic spirit of the Intermediates and the conversions they had had as the result of their meetings.

Others told of hospital work and the activities in these institutions. Problems of the high school, prayer circle, and Bible-study classes were also discussed. Many questions and answers were exchanged on this subject. One told how a group were informed that they could not hold a secret prayer circle, for secret societies were forbidden in the high school. They took their mothers into the circle and the organization was no longer a high-school organization. One delegate made it a special point to tell how in their prayer circle they had made the high-school dance a continuous subject of prayer until the dance was finally discontinued in the school.

Mr. Brown admonished the delegates to devote much time to consecrated prayer; saying that it is this kind of prayer that counts most in the service of the Master. A worker must watch for opportunities to talk to those he is praying for, and be very sure that he is first of all right with God himself.

Mr. E. P. Gates, field secretary for Illinois, made the closing address. He advised worth-while aims and then co-operation in working for those aims. Mr. Gates also spoke about his inability to advise the Intermediates because of the splendid testimonies he was permitted to hear while seated in one of the back seats, so that he suggested that they permit him to give them back-seat thoughts. He said: "Intermediates will do good work if their objects are worth while, and they will have a good time doing it, too. Nobody that is a sham ever has a good time. If you lower your standards, you will do nothing but sputter like a steam-radiator."

An extra session was held on Monday to meet the interest of Intermediate work. Practical questions were discussed, questions that touch the life of the young people—the theatre, card-playing, cigarette-smoking, and so on.

All the meetings were well attended, and bristled with good suggestions for making Intermediate societies count for Christ.

FIELD SECRETARIES' UNION.

MR. KARL LEHMANN, PRESIDENT OF THE FIELD SECRETARIES' UNION, PRESIDING.

Inspiration Point, better known as the assembly-room of the Hotel Alexandria, was the hotbed for practical Christian Endeavor Thursday and Saturday mornings between the hours of eleven and twelve. It was here where the men and women whose hearts are afire for Christian Endeavor, and better known as field secretaries, gathered with their friends to discuss the vital things pertaining to this great world-wide work. They are what one must call "the real thing" in Christian Endeavor, because it is this one thing that they do 365 days in the year.

They came to the Convention fresh from the firing line, where they are obliged to meet the stern realities of Christian Endeavor in all its various phases; and with these things in mind, and with the purpose to make the personal point of contact with their comrades, one can well realize that to meet with them was an exceptional opportunity. This conference included all the field workers, State, and district officers. These meetings presented a rare chance to discuss problems and to be helpful to one another.

On the first morning after the business of the organization had been transacted there were short addresses by Mr. E. P. Gates, field secretary of the Illinois Christian Endeavor Union, and Mr. A. J. Shartle, publication-manager of the United Society of Christian Endeavor. Mr. Gates spoke on "Making an Itinerary," and emphasized the fact that successful itineraries are planned well in advance and made to dovetail so that very little time is lost in covering the territory. He also spoke of not only making definite plans, but working them in all their details, and said that only by doing so can there be definite and lasting results.

Mr. Shartle spoke on "Advertising, Printing, and Literature," and emphasized the importance of the use of good literature and attractive, telling advertising. Among other things he said that it not only pays to advertise, but it pays well to advertise and one reason why some Christian Endeavor conventions, rallies, and conferences are perhaps not so well attended as they might be is the lack of intelligent, persistent, and attractive advertising.

During the period allotted for the second meeting on Saturday a number of short addresses were made by various field secretaries on subjects of great interest to all concerned in world-wide Christian Endeavor. Mr. H. H. Rottmann's talk on the Efficiency Campaign was especially interesting, while Rev. Edgar T. Farrill of Wisconsin spoke on "Financing State Work," and gave very many helpful suggestions that were eagerly jotted down by those in attendance. "The Kind of Meetings to Hold" was discussed by Field Secretary Jaeger from Colorado, and "The Right Kind of Addresses to Deliver at Meetings" was very efficiently presented by Daniel A. Poling of Ohio. California was represented by Mr. Paul Brown, who very ably presented methods on "How to Lead a Conference." His comrade in the work, Mr. Tom Hannay, Jr., spoke on "What to Present in the Pulpit on Sunday," and urged that the Christian Endeavor message be tied up tight to the Bible always. "How I Lead a Junior Rally," by Field Secretary Martin from Manitoba, brought out ideas new to many of the secretaries present. He was ably assisted by Mrs. Hutchison, the Junior field secretary from Ohio, who spoke along the same line. Mr. A. Hardy Priddy of Saskatchewan told how he organized a society.

On all of these subjects presented there was much discussion in general; and many real, up-to-date, helpful suggestions were made, which proved the solution to many problems in the States represented. The following resolution was presented and recommended to field workers:

Resolved. That the prayer circle which during the past two years was so successfully conducted, and which has proved so helpful to the workers at large and in the various States, be continued indefinitely.

This resolution was unanimously passed. The new officers of the Field Secretaries' Union elected to serve for the next two years are: president, Mr. Karl Lehmann; vice-president, Mr. Paul C. Brown, California; secretary, Miss Grace A. Townsend, Florida; treasurer, Mr. S. A. Martin, Manitoba.

PRISON WORK.

Swedish Evangelical Church, July 10-12.

MR. TOM HANNAY, JR., FIELD SECRETARY OF THE CALIFORNIA UNION, LEADER.

This conference was very ably conducted by Mr. Hannay. A very encouraging audience was present at each of these periods, and in view of the fact that the majority were Californians the conference dealt with the work in that State alone.

Christian Endeavor has almost free entry in all penitentiaries, and the California Union's superintendent of prison work, Mr. A. G. Muller, has been doing chaplain's work at San Quentin for nearly six months. California is vitally improving her prison laws, and her prison wardens are humane men. Warden Hoyle of San Quentin has reduced the use of the strait-jacket as a punishment from 7,911 hours in 1905 to 29 hours in 1912. Warden Johnson of Folsom has never used corporal punishment in any form, and the discipline of the prison has improved during his term.

There was much helpful discussion along the line of work suggested for county and city prisons, and it was impressed upon those present that Christian Endeavorers throughout the world have a great opportunity of getting in touch with the brothers back of the bars. The work in other prisons was discussed, and many opportunities for being of help to the unfortunates were clearly pointed out, so that much good is expected during the next two years in work along this line, due to this very interesting conference.

TENTH LEGION CONFERENCE.

Young Men's Christian Association Building, Thursday morning, July 10.

The conference of Tenth Legioners was both inspiring and helpful. Many practical points were brought out at this conference that proved a revelation to those present. California alone has five thousand members of the Tenth Legion. At this conference the Bible basis for tithing was presented, and the subject was discussed from many angles, such as the question of what tithing should include and the system of keeping accounts and giving beyond the tithe. Many instances were given of the effect of tithing on the individual and on the church. This splendid conference was led by Mrs. G. S. Brown, superintendent of the Tenth Legion department of the California Union. Mrs. Brown supplied convincing testimony to the blessing that follows the bringing of tithes into the Lord's storehouse.

In a discussion from the floor one of the speakers from Montana told of a church where nearly all members of the official board are tithers, and of the great power that they are for good in that particular church and community.

A pastor spoke of the emphasis laid on the tithing system in his church, and further related how during a course of sermons on this subject many new tithers were enrolled, thus proving that, when tithing is presented intelligently and in a way that the average man and woman can understand, it generally is accepted and put into practice.

It was told how, if we give of our substance to the Lord, He will honor us, not necessarily with a larger income, but He will open a way for us so that we can live better and more useful lives and make the nine-tenths go farther than the ten-tenths formerly used for ourselves.

It was clearly demonstrated in this conference by those present that the Tenth Legion movement is one of the remedies that will make the financing of the larger work of the church a possibility, and will ensure future success.

INTERMEDIATE QUIET HOUR AND BIBLE-STUDY CONFERENCE.

Immanuel Presbyterian Church.

PROF. HOWARD W. KELLOGG, OCCIDENTAL COLLEGE, LOS ANGELES, LEADER.

A great number of Intermediates met for their Quiet Hour at eight o'clock on three mornings during the Convention. The first morning the meeting was led by Professor Howard Kellogg of Occidental College. The second morning the meeting was led by Rev. E. F. Hallenbeck, D.D., and on the third morning by Mr. Thomas Hannay, Jr., California's beloved field secretary.

The Sunshine State makes much of Intermediate work, and the State officers make even more of the importance of developing young men's and young women's interest in the Bible and in spiritual life. The Intermediates are very responsive, and it is an inspiration to attend their meetings and to note the interest with which they follow the exercises. All these Intermediate Quiet Hour and Bible-study services were marked by the deepest reverence, and revealed the fact that the young people are ready for leadership along devotional lines.

Field Secretary Hannay, addressing the Intermediates on the topic "Service for Christ," among other things said: "You talk about doing things, but listen. You cannot live a life that you do not have. You cannot yield a life that you do not have. If you say you have had a transaction between yourself and God, and there is no difference in your life, there has not been a definite transaction. God demands that you shall have a definite change of life. You cannot go on dancing and playing cards. Gal. 2:20 gives a new life, a resurrection with Christ, that He may work in and through us."

Miss Viola Rich, California's Quiet Hour superintendent, sang a beautiful solo entitled "Lord, Help Me to Live," following which Mr. Hannay called for all those who had surrendered their all to the Master to stand, and he asked those who were willing to surrender their all to stand. The entire audience stood.

At the request of some of the Intermediates an extra conference hour was held on Monday morning in the Immanuel Church, from eight to nine o'clock. This was possibly the best and most important meeting of the Intermediates. Mr. Brown took Romans 12:1, 2, as a foundation for a very short and very strong talk. The Intermediates will long remember this closing message and this conference, and there is no doubt that great

good was accomplished during these intensely interesting and deeply spiri-
ual meetings of Intermediates and their devoted leaders.

QUIET HOUR WORKERS' CONFERENCE.

First United Presbyterian Church.

REV. G. C. CARPENTER, NATIONAL SECRETARY OF THE BRETHREN CHRISTIAN
ENDEAVOR UNION, WARSAW, IND., LEADER.

Large audiences attended the Quiet Hour Workers' Conferences. On
one occasion thirty-six Quiet Hour superintendents were present. This
special meeting was opened by a Quiet Hour service led by Rev. G. C. Carpenter, national secretary of the Brethren Christian Endeavor Union,
Warsaw, Ind. These opening devotions were a real quiet hour, and proved
a splendid preparation for the conference that followed. The leader gave
a brief address emphasizing the value and the necessity of proper spiritual
food. "The Quiet Hour," he said, "is the best plan yet to give young
Christians this spiritual culture so necessary for soul-growth. Two things
are necessary; first, that the Christian take wholesome nourishment; and,
second, that the Christian take that nourishment at regular intervals. Two
square meals on Sunday will not last until prayer-meeting night. We cannot store up enough at one time to last for days and weeks of spiritual
starvation. The Quiet Hour is the daily meal-time. Sit down and partake
of the bread of life. Meditate; read the Bible; and pray, that the soul
may be nourished."

The conference on methods followed this opening service. One of
the California delegates present told how they had secured definite results
in the work of the Quiet Hour by Convention opportunities, round-robin
letters, and pamphlets.

It was further suggested that the United Society of Christian Endeavor appoint some one from whom literature on the subject of the
Quiet Hour could be secured, and that a larger supply of such literature
might be developed.

The closing address of the conference was delivered by Rev. H. F.
Shupe, D.D., editor of The Watchword, Dayton, O. Dr. Shupe opened
his address by saying, "A noisy age needs a quiet hour." His address
was forceful and very convincing. He emphasized the need of the Quiet
Hour to get us acquainted with God, to keep us in touch with high
standards, to keep our bodies in tone, to increase our spiritual power, and
to help us practise the presence of God.

Note.—Dr. Shupe's address in full appears in the "Chapter of Addresses."

FLOATING CHRISTIAN ENDEAVOR CONFERENCE.

Chapel of St. Paul's Episcopal Church.

MR. JOHN MAKINS, SAN PEDRO, CAL., LEADER.

Floating Christian Endeavor work received careful and prayerful
consideration in the conference under the direction of Mr. John Makins,
San Pedro, Cal. The attendance and the great interest in this work proved
the fact that there is a growing interest throughout the country in
this form of Christian Endeavor work, which is too often neglected.
Workers from California ports, from the East, and from the lakes, as well
as others from inland counties, were present and participated.

It was stated in conference that a large number of the navy recruits
now come from inland States, where little information is obtainable regarding the life and temptations in the navy; and therefore great importance is attached to the work of Floating Christian Endeavor. It is further
desired that Christian Endeavor societies give their co-operation, and that

parents and friends and the young men themselves join in their effort to establish Christian work for the young men of the navy.

Miss Antoinette P. Jones, of Falmouth, Mass., was one of the speakers, and brought to those present a very interesting message regarding the great work. A resolution was passed, expressing appreciation for assistance rendered the workers engaged in Floating Endeavor throughout the world, and more especially in the United States, and expressing the hope that this good work might continue.

It was further resolved that the interior State unions be asked to cooperate with the work of Floating Endeavor in the more aggressive campaign to carry the gospel to the men of the sea, also that a committee of three be appointed to present a copy of these resolutions to Dr. Clark, Mr. Shaw, Miss Jones, and the daily press.

The key-note of the conference was the need of information about this form of work and a definite consecration to it.

STATE JUNIOR AND INTERMEDIATE SUPERINTENDENTS' CONFERENCE.

Parlor of the First Christian Church.

MRS. CHARLES HUTCHISON, JUNIOR FIELD SECRETARY OF THE OHIO UNION, LEADER.

This conference convened under the leadership of Mrs. Hutchison, and many problems of vital interest on this phase of Christian Endeavor work were discussed. Seven States were represented in this conference. During the discussion it was suggested that superintendents should reply promptly to all communications, and should always have at hand some good plans for both Junior and Intermediate societies, so as to be able to give aid when called upon.

The chief aim of the State superintendent, it was said, should be the training of workers, men and women; and a good plan for financing the work is to ask each Junior for a contribution of ten cents a year, and Intermediates for twenty cents a year. At least two Junior rallies should be held each year.

It also was developed during the discussion that the membership of this union should consist only of those actively engaged in this branch of the work of Christian Endeavor, and it was resolved to amend the constitution to that effect.

The secretary of the organization, Miss Lillian Hayes, who is now in London, England, taking up a special course in religious work, reported that during the year she had travelled 4,034 miles, had given 26 addresses, held 20 conferences, organized a number of Junior and Intermediate societies, and led Christian Endeavor prayer meetings. She further reported having spent five weeks in the field in Missouri, and most of her work was done attending and helping in a series of district conventions, addressing Christian Endeavor societies and local unions.

A special committee was appointed to recommend some form of organization adapted to meet the needs of this branch of the work, and one that will eliminate some of the non-essentials, which in the past have to a certain extent embarrassed the work.

At a later meeting this committee reported, and recommended the following: First, that the organization of a union for State and Provincial Junior and Intermediate superintendents be formed and made permanent. Second, that the officers of this organization shall consist of a president, a vice-president, a secretary, a treasurer, and an executive committee of three. This recommendation was received and adopted. The following officers were elected: president, Mrs. E. L. Condon, Le Grand, Io.; vice-president, Miss Helen E. Davison, Winnipeg, Canada; secretary, Mrs.

A. Brownlee, Hammonton, N. J.; treasurer, Mrs. Charles Hutchison, Toledo, O.; chairman of the executive committee, Miss Grace Hooper, Crete, Neb. The dues were placed at twenty cents a year.

SOCIAL PURITY FOR MEN AND BOYS.

First English Lutheran Church.

REV. E. A. KING, PRESIDENT OF THE WASHINGTON STATE UNION, LEADER.

Large audiences composed of young men, fine, stalwart fellows, attended the purity conference, conducted by Rev. E. A. King, author of "Clean and Strong," a book on purity, published by the United Society of Christian Endeavor, Boston, Mass. Mr. King described the great black plague as sex immorality, hard to eradicate because it is grounded in strong natural instincts. He told of the dangers connected with an immoral life, and named some of the agencies that should be used to combat it. Dr. King says, "First of all comes education regarding all that pertains to sex life." "Ignorance," he says, "is criminal. False modesty that prevents parents from instructing their children is a terrible source of danger to the child."

In connection with this address both the speaker and the audience enjoyed a stimulating testimony coming from a young man in the audience. This young man, unknown to both speaker and audience, rose and stated that he attended one of Dr. King's lectures to men some years before, in the city of Sandusky, O.; and as a result of that meeting the young man's life was transformed, and ultimately he became a thoroughly saved Christian. Mr. King's subject was "The Greatest Social Peril, and How to Meet It." He said, in part: "Everybody is acquainted with the phrase, 'the great white plague,' and all understand that it refers to the rapid spread of the disease of tuberculosis. So awakened are the citizens of every city and State over the fact that it is a preventable disease that they willingly submit to a tax in order that proper efforts may be made to eliminate the causes, prevent the spread, and prosecute the cure, of the disease. The gains made in these directions are wonderful, and we expect the time to come when the serious aspects of the disease will entirely disappear.

"It has been comparatively easy to carry on successful campaigns against tuberculosis because no serious personal moral questions have been involved; but it is altogether different with 'the great black plague,' of which I am about to speak.

"The great black plague is so called because it is a plague very much worse than tuberculosis, which is called 'the great white plague.' It is more difficult to describe and discuss because it has to do with the great problem of sex, and has been a subject of profound study and experiment from the beginning of time.

"It all grows out of sexual immorality, and is, therefore, one of the hardest problems with which to deal."

Continuing, Mr. King described the reasons for the modern movement in sex-hygiene education and social-purity reform, and gave a helpful review of what is being done to meet the problem and eradicate vice and correct viciousness. In explaining how the great black plague is to be met he said: "First and foremost in the list of agencies for the eradication of impurity and all its attending train of evils I would place the need for education in all matters pertaining to the sex life. It has been the custom for so many years not to mention the subject of sex in polite society that a lamentable ignorance has grown up among us. This is due largely to false modesty on the part of parents and teachers, but there is no satisfactory excuse for attempting to keep the knowledge of sex from the young. They are bound to discover the facts for themselves by blundering, or they are instructed from impure sources, to their physical and moral undoing."

As to practical suggestions he proposed that there be invited to the community a lecturer who can set before the public the facts and present the need for education. Perhaps there are capable persons already there who can be utilized for such work. One of the best agencies to accomplish the desired end is a Society of Social and Moral Hygiene similar to those in New York City, Chicago, Spokane, Seattle, and Portland. Through such an organization all the people in the community interested in the subjects could be co-ordinated and utilized for practical reform. Through such a society literature on the subject of sex could be secured and distributed, parents' meetings held, and authoritative information conveyed to the entire community. The city health department may undertake the task of popular sex-education as in North Yakima, Wash.

On the second day, Mr. King spoke at length of the new and important work being done along the lines of purity reform in his own home city in Washington. In this city of North Yakima the health department has published a series of five sex-hygiene pamphlets, and paid for them out of the public funds; and they are being distributed free to all the people. Perhaps one of the most important things said at the conference was this regarding the moral motif of the work: "In discussing the subject of sex-education it is worth remembering that knowledge is not safety, though it is power. Information concerning sex alone will not solve our great problem. There must be a moral motif running through all our endeavors, and for this reason we must be careful as to the choice of persons who are to impart sex-information, and also we must use the same judgment in selecting the books on sex-enlightenment that we place in the hands of young people. Many a boy or girl knows more than his or her parents and some of his or her teachers about the facts of sex. What such young people need, then, is not so much information as the creation of new moral ideals. Real personal religion, the kind that is linked with ethics, the sort that feels moral responsibility, is and has always been the best antiseptic against vice and passion. Any system of sex-instruction that ignores this element will fail to produce the much-desired result."

Any one desiring Mr. King's complete printed address may have it by writing to him at 4 South Sixth Street, North Yakima, Wash., and enclosing five cents in stamps.

SOCIAL-PURITY CONFERENCE FOR WOMEN AND GIRLS.

Young Women's Christian Association.

MRS. J. S. NORVELL, LOS ANGELES, LEADER.

A large and very enthusiastic, receptive, and responsive audience attended this great conference on social purity for women and girls. This audience was composed of delegates represented by mothers, public-school teachers, social-settlement workers, Young Women's Christian Association secretaries, Sunday-school teachers, young women in training for social service, physicians, women lawyers, nurses, juvenile-court workers, returned missionaries, prison workers, playground superintendents, and pastors' wives. It was a very enthusiastic and up-to-date congregation of women, wide-awake, well informed, having a clear vision of present-day social conditions, and striving to advance the cause of purity and clean living in every department of our social order.

Mrs. Norvell's address, which will be found in full in the "Chapter of Addresses," was clearly outlined, general in thought and teaching; and, while the outline was followed strictly, there were interpolated incidents, illustrations, and exhortations, bearing on the line of personal living, taking up the prevalence of bodily indulgences and habits that are sapping the strength and undermining the structure of the "temple beautiful" in which we are to serve our day and generation and honor our God. The questions of reading, amusements, recreations, athletics, vain imaginations, especially in the young woman of adolescent age, were impressed by thought, facts, illustrations, and incidents.

The conference further endeavored to show that all impurity, all weakness, all sin, all crime, all human wreckage, have been brought about by the old nature known as the "stony heart," and nothing can bring about the correction and fire the impetus for holy living save the impartation from God of the "heart of flesh," a pure heart.

The closing hour of this splendid conference was filled with wise, intelligent questions bearing on all phases of life and conduct such as the proper relationship of the sexes, as young men and women, as friends, escorts, lovers, betrothed, and married. Dangers of cheap and trashy reading; the danger from cheap picture-shows and variety theatres, cigarettes, smoking, Sabbath-desecration; methods to be employed in dealing with delinquents—these and many other practical questions were profitably discussed. From this conference, it is believed, all went away with the conviction that the many practical, helpful things suggested and explained would bear much fruit in helping to solve the problems of present-day Christian work.

STATE SECRETARIES' CONFERENCE.

Chapel of Christ Episcopal Church.

MISS ELIZABETH HALL, FIELD SECRETARY FOR EASTERN CANADA, LEADER.

This conference of the connecting links, connecting the State organization with the local, county, and district unions and the societies, was one of much interest and very ably conducted by Miss Hall. Some of the essentials to successful State secretarial work that were discussed were of the most up-to-date and very helpful kind. It was stated that a systematic secretary is one who is up to date in his methods and is accurate, who has the right aim in keeping records, keeping lists up to date and also so that they are accessible at any time. It was said that secretaries should be gracious at all times, and especially get into touch with those of larger experience. Personal letters whenever possible were suggested as the means of making the point of contact with individuals, societies, and unions, the sending out of report-blanks at stated times being one of the best methods by which timely reports may be secured.

One method used to secure replies to letters and postal cards was to send a card each day until a reply came. Every State and Province with an introduction department and secretary should be kept in touch with this particular work. The secretary should be in touch with the working of all the departments in the State. This would help the secretary to do the work of this office more efficiently. It was resolved by the secretaries present to do their best in keeping in touch with world-wide Endeavor, and especially with the individual who needs help.

WORK FOR BOYS AND BOYS' CLUBS.

Young Men's Christian Association Building.

REV. EDGAR T. FARRILL, FIELD SECRETARY FOR WISCONSIN, LEADER.

This conference awakened a great deal of interest, and attracted the attention of a large number of men to the great importance of the right kind of effort in behalf of boys and young men. Mr. Farrill, leader of this conference, has had a long experience with the up-to-date plans and methods looking to the development of the young. In his address and through the entire conference, discussing the varied questions asked, he sought to make very plain and to emphasize strongly that such work is not only desirable, but is the thing to do to-day. He further very strongly emphasized the fact that the thing to do to-day is to make the Christian Endeavor society a centre and source of a variety of schemes that look toward the growth of the whole being, mentally, morally, physically, and spiritually. Boys' Brigades, boys' clubs, organized Sunday-school classes, may all be parts of organized Christian Endeavor and bound up with it. Indoor and outdoor athletic meets, as well as lyceums and city governments, are as feasible as the prayer meeting of Christian Endeavor, and all are most closely and vitally inter-related.

Those present got a new vision of the attractive force Christian Endeavor may be made to possess for the training of youth for Christian service, and went away with a new idea of the need of Christian Endeavor to-day and the possibility for great work along this line in the future.

EVANGELISM.

German Baptist Church.

Rev. H. H. Rottmann, Interstate Field Secretary, Leader.

A very helpful and spirited conference on evangelism, its methods, intent, and purpose, was conducted under the careful and efficient direction of Rev. H. H. Rottmann. Mr. Rottmann spoke of public meetings, and advised that Endeavorers should follow the method of personal work.

Rev. Edwin F. Hallenbeck, D.D., of San Diego, Cal., delivered a very helpful address at this conference. He encouraged those present to consider briefly all forms of evangelism in public meetings, commending many of the methods used by Christian Endeavorers, but emphatically coming to the conclusion that the best method of young people's evangelism is personal work.

It was resolved that Endeavorers should seek to revive conversational evangelism, interesting others through daily conversation about the kingdom of God; further, that the leaders of the United Society be asked to give a two-word watchword, namely "Conversational Evangelism"; and also that the establishing of personal soul-winners' circles be recommended wherever possible with a view to training young people to win others to Christ. The resolution verbatim follows:

First, we recommend that the Christian Endeavorers be asked to make a strong, united effort to revive conversational evangelism, using the best up-to-date methods of work, bringing into their line of basic activity as much of our active membership as God will help us to enlist. Second, that the United Society leaders be asked to give us an international two-word watchword for general activity, namely, "Conversational Evangelism." Third, we recommend the establishing, wherever possible, of personal soul-winners' circles in our societies, who are to do practical personal work during the time of their training, making the class work be of practical value to every society undertaking it.

These recommendations were enthusiastically received, and after more discussion on the various means and methods of conducting this great world-wide work this splendid conference came to a close with a feeling that much good was accomplished.

STATE TREASURERS' AND FINANCE COMMITTEES' CONFERENCE.

Swedish Evangelical Church.

Mr. Walter R. Mee, President of the Illinois Union, Leader.

This conference of State treasurers and finance committees was led by

Mr. Walter R. Mee, president of the Illinois Christian Endeavor Union
Mr. Mee in presenting the purpose of this conference emphasized the
great importance of the office of the treasurer, its spiritual as well as its
material aspect. Among other things he said: "The treasurer should be
a man who is consecrated and also thoroughly businesslike. Promptness,
honesty, accuracy, neatness, tact, vigor, should be his watchwords. The
treasurer need not be timid in his approaches to his fellow Endeavorers
for funds, because he is seeking to further God's work, and it is therefore
a privilege to give; and with all eagerness and confidence the treasurer
should go forth to secure pledges." Said Mr. Mee: "Once the money
begins to flow into the coffers, the treasurer should keep most accurate accounts, pay out all money on proper orders, countersign checks, stimulate
and direct all State finances, and co-operate whenever necessary with
finance committees. All departments should refer their expenditures to
the executive committee before incurring the expense, and the treasurer
should not issue money unless this is done as a general rule, for this
method reduces to a minimum unwise use of the funds in hand."

Mr. Mee told how in the Illinois Union the budget system is in operation. Added to this, personal pledges are solicited, and through the year
an Illinois and Junior Day is planned. A special programme is sent out
through the State, and all offerings taken on these particular days are
forwarded to the State treasurer. The Illinois Union publishes a State
paper, and each month a list of all amounts sent to the treasurer from various societies and other sources is published.

Finally, Mr. Mee says, "The treasurer must be systematic, painstaking,
optimistic, and businesslike, constantly looking to the Master for help and
guidance."

Mr. H. N. Lathrop, treasurer of the United Society, made the closing
address of this conference, and suggested many practical plans for doing
a treasurer's work successfully. He said: "The paramount importance of
the treasurer or finance man is being alive, alert, and businesslike. No
haphazard method goes. The budget system is the ideal system. A
record of the societies' ability to pay should be kept. The various departments should tell what amounts they need for their work, and should
keep within their budget." "Businesslike methods," says Mr. Lathrop,
"ensure success. Keep tab on the members' standing in the societies.
Some can give fifty dollars, but give twenty dollars, and others can give
only one dollar. Most societies take pride in meeting their pledges and
exceeding them. Once the budget is secured, judge your various departments, their needs, and apportion the money accordingly. Make the
missionary, Floating, and various chairman keep within their allotment.
Teach them the necessity of handling money carefully. If the pledges
come in slowly after being made, send several letters to delinquents. Send
to the hopeless no less than five missives, and let the fifth be a night
telegram. Every society and individual must realize that a pledge is a
moral obligation and meeting it is as essential as paying a grocer's or
doctor's bill."

Mr Lathrop further said that, if a pastor or Endeavorer should become
angry because of the treasurer's persistency, he or she is perhaps not a
true Christian at heart. Be sure the telegram is sent at the psychological
time when certain heavy bills are to be made out, some particularly vital
to the health of the society or the State union. "Many helps are issued by
the United Society of Christian Endeavor," said Mr. Lathrop, "that will
suggest ways and means to assist the treasurer in his dilemma. Every
treasurer should secure these."

STUDY OF THE BIBLE.

First Presbyterian Church.

REV. JOHN BALCOM SHAW, D.D., PASTOR OF THE SECOND PRESBYTERIAN CHURCH, CHICAGO, ILL., LEADER.

The fact that at least eight hundred Endeavorers attended the first conference on Bible-study led by Dr. Shaw, shows the Endeavorers' deep interest in the word of God. Dr. Shaw is pastor of the Second Presbyterian Church, Chicago, Ill., but has accepted a call to one of the large Los Angeles churches. He is one of those men that are big in stature and large of heart, a man with a smile that illumines and wins. Dr. Shaw held three conferences on the general theme of "The Bible." His object was to establish faith in the word of God in spite of common criticism.

The first conference took up the history of the Bible. After the opening devotions Dr. Shaw led in repeating Scripture, which was taken up by the audience, scores repeating favorite passages with freedom and fervor, showing that the Bible is a vital and determinative force in the lives of Christian Endeavorers. Dr. Shaw then spoke upon the history of the Bible, and it was proved that the Bible has been more fully and variedly inspired than is generally supposed. His address was divided under these heads:

First, The Inspiration of the Writers of the Bible, thirty-six at least writing in different centuries and possibly at far-distant points, but all facing in the same direction, catching the same high vision, contributing to the same ongoing purpose, and coming out at the same goal.

Second, The Inspiration of the Editors of the Bible, by which they gathered these books out of the centuries in which they were written and put them into one united volume, which through all ages since, despite attack and criticism, has remained inviolably intact.

Third, The Inspiration of the Accessories of the Bible. First, its language, which under the providence of God was rendered unusually flexible and expressible; and, second, the material upon which the manuscripts were written, so perfect as to have proved almost indestructible, the oldest manuscripts having survived some fifteen hundred years without the least sign of decay.

Fourth, The Inspiration of the Copyists of the Bible, the copying being most difficult work because of the character of the letters, especially the Hebrew, and also because of the absence of punctuation marks and sentence-divisions, and yet so well done as to have made the Bible free from any vital and important errors.

Fifth, The Inspiration of the Custodians of the Bible. Who kept the Vatican manuscript, not brought to Rome until 1448, from the exigencies of fire and decay? God. Who guarded the Sinaitic manuscript, not discovered until 1849, all those centuries, and finally brought it into safe and interested keeping? God.

Sixth, The Inspiration of the Translators of the Bible, the Septuagint, the Vulgate, and the successive Anglo-Saxon translations culminating in the stately, vigorous rhythmic, apparently undying King James version.

Seventh, The Inspiration of the Distributers of the Bible, millions of copies outnumbering the editions of all other books, and increasing every year.

Having thus piled up evidence upon evidence, Dr. Shaw then concluded this first conference with a plea for a belief in a big Bible into which God has put more of Himself than into any other production given to men.

The second conference dealt with the story of the monuments as they confirm the Bible story. Dr. Shaw said, "Mr. Gladstone once entitled the Bible 'The Impregnable Rock of Holy Scripture.' It stands out like a Gibraltar in the midst of the ages; only it is more steadfast and secure than that. Gibraltar has been taken more than once, and the Bible has never yet surrendered."

"Some rocks get harder as they grow older. Such a rock is the Bible. While certain extremists have been trying to bore down into it as if with a view to blowing it up, other men have been digging down about it and showing us that it goes down deeper than any others have supposed, and that it is granite clean to the bottom."

Dr. Shaw then gave an account of the great discoveries in Assyria, Babylonia, and Egypt, devoting most of the time to those of Egypt. These in the main have been:

First, in 1881, the finding of the royal mummies in Deir-el-Bahari, confirming the history of Israel's dealing with many of the Pharaohs.

Second, in 1884, the discovery of the treasure city of Pithom, which was found to be built in part with bricks made without straw, ratifying the history of that part of Israel's sojourn in Egypt.

Third, in 1887, the Tel el-Amarna tablets, confirming much in the books of the Kings and Chronicles, where Israel's dealings with Assyria and Babylonia are recorded.

Fourth, in 1896, the finding by Flinders Petrie of the "Stele Israel," the only Egyptian inscription containing the word "Israel," Professor Ralf declaring that it would prove beyond a doubt that the children of Israel were in Egypt.

Fifth, the finding of Merenptah's body, he having been in all probability the Pharaoh of the exodus.

Sixth, in 1907, the findings at Elephantine, where wagon-loads of cylinders, tablets, etc., were unearthed, which Professor Driver of Oxford declares has done more for the Bible than any other discovery.

In the face of these confirmations the modern attacks upon the Bible are as futile as the firing off of a few crackers in front of Gibraltar, which does not hide the face of the rock even for a passing moment.

The third conference dealt with the testimony of experience to the inspiration of the Bible. Taking several passages, Dr. Shaw called attention to the impression made upon all, throwing a spell upon the company. He has tried all kinds of audiences, and found the same effect. Three reasons for this were given. First, they created an atmosphere which no other words did. Second, they made an appeal to the human spirit that evoked what no other literature did. Third, they carried with them an authority which all other utterances lacked.

Dr. Shaw then pleaded for a large place for the Bible in the life of the preacher, the Sunday-school teacher, and the individual Christian, ending with an incident of a Bible thrown into the ash-can as refuse by an apostate family, but afterward rescued and placed on a pulpit of a metropolitan church, from which the gospel has since been preached to tens of thousands of souls. Where is your Bible, Christian Endeavorers? In the place of command, or gradually slipping into disuse and abandonment?

ORANGE COUNTY, CAL., ENDEAVORERS AT THE LOS ANGELES
CONVENTION

DELEGATES FROM SANTA CRUZ
By the kindness of the Los Angeles "Examiner"

CHAPTER XII.

DRESS PARADE AND CONCERT.

Friday Evening, July 11.

LOS ANGELES had promised the Endeavorers in advance of their coming an electrical parade for Friday evening. For some reason the parade did not materialize. So Christian Endeavor rallied, generated their own electricity, and gave Los Angeles an electrical parade of their own that the City of the Angels will long remember.

Led by the mounted police, a brass band, and the members of the 1913 committee, clad in white, among them President John Willis Baer, they marched in front of automobiles carrying Dr. Clark and the officers of the United Society.

The metropolis of the Golden West will always remember this parade of thousands as it swung through the streets of the city. A respectable array of boys and girls, young men and young women, and many whose hair was streaked with silver, waving banners, pennants, flags, and mottoes. That was all there was to it, and yet it was a tense, radiating force, the embodiment of a cause, a pledge of loyalty, a proclamation of the vitality of a religious conviction. They marched four, six, and eight abreast, a breezy, cheering, singing line nearly two miles long. We have had processions at conventions before, but nothing like this for beauty, for enthusiasm, and for heartiness. Imagine hundreds upon hundreds of young girls dressed in white, and young men summer-garbed, and you may get a faint idea of the impression made upon many thousands of spectators.

When the front of the parade reached Auditorium Endeavor, more easily recognized when described as the big tent at Pico Street and Grand Avenue, the tail end of the procession was just starting from Sixth and Olive Streets and the intervening line stretched along Olive Street back to Fifth Street, across to Hill Street and along Hill to Pico Street, and thence over to the main entrance to the tent, beyond Grand Avenue, a distance of about two miles.

Every bit of this long way the young people were singing, and never dolorously. They were giving city and county and State slogans, not feebly nor haltingly, but with the tremendous enthusiasm of college crowds under the direction of hypnotic yell-leaders.

One of the astounding things about this parade was that many thousands of citizens waited for hours along the probable lines of march, which had not been definitely announced, and, in fact, was partially changed at the last moment because of police necessities, to see this comparatively unadorned parade pass. Hundreds of automobile parties ranged themselves along the curbs, and at many places the sidewalks were crowded. Thousands who have little personal knowledge of what Christian Endeavor means, looked on with sympathetic response to the uniform good humor and high spirits of Christian Endeavorers from many States and many lands.

Northern California discovered itself to Southern California in this parade, having the right of line, next to the officers. A score of county Christian Endeavor banners floated proudly at the heads of as many groups of young people—San Francisco, Alameda, Sacramento, Butte, many of them, from big counties and little, from the centres of population and from the remote and inaccessible mountain counties, all of them Californians, all of them of the sort to make every Californian proud.

"I love you, California," received a new stamp of approval at this convention. In the parade, as in all the big Convention gatherings, the song of California arose with stirring cadence, and visitors from a thousand distant communities sang it with spirit, in graceful recognition of the hospitality California has extended to them.

But these visitors did not fail to impress upon Los Angeles that they have things at home of which to be proud. State songs and State yells gave the parade the character of an interstate competition.

Illinois had in line a lusty delegation.

"Illinois, Illinois," a splendid song, written by a poet, a song to stir the heart of a Patagonian even, was sung by the Illinois troop as they marched.

The Kansas visitors, with a big sunflower at the head of the delegation, gave the Jayhawker yell with the vigor of a tornado.

Wisconsin, Michigan, Indiana, Ohio, Missouri, Colorado, Tennessee, Massachusetts, with the son of President Clark in the front rank—many States, all with proud banners, were in the line, all singing, all splitting the air at intervals with yells.

The young ladies from San Diego sang a song, the most distinguishing part of which was "San Diego is the place for me." Those from Orange County carried a great banner, on which was a great golden orange on a yellow background. The San Bernardino delegates also carried a large banner.

The nurses' corps, all in full uniform, followed by the emergency ambulance, which had been chartered for the Convention, presented one of the features of the parade.

A large group of Japanese Endeavorers, carrying lighted lanterns, was given a continuous ovation from the start of the parade to the finish, and when they entered the big tent they aroused so much enthusiasm that, had it not been an Endeavor crowd, one would have concluded a riot had broken out. The Japanese were given seats on the tiered seats back of the stage, at the right of the chorus.

All the delegations, as they passed along the streets, either gave their yells, which told the spectators who lined the sidewalks from whence they came, should their waving banners prove insufficient, sang as they marched. A half-dozen songs could be heard by the spectators, coming from different sections of the parade within a block. Some sang their State songs, while many joined in singing religious hymns.

As at a prayer meeting, where some voice sounding the opening notes of a well-known hymn brings with it the whole congregation, so one marching Christian Endeavorer would start a religious song well known to all, such as "Onward, Christian Soldiers," and all within range of the voice would immediately join.

It was indeed an impressive sight to see the delegations march into the Convention hall singing, cheering, and waving flags and banners. They came from East, West, North, and South, demonstrating one of the fundamental truths of Christian Endeavor, that all are one in Christ Jesus.

The Concert.

This was concert evening. Prof. William H. Mead was the leader of the orchestra, which, by the way, has an honorable history. It was started eighteen years ago by Mr. Mead and Paul C. Brown, California's field secretary; and it is good to think that after years of service in church and Sunday-school work it could come forward to the help of Christian Endeavor in the Convention. The players were equally at home in selections from Mozart and Handel and Wagner, playing with verve and understanding.

The Convention chorus of one thousand voices, led by Prof. L. F. Peckham, sang selections with remarkable purity, beauty, and unity of tone.

The Convention favorite undoubtedly was "I love you, California," the words of which were written by F. B. Silverwood and the music by A. F. Frankenstein. A special Christian Endeavor chorus was written for the song by Mrs. J. B. Brown, mother of Paul Brown, California's beloved field secretary. The bands played it, the girls hummed it, and the boys whistled it until it kept lilting through our very souls, and we caught ourselves singing over and over, "I love you, California," with the rest. And why not? California is here to be loved.

One of the soloists was Elmer N. Lafonso, the Indian tenor; another, George H. Bemus; and a third, Miss Ethel Foster, daughter of the song-leader, Mr. Percy S. Foster. Mrs. Robert A. Smith and Professor Peckham sang a duet. Mrs. Smith and the chorus gave a thrilling rendition of Rossini's "Inflammatus."

Three bouquets were given to the three men who were responsible for the music of the Convention, Paul C. Brown, Professor Peckham, and James G. Garth, the pianist.

In thanking the choir for their gift Mr. Brown told the secret of the unqualified success of the Convention singing. It was not only planned; it was *consecrated* and nourished by prayer. Every rehearsal was made a prayer meeting. The choir-leader was chosen because he is a sincere Christian, and the pianist, because he—a brilliant player—loves best of all to go to the slum missions and play for the men that are down and out.

This wonderful evening came to a close with the Hallelujah Chorus, sung by the choir with thrilling power.

THE ENTRANCE TO AUDITORIUM ENDEAVOR

THE RECEPTION COMMITTEE

CHAPTER XIII.

THE PEACE MEETING

Auditorium Endeavor, Saturday Evening, July 12.

The Relation of Christian Endeavor to Universal Brotherhood.

SATURDAY evening's peace meeting was introduced by a unique song by an American Indian chief in the full dress of his tribe, who gave a sample of the monotonous singing of his people.

He was followed by E. N. Lafonso, also an American Indian, who beautifully rendered "Nearer, my God, to Thee."

Three aspects of the peace movement were taken up. Rev. R. P. Anderson, associate editor of *The Christian Endeavor World*, led off with an address on the subject:

WHAT CHRISTIAN ENDEAVOR HAS DONE IN THE PEACE PROPAGANDA.

By Rev. R. P. Anderson, Boston, Mass.

The leader of the Russian Synod once remarked that dynamite is powerless compared with the force of a new idea. In our own day an old idea has awakened to new life. Ever since the angels proclaimed peace on earth and good will among men the upward push of clarifying human intelligence, vitalized by this idea, has been preparing the way for the abolition of war.

Now what has Christian Endeavor done, what is it doing, to advance international peace?

First, note the influence exerted by its ideals.

Perhaps one of its greatest services, and one that cannot be measured, is the steady influence it exerts through its ideals, its methods, and its world-wide fellowship upon the common people of every country in the world. Week by week Endeavorers in all parts of the globe are repeating their covenant to do whatever Christ would have them do; week by week they are reminded that their brothers in all lands are thinking the same thoughts, studying the same topics, pursuing the same aims, and praying to the same Lord; and, as these ties of brotherhood are drawn closer, nations are no longer considered "foreign," but all are one in Christ Jesus.

Second, there is the influence exerted by its founder.

Dr. Clark is a peace society in himself. All his missions have been peace missions. You may remember that, when war threatened between Chile and Argentina, two bishops, one in each country, started a crusade among the common people, and aroused so strong a sentiment in favor of peace that the rulers were led to submit the differences between the nations to arbitration; and that figure of Christ on the border, "The Christ of the Andes," as it is called, stands as a testimony, net only to the power of international Christian sentiment, but to the work that two men accomplished. In his writings and his wide travels Dr. Clark is doing a similar work among the young people of the world. If any living man ought to receive the Nobel peace prize, Dr. Francis E. Clark is that man.

Third, there is the influence that goes forth from

our international conventions, which are peace meetings. One think of Agra, India, where for the first time in the history of missions in India men of many nations and of many denominations were brought together on one platform; or of Geneva, Switzerland, where more than thirty nationalities were represented. At such gatherings race differences are forgotten. One emotional French brother at a convention in London said, as he grasped the hand of a German Endeavorer, "I did not know that Germans were so nice." So Christian Endeavor is fostering the spirit of internationalism and world-brotherhood and preparing the path of peace.

At the last British convention it was voted to hold the British national convention of 1915 in France. Think of it! A British convention in the home of Britain's traditional foe! Surely we have progressed far beyond the days when Shakespeare could make Bedford say in Henry VI.,

> "Bonfires in France forthwith I am to make;
> Ten thousand soldiers with me I will take,
> Whose bloody deeds shall make all Europe quake."

And now a peace army of Christian Endeavorers is going to France to draw the nations together in the bonds of friendship.

Fourthly.

Christian Endeavor is developing the interest of one nation in another, and thus furthering the cause of peace. Cleveland Endeavorers have borrowed the very name of their union, the Sunrise Union, from Japan; and they donate $1,000 a year toward Christian Endeavor work in the Land of the Rising Sun. Missouri has undertaken to aid China, and has not only given to that land two splendid field secretaries, Rev. and Mrs. Edgar E. Strother, but generously supports them in their labors. These things are but beginnings. One is tempted to ask what State will now interest itself in and help Mexico or Brazil or Spain or Italy or Korea or our own Alaska.

Fifthly.

The Christian Endeavor World has been consistent and insistent in its advocacy of peace. On June 4, 1904, there appeared in its pages an article from the pen of Professor Amos R. Wells, suggesting in connection with a peace topic that each society send to Congress a petition urging the government to take steps to induce the governments of the world to establish an international legislative body, a permanent parliament of the world. A suggested form of petition was printed, and 1,642 memorials were sent from as many societies to each branch of Congress. The hearts of the young people are right on the peace question, and Christian Endeavor is seeking to keep them right and to direct their energies.

Sixthly, there is the personal influence of Endeavorers.

It is not generally known that the man who under God was instrumental in bringing about peace in China and averting a long and disastrous civil war is a Christian Endeavorer, the treasurer of the United Society of Christian Endeavor in China, Mr. Edward S. Little. During a residence of many years in China Mr. Little had come into personal contact with the men who happened to be ranged on both sides of the Chinese question; and, when war broke out, he was therefore in a position to correspond with them all. At the darkest moment he proposed to Yuan Shi Kai and to Sun Yat Sen that they appoint commissioners to discuss terms of peace, and he offered his house in Shanghai as a place of meeting.

His offer was accepted. The meeting took place, and lasted for six weeks, one of the commissioners and his staff being entertained at Mr. Little's house all the time. During the negotiations Mr. Little acted as middleman, according to Chinese custom. It is a matter of history how an armistice was declared, the revolution ended by Sun Yat Sen's nobly and unselfishly withdrawing from the presidency, and the new republic came into being. One might almost say that the Chinese republic was born in Christian Endeavor. At any rate, Christian Endeavor had a large and important part to play in bringing in the dawn of China's new political day.

And now what can we as Endeavorers do to advance the cause of peace still further?

I would suggest that we can have more international correspondence. Our societies might send greetings to Endeavorers in many lands. Think what it would mean for good will to send messages to Mexican societies just at this time. If the language difficulty seems too great, it may be overcome by learning Esperanto, the international language.

Then we might observe Peace Sunday more generally than we do. A great topic like this ought to have our best attention at least once a year.

Once more, we might form a Christian Endeavor League of Peace, somewhat similar to the Comrades of the Quiet Hour. The members might be bound together by a pledge something like this:

"Trusting in the Lord Jesus Christ for strength, I will seek to promote good will among men and peace on earth, and I will work as I have opportunity toward the abolition of war."

Furthermore, we should have peace committees in every society to keep abreast of the peace movement and bring information about the progress of peace in all the world to the members at least once a month. The present information committee could very easily be called "the information and peace committee."

Looking back through the years, one sees that great waves of reform sweep periodically across the world. One of these waves rolled over slavery, and carried it away. We have had prison-reform, and we are now in the midst of political and industrial reform. A mighty wave of temperance reform has also arisen during the last two or three decades It is time that the nations reformed their war propensities. The peace wave is upon us, and when it has done its work war will be no more.

It requires no stretch of the imagination to believe that Victor Hugo's prophecy will be realized at no distant day.

"A day will come," says Hugo, "when a cannon-ball will be exhibited in public museums just as an instrument of torture is now, and people will be amazed that such a thing could ever have been. A day will come when these two immense groups, the United States of America and the United States of Europe, will be seen placed in the presence of each other, extending the hand of fellowship across the ocean, exchanging their produce, their industries, their arts, their genius, clearing the earth, peopling the desert, improving creation under the eye of the Creator, and for the good of all uniting these two irresistible and infinite powers, the fraternity of men and the power of God."

We also have the peace question at home, the question of the relation of the colored and the white races in the United States. Bishop Alexander Walters, D.D., one of our trustees, spoke inspiringly on

THE FRIENDLY ATTITUDE OF THE NEW SOUTH TOWARD THE NEGRO AND THE PROMISE OF HIS FUTURE UPLIFT.

By Bishop Alexander Walters, D.D., A. M. E. Zion Church.

Mr. Chairman and fellow Endeavorers, in His name, the Christ, and on behalf of twelve million Afro-Americans I greet you.

This is our year of jubilee. Fifty years ago the great Lincoln, the heroic leader, the wise statesman, the sympathetic friend of humanity, issued his Emancipation Proclamation, which liberated more than four million bondmen and the consciences of more than thirty million white men and women. It was a wonderful feat. And, following the injunction of Holy Writ, which says, "And ye shall hallow the fiftieth year . . . ; it shall be a jubilee unto you," we have proclaimed this our year of jubilee. We come on this glad occasion to report the progress we have made during our fifty years of freedom.

The past half a century has witnessed a wonderful change for the better in the life of the black man and in the development of the white man of the South. At the surrender at Appomattox the Old South with its cruel system of slavery and its non-progressive spirit passed away, and a new South was born; and on its banner is written, "Liberty for all men regardless of creed or color."

The Old South was satisfied with its large plantations and its slave labor to operate them, contented with its leisure class and far-famed reputation for chivalry and hospitality.

The Old South was willing that the North should own and operate the great factories and iron-furnaces. The hum of the wheels of commerce had but little charm for it.

The New South has turned its face to the rising sun; its spirit is aggressive and its motto is, "Onward."

The Old South closed the door of opportunity against the negro; the New South has opened it to him. It is a great pity that the New South has in it a place for lynching and burning of human beings; and the sooner these demoralizing and brutalizing agencies are eliminated, the better it will be for all concerned.

The friendly attitude of the South is seen in the large amount of money expended in the erection of school buildings for colored children and salaries paid to our teachers. While it is true that we contribute considerable toward our own education, the fact will remain that the large majority of the public-school funds is paid by the white people.

The friendly attitude of the New South is seen in what it is doing to aid the negro in his material advancement.

Whether we agree with it or not, the standard of worth of this nation is the almighty dollar, and I am afraid that the negro will in the last analysis be judged by that standard; understanding this, he started out fifty years ago to get hold of some of the substantial things of earth; and his white neighbor of the South, appreciating his efforts along this line, encouraged him by selling him land and lending him the money with which to pay for it.

According to the census report of 1900, the negroes own 176,485 farms valued at $230,000,000, the average value of a farm being $300.

The negro has not become a white man, and cannot become one. Indeed, he will perhaps never be just like the Caucasian. God no doubt did not intend him so. And, if the negro is sensible, he will conserve his virtues and refuse to imitate the white man's vices.

The friendly attitude of the New South is witnessed in what is being done in some quarters to improve the moral and spiritual condition of the negro. The white denominations of the South are doing more to-day than ever before to aid in our moral uplift.

Those who were present at our Atlantic City meeting have not forgotten the eloquent and thoughtful addresses of Doctors Landrith and Darby in the interest of our uplift.

The Christian Endeavorers of the South are extending a helping hand.

There are rifts in the political clouds that bespeak for us a brighter day along the political lines. We have the proof of this in the invitation to align ourselves with the Democratic party by such great journals as *The New York World, The Charlotte Observer, The Columbia State*, and *The Louisville Courier-Journal*, whose great editor, Colonel Henry Watterson, says in an editorial in that paper: "A new generation of blacks has come upon the scene. These blacks are better educated. In the North they understand the situation."

We ask to be aided in our development as black men and not white men; we are satisfied with our color and with our race.

The black people form one of the three great families of the world; Shem represents the Mongolians; Ham represents the Africans; and Japheth represents the Caucasians.

I believe that each of these great peoples has a destiny, some great work to do; and under God each should fulfil its destiny.

We are preaching the birth of a new era, proclaiming that superstition has given way before the light of Christianity, that sentiment is subservient to reason, that emotion has given way to restraint, and that the dawn of a glorious day is at hand, a day when universal brotherhood will be recognized by both white and black.

Rarely have we listened to so inspiring a speech as that of Hon. J. A. Macdonald, editor of the Toronto *Globe*. It was the utterance not only of a statesman, but of a citizen of the world who thinks in terms of empires and continents and movements embracing the world. His subject was:

YOUNG AMERICA AND THE WORLD'S PEACE.

By Hon. James Alexander Macdonald, LL.D., Editor of *The Globe*,

Toronto, Canada.

It is a great thing to be young, greater still to be young and in America, greatest of all to be young, to be in America, and to have a vision of the world.

Gathered here from the farthest ends of the United States and Canada, here on the shores of the Pacific where East and West front each other and where the lines go out into all the earth, there comes to Young America so loud a calling of the great world that they are dead who do not hear. That the world's loud calling may come to you young Americans, and may come with a world message and in the accent of world power, I venture to challenge you with the thought of America's supreme obligation to seek the fulfilment on a world scale of the prediction and promise of peace and good will for all nations.

The World's First Vision.

The world's first vision of America was a vision of freedom and peace and a great new chance for the race. More than four centuries ago that vision came to Europe. With the fall of Constantinople the eastward look of Britain and Europe was closed. The eastward currents of trade and of life were turned back. Then all Europe faced about, and peered into the darkness of the unknown Atlantic. Dreamers dreamed of westward seaways to China and the Orient that would compensate the nations trading with Europe for the fall of Constantinople and the blockade of the Dardanelles For them the vision shone over the dark water. They were not disobedient to that vision. They followed the gleam. They found not China, but America. For Columbus, for Cortes, for Cartier, America spelt trade. Through the centuries for the down-trodden peoples of Europe America meant freedom, peace, and a new chance—freedom from the autocracies of Europe, peace from the military disposition of the Old World, a new chance for the common man to get a man's chance for himself and for his children.

That was the world's first vision of America. That vision has never faded. It still glows in the souls of the emigrant and eager newcomer from Britain and the nations of Europe. From their crowded cities, from their historic valleys, from their mountain outlooks, they still see afar the vision of America. They see, and across the wide Atlantic they follow, eager, wondering, hopeful as of old. Tell me, you young Americans, has that beckoning vision of America died down and faded out of our souls, we who are American native-born?

America's First Promise.

Europe's great vision was answered by America's first promise. New England, inheritor of Britain's democracy, gave the pledge of freedom, "freedom to worship God." Virginia, with the best blood of Cavalier England in her veins, promised to conserve what was best in Anglo-Saxon institutions and life. Both gave the promise that America would offer to all comers freedom and equality—equality in birth, equality of opportunity, freedom of conscience, and the full enjoyment of "life, liberty, and the pursuit of happiness." When the time came, when there seemed no other way to freedom, the colonies of America struck for independence. By the mouth of Washington and of Jefferson. and in the great words of their Declaration, their high pledges were given for all time to all mankind.

How the nations of Europe marvelled! How their arrogant autocracies mocked! How their children born in oppression hoped it might be true, and stole away across the seas to America's sacred soil! The colonist patriots sacrificed for freedom's sake ties of kinship and America's national background of a thousand years of Anglo-Saxon history. They made a new start that they might be free. Tell me, you young Americans of this great republic, is that passion of freedom the dynamic of your lives?

Canada's Contribution.

Nearly a hundred years after the Declaration of Independence the colonists in the remaining British Provinces were astir. They, too, were men of the British breed. In them throbbed the old Anglo-Saxon impulse. For them, as for their brethren in Massachusetts, Virginia, and the Carolinas, life was not worth while that was not just and free. They were told that they too must cut the painter and strike for independence. They could have had it for the asking. Gladstone and Beaconsfield and the British public opinion would have granted Canada's independence, had Canada demanded it.

But the fathers of the Canadian Confederation had another vision. They dreamed of freedom, not through separation, but by the larger unity. They did the new thing, the unique, the original, the absolutely unprecedented thing; they rose from colonialism to nationhood without war or bloodshed. For the first time in the world's history a colony came to political freedom and national self-government by the peaceful ways of its own Parliament and without the loss of any worthy tradition or the sacrifice of any national heritage.

More than that, Canada not only blazed the trail to a new freedom, but through her achievement the British empire of to-day was made possible. Canada having come to national autocracy through development and not through separation, Australia followed, and then New Zealand; and in our own short day the colonies of South Africa emerged into the free self-governing South Africa Union.

The Dominion of Canada, the Commonwealth of Australia, the Dominion of New Zealand, the Union of South Africa, and the self-governing colony of Newfoundland! There are, the five free nations of the British breed. Five heirs of British civilization. Five fingers of the great British hand. They are all free. They are all related by blood and interest and a common purpose. In any great time of stress they all close toward the palm. And that hand of British power is stretched over the seven seas, never again the mailed fist of oppression, but the open right hand of freedom and justice and peace. And on the stretched forefinger of that hand the name "Canada," brightest jewel of them all, sparkles forever.

Tell me, you Americans of the Canadian breed, have you learned the Canadian secret? Are you obedient to the Canadian vision? Are you ready to rise worthy of Canada's share of America's greatest achievement, and to join with the United States in the supreme obligation which America owes to the world?

America's Greatest Achievement.

And what is America's greatest achievement? It is not in literature or art. It is not in commerce, in industry, or in mechanical invention. In all the achievements of which we are quickest to boast we but share with other continents, and often follow where others have led. But in one thing America leads the world. One American exhibit has no competition. We can show, we of Canada and you of the United States together can show, two proud nations, rich in all that makes nations arrogant, in our veins the blood of all the proudest and most dominant races of history; and yet across this continent runs a common international boundary line, separating the sovereignties of these two nations, but over all the 4,500 miles of that boundary there stands no fortress, there sails no ship of war, there yawns no gun, there stalks no sentinel on guard. Four thousand five hundred miles of river and lake and open prairie and mountain gorge, and every mile of it a bond of international unity and a pledge of international peace!

That is America's greatest achievement. That American exhibit is without precedent or parallel in all God's world. Tell me, you citizens of this continent of peace, are not we, you and I and all of us, under obligations to put first things first, to leave to the lesser breeds such boastings as the Gentiles use, and to make America's proudest boast before the nations this 4,500 miles of civilized boundary line, and our one full century of unbroken peace?

The Republic's War Lesson.

America stands for peace, but America has learned by bitter experience the futility and the horror and the waste of war. This great republic, pledged to the highest ideals of freedom and peace, went out into the awful and unimagined conflict of the Civil War. For those ideals South and North paid the full measure of devotion. It may have been to save the Union, as the North declared. It may have been to preserve the sovereign rights of the States, as the South protested. It may have been, as many judged, to decide whether in this republic and on what terms white and black might live together. Whatever the issue, that Civil War was of all wars in history the most unflinching in its devotion, the highest in its ideals, the most unselfish and heroic in its motive.

And what is its lesson? This: that war did not settle the questions at issue. Those questions were left to be solved by reason and intelligence and the Christian method of love and service. And this lesson too: that the piled-up burden of war debts rests heaviest on the man lowest down, and the nation's increasing war budgets wastes the taxes of the people that ought to go for the causes of education and social betterment and the lifting of the burdens of the poor. The fact that this republic in these years of peace spends seventy per cent of its entire federal revenue on war debts and preparation for war tells its own story and teaches its own lesson. And this third lesson America also has learned: that the most disastrous, the most ruinous, the most irreparable, of all the waste of war is the waste of men, the wanton destruction of the flower of our civilization, the slaughter of the fittest of our human breed, and the loss to the nation of those generations of heroes and patriots who never had a chance to be born.

Tell me, you men and women from North and from South, who in love and life have suffered the loss in which there is no gain to match, is not this republic's war lesson stern enough to justify America in standing up among the nations with a plea, that shall have the accent of a demand, that in the world's neighborhood of nations there shall be no war, and that hate and brute force shall yield to reason and the power of Christian civilization?

The Dominion's Peace Message.

And Canada has its word, a word for peace. That new nation stands almost alone with no war page in its national history and no war debt burdening its people. Once on the veldtside, in the trenches on the march to Mafeking, through the rush at Paardeberg, the sons of Canada proved themselves sons of the British blood, not unworthy of the American breed. But Canada rises unblemished by war's taint, unwasted by war's loss, holding no enmity against any nation, and stirring in no nation's heart resentful memories of cruelty and wrong.

Tell me, you from Canada, is not Canada's peace message worth keeping unbroken by war's harsh notes, worth carrying to all the dominions of the king, worth sounding in trumpets around the world?

America on the Pacific.

President Taft once said, "The situation on the Pacific for all America is safer because two flags and not one are afloat on its shores, representing English-speaking interests, civilization, and power." His successor in the presidency of this republic stands true to that international obligation.

Secretary of State Knox once expressed the true American idea when he said: "Instead of the United States desiring political union with Canada, it is in the interests of this republic that Canada should remain a free nation within the British Empire, and for this reason: the power of America to-day is the power of the United States and the power of Canada, plus the power of Britain. Were Canada to become either an independent power or States in the American republic, there would be for America no 'plus Britain.'" The new secretary of state will not deny the significance of that "plus Britain."

And from the point of view of a Canadian it is a matter of moment that, with the United States and Canada on one side of the Pacific, sharing each with the other all that may be involved for American integrity in the Monroe Doctrine, there rises up at the far gateway of the Pacific the Commonwealth of Australia and the Dominion of New Zealand, both of them bound up with America in responsibility for English-speaking interests and civilization; and behind them all, under the Southern Cross and under the Northern Lights, there stands the pledge of the English-speaking fraternity, "plus the power of Britain."

Tell me, you children of the world's Anglo-Saxondom, does not the fact of English-speaking civilization, and the thousand years of its history, give to America and to young Americans a place to hold and a part to play which challenges all that is aspiring and strong in our common American life?

America in the World.

Not for conquest, not for their own aggrandizement, not that they may lord it over others, have these nations of America and of Britain come to their place of prestige and power on the Pacific. It is given to America to lead the way to the larger freedom for the nations beyond the Pacific. American service in Japan, the leadership of American ideas and examples in China, have given this republic the place of honor in the Orient. That honor is itself a new obligation. It is a call to all true Americans, in Canada and in the United States alike, to rise to this new opportunity. If America will stand by China in these days of peril, and will secure the integrity of that newest republic, the problem of the Far East will be solved in peace.

The call is to Canadians as subjects of Britain to demand that the curse of the hatred and blighting opium traffic be lifted at once and forever. The call is no less urgent to Americans as guardians of the honor of this republic to demand that America's exportation of the cursed rum traffic and tobacco traffic in the Orient be swept away. It is a call to Young America to turn back Christendom's age-long shame, the pagan and barbaric glorification of war.

This was the world's first vision of America. This was America's primal promise. For such a time as this America came into the kingdom and was isolated from the war nations of the world. To rise in such a crisis and make America's dream come true the United States and Canada are bound indissolubly in one supreme obligation.

> "Two empires by the sea,
> Two nations great and free,
> One anthem raise."

That anthem is the angel-song of Bethlehem. Its note is peace and good will. Its motive is the redemptive love of Christ. To make its theme the marching-music of all nations is the world's loud call to Young America.

Dr. Lapsley A. McAfee closed with a decision-service, the whole audience rising to indicate that they would become advocates of peace and would seek to follow some of Mr. Anderson's suggestions for furthering international amity.

CHAPTER XIV.

WITH "BILLY" SUNDAY.

REV. WILLIAM SUNDAY, better known as Billy Sunday, was at the Convention three days. All his meetings were packed to the doors. Thousands were turned away from the Theatre Beautiful the first night. The next night an overflow meeting was addressed by Dr. Charles M. Sheldon and Dr. William Patterson, of Belfast, and even then hundreds upon hundreds went away disappointed because they could not get in. On Sunday morning, at nine o'clock, an audience of nearly ten thousand listened to the evangelist in Auditorium Endeavor. In the forenoon, in one of the churches, he again addressed a great multitude, but only a fraction of those that wanted to hear him. Once more, in the afternoon, the human tide set toward Billy Sunday's meeting, filled the hall, and had to be turned aside. And an evening meeting accommodated only a tithe of those that stormed the doors.

What is there about this man that attracts the crowd in this fashion?

In appearance he is thin and wiry. When he walks, his head projects forward, and his eyes are apparently fixed upon an invisible goal. The face is the keen one of a hunter.

On the platform he is transformed. A great avalanche of words flows from his lips. He is a master of common speech, with a huge vocabulary at his command. He is colloquial even when telling a Bible story, and this fact makes him popular. He speaks so that the common man can understand.

Then, the most somnolent cannot go to sleep when Sunday preaches. He is always doing and saying the unexpected thing. One moment he is at one end of the platform; then with a rush he is at the other, gesticulating, leaning over the rail, thrusting his fist into the face of the audience. His arms are not enough for gesticulative purposes. He uses his legs, too.

But these things are mere externals. One sees at a glance that the man is aflame with a passion for souls. He is a fighter. He is fighting the world's biggest enemy, sin. He wants to arouse the church to take part in the battle. He believes and says that, if church-members would do their duty, they "could put the devil into the hospital before Christmas."

On Sunday morning the preacher's subject was the groups that surrounded the Lord on the night before the crucifixion. There were Judas and the Pharisees. There were eight disciples in another group, to whom Jesus merely said, "Sit ye here," and left them. There were Peter, James, and John, whom Jesus took with Him farther into the garden, and to whom He

A GLIMPSE OF AN AFTERNOON AUDIENCE

said, "Watch and pray." And then, last of all, there was Christ Himself, alone, in an agony of sweat.

At one point in his address when he had been particularly explicit in pointing out the short-comings of the negligent, he said: "I'm not here to give you what you want. I'm here to give you what you need. If you don't like it there are plenty of exits and it won't take you long to get out."

The theme of his discourse was the story of the betrayal of Jesus and His hour in Gethsemane, told in rough and ready vernacular. He likened the twelve apostles to the church-members of to-day with startling comparisons.

"When the mob was hunting for Jesus to crucify Him," he said, "Judas was away from the other apostles. He was out in the world, mixing with the world and the devil. He was a church-member, mind you, but he was a long way from the church and from religion.

"Eight of the disciples were at the borders of Gethsemane. They didn't amount to anything in the emergency. They were about as useless as a good many church-members. Three, Peter, James, and John, were farther in, and Jesus was alone.

"To Judas, Jesus had nothing to say. To the eight He said, 'Sit ye here.' That was about as big a job as they were capable of tackling. To the three He said, 'Watch and pray.' Remember they were the best He had, and they fell down, for He found them asleep.

"Peter thought he was strong enough to make good. 'I'll never deny you,' he said to Jesus. Jesus said, 'I'll just call that bluff.' And you all know how Peter fell down. It's always the fellow that does the most wind-jamming that gets cold feet first.

"What we need to-day to save souls is more spiritual fervor, more work, and more sincerity. Some of the people whose names are on the church records are doing nothing for God. They are the good-Lord, good-devil, milk-and-cider sort of members. When they die, they'll leave nothing behind them but an epitaph on a tombstone.

"The church to-day isn't much more than a mere social organization. The old-time fire and spirit is lacking. Some of the women in it are nothing more than something to hang a dress on, digest expensive food, play bridge whist, and go to the devil.

"The society woman is about the most useless person in the world. When you have a prayer meeting and a whist party the same night, you'll find most of your bunch playing bridge.

"Some people think I'm talking against them when I'm talking against the devil. You've got to be more alert. You must look after your children. If you'll keep the devil out of your boys and girls, he'll soon bank his fires, put crape on the door, and tack up a sign, 'Hell for Rent.'

"The hypocrisy of the church is breeding infidels. I wonder

that God is doing as well as He is with the bunch He has to
work with. We're too much of the cream-puff and charlotte-
russe sort. When you have a saloon election, lock up the
church-members and maybe you'll carry the day. A tidal wave
of old-time religion would do the world more good than all the
doctrinal preaching.

TO HEAVEN BY PULLMAN.

"To see one of these hypocritical church-members, you'd
think he had a through ticket to heaven with a seat in the Pullman car and a call for the porter to wake him up when the
train began to slow down in the yards of New Jerusalem, but
you'll find that he'll likely get side-tracked.

"You may not like that kind of talk, but I can't help it and I
don't want to. I'm no religious masseur, no spiritual osteo-
path. I'm a surgeon, and I believe in striking the knife into the
root of the disease.

"Four out of five church-members are doing nothing to help
Christ. Some of them think they are getting by when they observe Lent. What a silly idea! It is a travesty to say that men
can store up enough piety in forty days to enable them to live
like the devil for the rest of the year.

"The church has degenerated into a third-rate amusement
bureau with the religion left out. Half its members could die
and it wouldn't lose anything. When you have five hundred
members in your church, you think you are doing well if you
can scare up an attendance of seventy-five at a prayer meeting.

"You hold socials. I believe in socials, but they ought to be
free. They could be if the members contribute what they
ought. The Mormons get the money because they keep tab
on their members. When you try to do it you get it where
Queen Elizabeth wore the ruff.

"Multitudes in the church are nothing but bench-warmers.
To get them to do anything is like trying to drag a cat back-
wards by its tail over a carpet. I believe there are thousands
in this tent who would make sacrifices, who would die for
Christianity as quickly as did the martyrs in the Coliseum of
Rome, but there are other thousands who don't care a snap.

"In many respects the people are ahead of the preachers in true
religious spirit. If God Almighty could convert the preachers
we'd give the devil a run for his money and have him in the
hospital before Christmas."

Sunday believes that the church is sick. He does not think
that tender massage will cure her. He's a surgeon. He says
so. "Yet, when I plunge my scalpel into the putrefying ab-
scess," he cried, "some salaried quack shouts, 'You've stabbed
the church.'" Then with indescribable scorn the preacher

shouted back, "You *lie.*" The effect was dramatic. One man called out, "Amen." "I'm an 'Amen' Christian myself," smiled Billy. "Amen," from various quarters. *"Don't shout, 'Amen' unless you live it,"* shouted back the preacher.

Billy Sunday clothes truth in homespun. "The less religion a church has, the more oyster soup it takes to run it. I believe in socials, but they should be free; and if all the members gave a tenth of their income, as they should, the socials would be free, too."

"Jesus," said Mr. Sunday, "had a different message for each of the groups. To Judas he had nothing to say. To the group of eight He said simply, 'Sit ye here.' It was all they were good for; it's all some people are good for to-day—seat-warmers, listening to a sermonette."

But Billy Sunday is not all invective and scorn. There are depths of tenderness in him. Few eyes were dry when he told his experience as a boy on his way to an orphan home, his father having been killed in the Civil War.

He speaks with a note of conviction that grips the heart. When at this meeting he gave an invitation for those to stand who wished to live wholly for Christ, the entire audience rose. Then the preacher sprang up on the rail in front of the platform, and made the closing prayer. It is safe to say that few that were present will forget his message.

One of the Daily Sermons During the Convention.

David's brothers were princely young men and in King Saul's army and they were away to war. I imagine his father saying to David: "Say, son, I wish you'd go to the army and see how the boys are. Your mother is worried about them and they have not phoned nor wired nor written a word for weeks."

When David reached the camp, Goliath came out, as was his custom, and defied the God of Israel. Imagine David saying, "Who is that big lobster putting up that stiff line of talk?"

"Oh, he is the main works of the bunch of Philistines over on the other side of the Cañon."

"Well, why don't some of you fellows go out and give him what's coming to him?"

"Oh," replied one of the brothers, "the gang all get 'cold feet' whenever he shows up. He does that stunt every day."

David might have replied: "You fellows make me tired to let that four-flusher and false alarm get away with that hot air. I'll call his bluff."

David goes to the brook and picks out five smooth stones, and puts one in his sling and blazes away. He soaked the giant on the coco between the lamps, and he went to the mat and took the count. David drew the giant's sword and chopped off his block and the gang all beat it.

Some self-opinionated highbrows call this SLANG. I don't; it's simply preaching the gospel in the language and vernacular of millions of people. It was my language until twenty-seven years ago.

One dark night in Chicago I found Jesus Christ as my Saviour, and with the Holy Spirit as my guide I entered this wonderful temple of Christianity. I entered at the portico of Genesis and walked down through the Old Testament art gallery, where pictures of Abraham, Jacob, Isaac, Joseph, Isaiah, David, Daniel, and a multitude of others hung on the wall. Next I entered the music-room of the Psalms, where the Spirit swept the keyboard of my nature and brought forth a cry of sorrow for my sins. Next I entered the business office of Proverbs and heard the wise man of old say, "The way of the transgressor is hard."

I next strolled into the chapel of Ecclesiastes where the voice of the Preacher was heard. Then I passed into the conservatory of the Song of Solomon, where the rose of Sharon and the lilies of the valley perfumed my life. I walked into the observatory, where there were telescopes of various sizes, some pointing to near-by stars, some to the far-off stars, but all centred on the bright and morning star which was to rise above the moonlit hills of Judea.

I entered the audience-room of the King and caught a vision of His face from the standpoint of Matthew, Mark, Luke, and John.

Next I entered the room where the Spirit was forming the infant church through the Acts of Apostles. Then into the correspondence-room where the apostles sat writing their letters and the epistles to the churches.

Last I entered the throne-room, where all towered into a glitering peak in Revelation, and I am glad, and thank God, I can say I was a sinner, but Christ made me whole.

Hon. J. A. Macdonald

Rev. Charles M. Sheldon, D.D.

Superintendent roling

Rev. "Billy" Sunday

Dr. Recard

Dr. Goodchild

CHAPTER XV.

GREAT SUNDAY-AFTERNOON MEETINGS.

Auditorium Endeavor, Sunday Afternoon, July 13.

MEN'S meetings at International Christian Endeavor Conventions are always a mighty feature for good, and Los Angeles was no exception. Sunday afternoon, Auditorium Endeavor, the palm garden of the Convention, was the rallying-point for nearly five thousand enthusiastic, plain, average working men, the kind that do things. They came with great expectations, and that their expectations were realized was fully demonstrated by their magnificent support of the speakers.

Dr. Clark presided at the meeting. The praise service was led by Prof. Percy S. Foster. A combined chorus of men rendered splendid music. The devotional service was conducted by Rev. Clarence J. Pinkerton, pastor of the First United Presbyterian Church, Los Angeles.

The first speaker introduced by Dr. Clark was President R. B. Peery, D.D., Ph.D., Midland College, Atchison, Kansas. President Peery delivered a clean-cut, convincing address, that held every man, on the subject,

DOES MAN NEED THE SABBATH?

BY PRESIDENT R. B. PEERY, D.D., PH.D., Atchison, Kan.

Apparently many think not. For they are doing all they can to destroy it, by letting business and pleasure continually encroach upon it. Should they succeed in abolishing it, what would be the result?

Man's physical nature demands a day of rest. Night does not quite repair the waste of day, and a weekly rest is needed to keep the body up to its full measure of efficiency. When Japan first began her intercourse with the West, she noted with envy the superior physique of our people; and, starting out to find the cause, she rightly attributed it to their rest-day. Hence she at once adopted the Christian Sabbath, in spite of a deep dislike of Christianity, in order that her people, too, might be strong. Glance at a map, and you will see that the Sabbath-keeping nations are the leading nations of the earth. Three-fourths of the world's mail is in the English language, and the English-speaking people most closely observe the Sabbath.

Blackstone says, "The keeping of one day in seven as a time of relaxation and refreshment is of inestimable benefit to a state, considered merely as a civil institution."

A general neglect of the rest-day would be swiftly and surely followed by bodily weakness, decay, and premature death. If we would live long and be strong, we must have a Sabbath.

Man also needs a Sabbath for the development of his social nature. For he is a social creature, and attains his highest development in proper social relations. The stress of modern commercial and industrial life is so great that the average man has little time for society. He is almost a stranger to his own children. The Sunday holiday gives him an opportunity to know family and friends, and cultivate his social nature. If deprived of this opportunity, he would become more individualistic and of still less worth to society at large. Thus the Sabbath is imperatively necessary for the exercise and gratification of the social instinct.

So the Third Commandment is not an arbitrary religious enactment resting upon divine fiat alone, but is a benevolent provision for human welfare, resting back on a deep original necessity of nature. It is not a restriction upon activity, but a safeguard of life and energy. The Sabbath did not originate with Moses, but has existed from the beginning.

While a day of rest is needed for proper physical and social development, it is even more demanded by man's religious nature. Undoubtedly religion is for the whole week, and the Christian is always a Christian. But religion must take visible shape and form in the church, with public ceremonies and worship; and for these a special time is absolutely essential. At best, we are none too ready to worship, pray, read the Holy Word, and meditate upon it; and we must have a time set apart for this special purpose as a continual reminder and an incentive to the cultivation of the spiritual.

Without our Sunday the visible church would not long survive, and Christian morality would rapidly decline. The experiment was once tried in France, with this actual result; and it must needs always be so. No Sabbath, no worship; no worship, no religion; no religion, no morality; no morality, no permanent freedom and liberty.

When we think of the many strange things witnessed at former International Conventions of Christian Endeavor, strange because of their unexpected and most timely injection, we must admit that here also Los Angeles gave us one of the most thrilling incidents we have experienced in a long time.

Veterans of the civil war, some who wore the blue and others who wore the gray, stormed the meeting in friendly assault, and for a time the meeting was theirs.

Dr. Clark, stepping to the railing of the platform, stated that he had been informed that a considerable number of the old soldiers were in the audience. He asked them to stand, and in in response thirty veterans of the Union army and seven of the Confederate army stood.

At the invitation of Dr. Clark, they went up on the platform, and the audience of nearly 5,000 men applauded and cheered until they were seated. Then as Dr. Clark asked all to rise and sing "America," the great audience rose, and there was enacted a scene never before witnessed at a Christian Endeavor Convention. The old veterans, with tears streaming down their cheeks, embraced. The blue and the gray met as one. They kissed the flag and in many ways vied with each other in demonstrations of loyalty to the flag and country.

The next speaker was our own and much loved Daniel A. Poling, national superintendent of temperance and Christian citizenship. From the moment Mr. Poling began to speak, he gripped his audience, and his strong, masterly effort thrilled the men to action.

The close of the address was tremendous. Mr. Poling called on every man in the great audience, who would promise to join in an active campaign for the destruction of liquor, to stand. To a man the audience arose. Mounting a chair, the speaker asked the great audience to raise their right hands and close their fists. With their hands raised and fists clinched, they repeated a pledge to make their votes count on every occasion for the final extermination of the liquor traffic. It was a dramatic close to a never-to-be-forgotten address. Mr. Poling's address follows, and the subject is,

THE LIQUOR MENACE AND HOW TO MEET IT.

EDUCATE AND EXTERMINATE.

By DANIEL A. POLING, National Christian Endeavor Superintendent of Temperance and Christian Citizenship.

Two years ago ten thousand young people gathered in the International Convention at Atlantic City electrified the continent with the resolution, "A saloonless nation in 1920." And like the echo of that challenge rang from East and West and North and South the answering challenge, "A saloonless nation in 1920—how?"

To-day on the sunset slope of America the Christian Endeavor host makes reply, and the reply is a call to arms,—"A saloonless nation in 1920; educate and exterminate."

There stand revealed to-day two vital weaknesses in the anti-liquor programme.

We have not had adequate information as to our enemy, and we have failed, therefore, of being properly armed against him. While it is generally agreed that John Barleycorn is a very devil when left loose in a life, the nature of alcohol and the place of liquor as an institution in the state, its insidious relation to government, its criminal grip on public affairs, and its demoralizing effects on industrial life—these are not generally known. "My people perish for lack of knowledge," and America staggers to-day beneath the accumulated weight of fifty years of licensed liquor blight because the citizens of the republic have not known their foe. "Ye shall know the truth, and the truth shall make you free," is prophetic of politics and government as it is true in religion. The victory of faith is the perfect fruit of knowledge of a righteous cause.

We submit that the statement of this first weakness suggests the solution to the problem presented by the second weakness, which is the lack of a comprehensive, nation-wide programme participated in by all temperance organizations. We shall never reach our goal, national prohibition, or achieve practical results commensurate with the time, money, labor, and sacrifice invested until, without prejudice to the fundamental principles and policies of any particular organization, we find and occupy a fighting platform of common agreement. And we are profoundly convinced that in a militant educational campaign, carefully wrought out and nation-wide in its scope, we find such a programme, we have presented by the providence of the hour such a platform of common agreement.

Let this educational campaign begin in a national council convened at the call of one hundred and fifty men and women, representative of all the temperance organizations of the country, and drawn from all walks of life, religious, industrial, educational, and political. Let the call be specific and define clearly the bounds of the council, so that no man need fear the coercion of numbers, so that no organization shall hesitate at the thought of the possible pressing of partisan policies and methods. The very inspiring of confidence between men and between organizations would make the assembling of such a national council epoch-marking in its results.

While no man is a prophet to announce the work that such a council would perform, the specific programme that such a council would declare, we will agree here to-day that it might well begin by compiling a reliable temperance literature, culling from the hopeless mass of contradictory speeches, reports, pamphlets, and books a standard library, and recommending it to the whole temperance world. With this literature there should go comprehensive, practical plans for its continuous presentation attractively and convincingly. We refer not to literature dealing with methods and principles of organizations, but to that class of publications unanimously withdrawn from the partisan field.

Necessarily such an educational campaign will begin with the nature of alcohol itself, and go on until men generally know and publicly agree that it is poison; that it destroys brain cells, beginning with the most delicate; that its ultimate effects on every part of the system are baneful; that alcohol makes all natural instincts stronger, and weakens reason, judgment, and will, through which natural instincts must act. Let this campaign of education go on until the nation has been aroused to her danger, and smites the foe that leaves in his train brain-disintegration, bodies receptive of disease, and perverted souls.

But alcohol involves a traffic, an organization, an institution, and as such comes into contact with the duly constituted authority of the State law. The liquor traffic respects no law that stands between it and financial gain. It is the red-mawed anarchist of them all. Here is a challenge to every patriotic American citizen. Upon his innate respect for law and order the Anglo-Saxon has established his every sacred institution. When this respect has been sacrificed to lust and greed of gain, he goes the long way of ruin travelled by the red man when he lost the freedom of his ten thousand hills.

America travails to-day in the throes of a stupendous industrial crisis, and the liquor institution must be revealed to the laboring man as the cheapener of labor, the one unrivalled cause of child labor, the supreme impairer of labor's earning power, the working man's fiercest foe. No longer dare we exempt the liquor traffic from the national application of the sound economy of business and morals.

There is still ringing in our ears the political slogan of last fall, "Let the people rule." And the people must rule or we perish. The liquor traffic is everywhere the foe of free government. The liquor traffic has become the master corrupter of politics. Whenever a city strikes for civic regeneration and freedom from municipal corruption, its blows fall on "John Barleycorn." Whenever great interests desire to secure legislatures friendly to themselves and at the expense of the public, they form at once a thieving partnership with the liquor traffic. Keep the saloon out of politics? It cannot be done, because the saloon is already in politics. The question of the hour is: "Will clean men dominate politics? Will clean men go where the liquor traffic is, and fight it to the death?" Let us sign the new declaration of political independence, and calling on God for strength, go forth as did the Covenanters of old with no fear of failing to do our whole duty.

But the liquor traffic reaches its full height in infamy when it smites and befouls the individual citizen, the voter of the State, the man of business, the father of the family, the mother of the home, the child on my knee. Thus does America tremble and stagger. Give her clear heads, clean bodies, and an untainted spirit, and she will conquer foes without and foes within. But the liquor traffic smites at these very vitals of life. Church of God, in the name of the Christ of little children, awake! For the perpetuity of the state, with word and prayer and purse and vote, fight back into the hell of its birth this monster of infamy.

We have scarcely outlined the beginnings of an educational programme that in the hands of a united temperance army would in less than one year sweep the North American continent as a cleansing fire. Do you say that already these things are known? From first-hand information of every great city of the nation I say that these things are not known, that millions have never heard, and that other millions have heard in part, only to deny.

Christian Endeavor will set a heartening example to all divisions of the conference army by its adaptation of the special literature of the Voter's Information Bureau, which has already received official recognition from the Sunday-school, the Woman's Christian Temperance Union, the Prohibition party, and the Anti-Saloon League. The monthly posters of this Bureau should speak from every roadside fence, every wayside tree and watering-trough, every crossroad store, every city bill-board, and as nearly as possible every factory, barber shop, Sunday-school, and railroad caboose of the land. Let the young people's societies organize touring parties and cover the land with the trial of "John Barleycorn," condemning him to political destruction, national prohibition on the unimpeachable testimony of science, church, home, business, labor, and good government, in every hamlet and city.

Let us make Good-Citizenship Day, first adopted by the Nebraska Christian Endeavorers, and officially indorsed at the Atlantic City Convention, truly a national day. The Sunday immediately preceding the Fourth of July should command every pulpit, every newspaper, every patriotic society, every fraternal and religious organization in the land, until the united voice of a free people shall lift to high heaven a tocsin for peace, brotherhood, Christian citizenship, and freedom from rum.

Let us give a new impetus to the total-abstinence pledge-signing crusade of forty years ago, for in the warmth of brotherly hand-clasp the temperance forces of the nation are discovering that no plan of merit need be superseded, can indeed be spared, but that all plans must be harmonized into a fighting whole and supplement every onslaught of the political advance, as the wings of an army safeguard and strengthen its centre. Such a pledge-signing crusade should incorporate the "Catch-my-pal" plan of the Irish Total Abstinence League, by which every individual signing the pledge agrees to promote the cause of total abstinence by getting others to join the movement. Thus he becomes part of the fighting advance. But as Mr. Patterson, originator of the "Catch-my-pal" idea, himself declares, total abstinence is only the first step. It is of supreme importance that the fruits of this new total-abstinence crusade be conserved before the movement wanes as all other purely moral-suasion movements have waned, and that these efforts be directed into political action.

On the sixteenth of April this year General Secretary William Shaw of the United Society of Christian Endeavor spoke with the voice of a prophet to a Boston audience, and electrified it with the new political covenant. "God helping me, no candidate or party not openly declaring for the destruction of the liquor traffic can have my support or vote." Its acceptance was as spontaneous as was its conception and presentation, and it has already been indorsed by the temperance society of the Methodist Episcopal Church, and is enthusiastically received wherever presented. It is the new Declaration of Independence of which the Atlantic City Convention had a vision when it declared, "A saloonless nation by the Fourth of July, 1920, the three hundredth year from the landing of the Pilgrims at Plymouth." Here we find a common fighting-ground in politics, an opportunity for men and women of every political affiliation to enlist effectually against the liquor traffic, and to make their political sovereignty count for the destruction of the saloon.

And, Christian Endeavorers of North America, shall we not catch a vision to-day of national anti-alcohol congresses covering the continent in a mighty chain of educational and inspirational councils? Let the national council of temperance leaders announce to the world a programme even more extensive and intensive than that of the Men and Religion Forward Movement, which so blessed the churches of America. One hundred conventions, thoroughly prepared for and equipped, bringing into the centre of every State of the Union the temperance leaders of the nation, and sending out into every hamlet of the adjacent territories temperance deputation committees to instruct, organize, and inspire, would, I am profoundly convinced, do more than any other one thing that could be devised, to enact into government the challenge of Atlantic City, "A saloonless nation in 1920."

Such a united educational movement would give to every temperance organization of the country an unparalleled opportunity to direct public sentiment, and to win men, now thoroughly informed and aroused, to its distinctive methods and fundamental policies. And it is our sober judgment that organizations not big enough to accept such an opportunity, too small of vision to welcome such a fighting chance, are too infinitesimal, in these pregnant days of momentous crises, to command the time, money, and labors of any portion of the militant host that cries, "The saloon must go."

We stand to-day in the midst of destiny. God make us worthy of the hour! From the slough of bitterness and mean speech we have lifted ourselves to the firm footing of brotherhood in a common cause, and the broken step of divisions becomes the rhythm of a united army. Behind us are the burned bridges of selfish prejudice and partisan hate, but behind us are the beacons of our comrades who showed the way. Behind us is the wilderness where we wandered, but behind us are the trails blood-red from the trampings of the Haddocks and St. Johns and Willards and Finches and Goughs and Dows, who led the march out of Egypt. 'Tis the hand of yesterday that thrusts us forth, and as fighting men to men who fight we cry all down the line, "All hail the past!" "All hail the past!"

And now I hear the challenge of the embattled hosts, and where but yesterday a thousand discords rang it rises a united shout. The mingled voices of women and little children, of blue-clad veterans and of men in gray, of sturdy toilers from mill and farm, of church and school, of science and politics, of Woman's Christian Temperance Union and Good Templars, Anti-Saloon League and Prohibition party, proclaim in all the land between two seas: "A saloonless nation. National prohibition, an amendment to the Constitution of the United States." We sound a new Declaration of Independence and a call to arms. The command is, "Forward all along the line." The destination is Washington. This is a war of extermination! Who stands to fight for God and home and native land?

After listening to a beautiful selection by the male chorus, Dr. Clark introduced one of the most noted speakers of the Convention, the Hon. James Alexander Macdonald, editor of the Toronto *Globe*, Toronto, Canada. Mr. Macdonald made a timely and very convincing address on, "Jesus and the Social Problem."

He defined the social problem as the problem of living with other people, which involves our relations in the home and in the workshop, and touches the duties of both master and servant. It takes in economic questions, capital, labor, wages, and international questions of war and peace.

Jesus faced that problem not in the form in which we face it, but in such a way as to leave great principles for our guidance. The Gentile principle of selfish ambition produces great over-lords and masters. Is our civilization Gentile or Christian? Is its chief output a few millionaires, or captains of industry, or plutocrats; or is it levelling up the common people, and touching life with beauty and greatness?

Jesus saw a new social order in which service alone prevails. This idea is sinking into the heart of the nation to-day.

Some years ago Dr. Macdonald visited the glen where his forefathers lived in Scotland. An old man spoke to him one day, not about the American millionaire that owned half the glen, nor of politics, nor of world-movements. He spoke about the schoolhouse. He said, "We have seven teachers, and four of them are A.M.'s"; and he was proud of the fact that the glen had a school that could prepare the boys for the greatest colleges in the land.

He was asked whether it did not cost a good deal of money. He admitted that it did. "But," said he, "we try to give our boys a good schooling. There is nothing for them in the glen. Some of them will go to Glasgow, and some to Liverpool, and some to London, and maybe some to America; and we are glad to have them go. The only thing we export in this part of the country," he concluded, "is educated people." Here in a remote Scottish glen was a people serving the world by exporting educated boys. Is not that splendid?

Service! That is the new note being struck to-day. "When King George was crowned," said the speaker, "I was there. I saw the crown of Edward the Confessor placed upon his brow. But the most significant thing in the ceremony was the text from which the bishop preached. Looking squarely into the eyes of the king and queen, he quoted a text which embodies the aspirations of the age, 'I am among you as he that serveth.'"

At the close of the meeting Alford F. Judson, who was a major in Lee's army, asked to be heard for a few minutes. He mounted the speaker's platform with an American flag, and said that, though he fought to destroy that flag, he loved it now and honored and loved the boys in blue who had saved it. He kissed the flag while the audience cheered, and then invited one of the grizzled Union veterans to stand, and, grasping his hand, recited a poem of patriotic tenor.

This closed what was probably the most wonderful and most

effective men's meeting held during an International Convention of Christian Endeavor in many years.

THE WOMEN'S MEETING.

The Theatre Beautiful.

Hundreds of women were sadly disappointed in their efforts to secure admission to the Christian Endeavor women's mass-meeting in Temple Auditorium. Choral Hall fell far short of taking care of even a third of the overflow that clamored with the police for entrance to this one great congregation of women during the convention.

It was an outpouring of the femininity such as Los Angeles has seldom if ever witnessed. Every available seat in the vast theatre was occupied. The stage was crowded and even the orchestra space had its quota of the fair sex.

It was a meeting of real Endeavorers, women anxious not only to help themselves and their own little communities, but to help the world at large in the achievement of better things. The great room vibrated with the thrilling songs of that feminine choir that raised its voice in praise and thanksgiving at the opening of the meeting.

Mrs. Robert J. Burdette, Pasadena, Cal., presiding, first called for a short prayer; and then came a song led by Prof. L. F. Peckham, director of the combined choir of Endeavorers, in which the great audience joined in the chorus that went swelling out through the open doors, a message to the passing throngs and the loiterers in the park across the way.

Mrs. Burdette gave the visiting women a special welcome to the State of woman's achievement, a land that originally was a homeless, womanless coast, but to-day, as if by the law of compensation, the land of women voters, women farmers, and women of wealth and success in every line. "To crown our achievements here, we have the largest Y. W. C. A. in the world and we hope that your presence with us will inspire us with new ideals and increase our many worthy activities.

"While the movement along educational, philanthropic, civic, and political lines has been going on for several decades, the movement in the church has been going on for 2,000 years. There will always be a man's way and a woman's way as long as there is the everlasting masculine and the eternal feminine, which is as God wills it. There is but one thing more disgusting than the mannish woman and that is the womanish man. Woman's work for the kingdom of God must be equal to that of her brother but need not be identical.

"Upon woman is placed the moral responsibility of constantly advancing ideals in public opinion, private life, and Christian citizenship. No organization entrusted to the church has done more for the development of women than the Christian Endeavor and kindred societies. If every woman here would leave with the determination to live a life of absolute Christian citizenship, there would be less need of home-missionary work, of the care of the criminals and the unfortunates."

Mrs. Burdette then introduced the first speaker, Mrs. J. S. Norvell, of Los Angeles. She spoke on "Who Should Respond to the Cry of the Outcast?"

"A mother always comes first in the work of the world. God created woman as the last of his work to crown it all. He stopped his creative work to turn it over to woman, and consequently this great mother-instinct has led the world," she said. "Mother-instinct made it impossible for the mother of Moses to turn him over to the Egyptian masters. The sister of Moses, who assisted her in hiding the infant, stands to-day for the big sisterhood movement of our great Endeavor Society. It is the prototype of a great impulse, of a life force that we are developing.

"The daughter of the king, who found the child, proud in the royalty of her birth, was not too exalted to pick up the outcast and minister to his wants. Her boast of blue blood did not prevent her from ministering to the needy. The girl child with her saw the example and was taught its great lesson. To-day when we hear the call of the needy, the downtrodden and the outcast, we should rejoice in the privilege of service."

Mrs. J. A. Macdonald, of Toronto, Canada, wife of Hon. James Alexander Macdonald, editor of the Toronto *Globe*, was the next speaker. She had for her subject

THE APPEAL OF THE HOME FIELD.

By Mrs. J. A. Macdonald, Toronto, Canada.

"The field is the world." When Jesus made that statement, He intended His followers then and now to take the world-wide vision of life and its opportunities. Very plainly He said, "Go ye into all the world." The gospel message that He gave to His apostles was a message, not for the Jew alone, but for all people. He made it a mark of discipleship that those who believed in Him and His kingdom should set no bounds to their Christian sympathy, and should make their Christian endeavor as wide as the world.

And yet Jesus had those first disciples begin their world-wide mission at points nearest home. "Beginning at Jerusalem" was their marching-orders. The uttermost ends of the earth could not be reached if Judea, Samaria, and Galilee were neglected. Had no church been organized in Jerusalem or Antioch, no efficient missionary work would have been done in Rome or Spain or Gaul. All history has proved the wisdom of "beginning at Jerusalem." And all history has also proved that real Christian love and real devotion in Christian endeavor for those at home will carry both the individual Christian and the organized Christian church into the regions beyond.

When it is seen that the field is the world and that the gospel message is for all the world, there will be no conflict between work in the home field and work in the foreign field. Work at home cannot be confined to home circles. If it is a work of love for love's sake, it will go out wherever love is needed and do whatever love demands.

That is the real meaning of Christian Endeavor. First of all, it is Christian. It takes Christ's point of view. It works for His ends. It is inspired by His motives. It goes where He has gone. It does the things He would do.

If we speak, therefore, of the home field and of the foreign field, it is not because home and foreign are separated one from the other; but we must begin where we are, do the work nearest at hand, organize the Christian life and Christian effort where it has already begun. Make it strong and efficient at home, and so it shall go abroad to the circles outside, and make the fields that now are "foreign" the "home" fields of our larger Christian Endeavor.

In this twentieth century, when all the world is open, when every country touches every other country, when the life of one race helps to make or to mar the life of every other race, no field of Christian Endeavor can be a foreign field. All the world has become a home field. Its ignorance is home ignorance; its vice is home vice; its sin is home sin; its heathenism is home heathenism. Our homes in America are not safe for us or for our children if ignorance and vice and sin and heathenism are allowed to flourish in Europe or Asia or Africa or the islands of the sea.

There are those in all our churches interested by the unusual conditions of work in the foreign field. The hopelessness of heathenism makes its appeal to them. The emptiness and blankness of the heathen life, and especially the life of heathen womanhood, give emphasis to that appeal. No word ought ever to be spoken anywhere that would cut the nerve of what is called foreign missions. In the long run, and in the commingling of east and west on both shores of the Pacific, foreign missions become home missions.

But in order that foreign-mission work may be strong and carried on strongly the work in the home field must be made vital, thorough, and aggressive. It is, therefore, in order that our minds may be stimulated and our hearts moved by the situation in America that this subject has been put on the programme for this afternoon. The committee was convinced that the Christian Endeavor movement must first be a home endeavor, must first be an American movement, if it is to be effective abroad and reach the world. We are, therefore, asked to face with open eyes the home field as we each may see it, to consider the home needs as we each may know them, and to respond to the home appeal as it comes to us out of our experience and knowledge in the local societies and local churches to which we belong.

We shall not rightly understand our local needs, nor shall we justly appreciate the value and the power of our local endeavors, if we do not have in mind in all these local affairs the larger life of the nation of which we are citizens.

The mistake is often made of thinking only of the local society and the local community. That mistake instead of making the local society strong, makes it weak. It tends to make our efforts seem small and insignificant. It is only when we set our Christian Endeavor against the background of the big life of the nation that our efforts are seen in their true light. I have known Christian Endeavor societies to dwindle and die because they were self-centred. I have known other societies to take on new life and become sources of great influence just because they felt themselves a part of the great life of the country. I have known missionary associations that lost their missionary spirit because they lost the national outlook. It is when we feel that our work is not ours alone but the country's and the world's, that we take it up and carry it on bravely and with confidence.

If I had but one word to speak, it would be a word for the widening of our outlook, a word that would make the least service we render seem to be a part of all the large work that is being done, a word that would make the individual worker, alone in the obscure corner, a needful member of the great army, a word that would make our little congregation and its little society a real force in the redemption of America.

It would be a great thing for us, it would be a great thing for the womanhood of America, if we and all other American women could feel ourselves to be a part of the power which America ought to be in all the world. It would lift us out of the littleness of the average woman's life. It would make social and selfish ambitions seem too small, social rivalries and conquests too petty, for us really to care about them.

If to this generation any one appeal is made, it is an appeal to us and to all the women of America. The doors are open to us through our churches and our church organizations to do a great work in redeeming America, not only from the social evils that threaten our very homes, but also from all other evils in the life of the country which make for the country's weakness and shame.

In the United States and in Canada there is much talk about votes for women. In some of the States women now have the franchise on equal terms with men. The day may come when everywhere in America a woman shall have the vote because she is a woman, just as a man has the vote because he is a man.

That question is not of the first and highest importance. What is of importance is that women, whether they have the vote or not, should feel that they have a share in the life and work of their country and that they may do a service which cannot be done except by women.

For myself I have learned that there is almost no kind of work that is really effective which may not be done through the church or through societies and organizations which the church maintains and inspires.

Too often the church is the victim of mere church custom. It is slow to change its methods and to enlarge its operations to meet the needs of new conditions. One of the good things done by the Christian Endeavor movement is in breaking up these old limitations of church activity. The churches are now taking an active interest in the social problem, in the house problem, and in all the problems that are raised by the incoming of great masses of aliens and foreigners. The old style of church-work has proved utterly inadequate to meet the new conditions of America.

The women have come to take a very large share in the missionary work of the church. At first that work was mainly in the interests of the foreign field. Now it is just as eager about work in the home field.

You who live in United States know the conditions in this country, and hear the appeal of the home field as it comes from the new communities all over the land. My own experience has been confined very largely to work in Canada. As a member of the Women's Home Missionary Society in the Presbyterian Church I have learned some of the needs of the home field. I have heard its appeal, and I know through the knowledge which experience brings that the work which is done by the women of Canada in the pioneer districts, and among the foreign people in the cities, and in the great foreign settlements throughout the country, is not only a great blessing to Canadian womanhood, but is also an important service in the making of the Canadian nation. All the churches of Canada are organizing their women for work in the home field. The congregations are organizing women's missionary societies, young women's missionary societies, and mission bands for girls. Training-schools are being established in the larger cities, and from them trained women workers are being sent out as Bible-readers, pastors' assistants, trained nurses, and helpers of all kinds, who carry the gospel message into the homes of the people and make the foreigner and the stranger a citizen and a neighbor.

The work of which I have the most intimate personal knowledge is the work among the new settlers in New Ontario, and in the great western Provinces of Manitoba, Saskatchewan, Alberta and British Columbia. We have one Women's Home Missionary Society that organizes and directs all this work from Ottawa and Montreal on the east to Victoria, Vancouver, and the Yukon on the west. Our work has to do with the foreigners and the pioneers in all that wide area. Our society serves under the home-mission committee of the General Assembly. We maintain hospitals and homes for children among the Ruthenians, Hungarians, Bulgarians, Austrians, Swedes, Germans, Icelanders, Poles, Galicians and people of almost every other nationality of Europe. We maintain hospitals equipped for real hospital service, with doctors and nurses trained for their work. We take an active interest in the lumbermen and the miners, and send large quantities of reading matter to their camps. The loggers' mission in British Columbia, with its missionary boat, its missionary and its doctor going up and down the inlets and rivers along the coast, is one of the most picturesque and one of the most useful services in which women in Toronto and eastern Canada are engaged. It carries almost the only gleam of light from home that comes to thousands of men and boys whose daily life is hard and dull and deadening.

What I have said about the work of the Presbyterian Church might be said about the work of the Episcopalians, the Methodists, the Congregationalists, and others. All those churches are devoting themselves with great ability and great enthusiasm to bring the gospel of salvation from sin to the strangers of other races and other languages that have come to Canada. Each one has its own peculiar methods and lines of work, but we are all one in sympathy and in purpose. The motto of the society with which I am connected might be the motto of all other similar societies. That motto is, "Canada for Christ."

Unselfish service is always educational for those who engage in it. It develops the mind; it broadens the sympathies; it quickens all true emotions; it makes the whole woman a better woman, better for her home and family, a better member of her own social circles and a better citizen of her country. All the women I know, who have given themselves unselfishly even to the routine and humdrum work of their little societies and ordinary programmes have reaped a harvest that has enriched their lives, and who can tell how much the service means for the country and the nation? No matter whether we have the vote or not, we have the power of life, and that power is far greater than the right to vote.

The organized womanhood of the United States and Canada could evangelize and Christianize America by making the homes of America truly Christian.

"America for Christ" should be the motto of all Christian Endeavorers on this continent, "America for Christ" would mean "Christ for the World."

The last speaker of this most remarkable meeting was a returned missionary from China, Mrs. Edgar E. Strother. Her subject was

OUR SISTER ABROAD.

By Mrs. Edgar E. Strother, China.

Women in the Occident can hardly realize the condition of their sisters in lands where Christ is not known. Far too often girls are unwelcome at birth, betrothed in infancy, and later the slaves of relentless mothers-in law, without hope in this life or for that which is to come. They have had no opportunities or advantages, and very little to relieve the monotony of their daily round. Oh, the unutterable hopelessness of a heathen woman's life! Some have made pilgrimages to the great idol shrines and fulfilled all the demands of their code of ethics, but have failed to find the peace they sought.

Some women in these Western lands, constrained by the love of Christ, lifted up their eyes and looked on the whitened harvest-fields, and went with the simple story of the gospel to their sisters abroad. By believing the message about the Lord Jesus Christ these found the peace they had so long sought. These Chinese Christians were ready and willing to help, but lacked the training. Christian Endeavor came to their aid, showing them what they could do for Christ and how they could do it.

Some missionaries have told us that before Christian Endeavor was introduced they had to come in from their itinerating-trips to lead the prayer-meetings, but now the young Christians have been trained in Christian Endeavor how to prepare for a meeting and lead it. The best Christian Endeavor rallies and meetings we have ever attended were in China. The Chinese Endeavorers come to the meetings well prepared, for they use the daily Bible readings in their family worship or in their personal Bible-study. They bring their Bibles and hymn-books to the meetings. We heard fifty-seven participate in fifty-three minutes. At the opening of the meeting some societies put up the names of the first eight or ten who are expected to take part. Often a new leader is assisted by an experienced one.

In some Christian Endeavor societies in mission schools the older girls go out two by two, on two afternoons each week, with the missionary, teacher, or matron, to visit in the heathen homes, give the gospel message, and invite the women to the chapel services. One Sunday we saw a Christian Endeavorer surrounded by seven women who had responded to her invitation.

Chinese Christian Endeavor societies not only have the usual committees, but have introduced others to meet their special needs. The "instruction committee" is almost universal in Chinese societies; those who have had the advantage of an education are appointed on the instruction committee to teach the unlearned how to read their Bibles and hymn-books. The "chapel-order committee" has been helpful, as members of this committee are stationed in the different parts of the chapel, and tactfully deal with the heathen who come to the services and are disposed to speak aloud or otherwise disturb.

We can scarcely realize the value of Christian Endeavor training to some of the pupils in mission schools when they return to their homes and are practically the only witnesses for the gospel in their neighborhood.

There is no more effective way of winning China for Christ than to train the Chinese girls and women in Christian Endeavor societies.

First Congregational Church.

Sunday Evening.

Twelve hundred people were at the First Congregational Church on Sunday evening when Dr. John Willis Baer presided. Rev. A. B. Patten, of Sacramento, delivered an inspiring address on "The Social Message of Jesus," which, he said, is really one with Christ's message to the individual; for there are not two gospels, but one for the whole man and the whole world.

The social message of Jesus is for souls in society, and we

must remember that saved souls are always socialized souls. God was in Christ reconciling the world unto Himself. Human character and citizenship were out of tune with God. Jesus brings them back into harmony. He builds character into citizenship. His ideal is a federated humanity.

The second address, "The Spiritual Message of Jesus," was given by Rev. George E. Burlingame, D.D., of San Francisco. Jesus, he said, is the advocate of spiritual values, and we cannot understand His social message without first grasping His spiritual message. The one is a part of the other. Jesus presents spiritual ideals as the goal of life. That ideal is the will of God which is expressed in individual life as holiness, and from this centre works itself into all social relationships.

These spiritual ends are attainable only through the use of spiritual means, the ministry of prayer, the word of God, and the gift of testimony. But more, Jesus shows us vast spiritual forces through these spiritual means, by which we are enabled to attain the goal He sets before us. An ideal without a dynamic is not worth much; but Christ provides both, so that the church may become "Christ's agent in the world."

First Christian Church.

Treasurer Lathrop presided over the meeting on Sunday evening at the First Christian Church. The unusual combination of speakers and subjects made it take on an international, interracial, and interdenominational character.

First came Rev. C. T. Scott, D.D., of Victoria, B. C., on the theme "Thy Kingdom Come." Although uttered by a Methodist from the Dominion of Canada, his presentation of the social message of Jesus Christ was essentially the same as that given by the speakers from the United States.

Rev. W. T. Johnson, D.D., our colored Baptist trustee from Richmond, Va., spoke on the subject, "Wanted—An Opportunity to Rise." Dr. Johnson eulogized the negro as a home-maker, and referred to the fact that he is paying taxes on property worth seven hundred million dollars.

That negroes love Christian Endeavor is shown by the fact that there are 5,567 colored Christian Endeavor societies.

Dr. J. Percival Huget's subject was "The Spiritual Dynamic, the Essential of Progress." Three things govern progress: the law of struggle, the law of power, and the source of power. No power is sufficient that does not come from God, and the one who is working with God works with limitless power.

Each of the three addresses was splendidly and enthusiastically received by the large audience, and at the close Canadians and citizens of the United States listened to Dr. van Dyke's new "Home, Sweet Home" and the singing of "America."

Immanuel Presbyterian Church.

A large congregation gathered on Sunday evening in Immanuel Presbyterian Church, where Rev. Alexander Gilray, D.D., of Toronto, presided.

The first subject, "Enlargement for Efficiency," was ably treated by Rev. E. A. Watkins, D.D., president of Palmer College, Albany, Mo. The speaker pointed out that any real efficiency in service for Christ depends on time and adequate enlargement of mind. An abidingly useful life or ministry can only follow devoted study along the best lines of reading and thought. Then, only as there is spiritual enlargement by devotion to the meaning of the cross, and much searching of the Bible in close fellowship with Christ, can there be a growing and abiding efficiency. The second speaker was President Henry Churchill King, of Oberlin College. He spoke with rare skill and interest on "The College Man and the Church." "The college man," he said, "needs the church, the pillar and ground of the truth. It is only as the student remains loyal to the claims and call of the church at home and abroad that he can rise to the full meaning of the vision of service and life. Moreover, the college man can be of immeasurable value to the church. Pity the student or man of thought that does not know his responsibility and his opportunity in the church."

Note.—Addresses delivered at these meetings appear in full in Chapter of Addresses.

CHAPTER XVI.

A CHAPTER OF ADDRESSES.

BY grouping the majority of the addresses delivered during the Los Angeles Convention we endeavored to facilitate matters for the reader in locating these very enthusiastic, helpful, and inspiring addresses. This chapter is really a feast for those who desire to know of the many good and timely things spoken during the convention. Through it all the reader will find running the threads of hope, cheer, encouragement and life. We, therefore, call your attention to the following addresses delivered by consecrated men and women whose hearts are afire for God, with the hope that much good may be derived.

INTERNATIONALISM AND THE CHURCH.

By Hon. James Alexander Macdonald, LL.D., Editor of the *Globe,* Toronto, Canada.

In this new continent of America we and our churches have come into vital touch with the larger issues involving the world. By the force of the great facts of the American situation we are compelled to think internationally. For this reason I venture to speak to you to-day, first, on the fact of internationalism, and then on the duty and privilege of the church in relation to that fact.

The Fact of Internationalism.

No nation ever again can live to itself or die to itself. It was once the dream of American statesmen that this republic might live in comfortable isolation from all alliances and antagonisms with Europe and the world. Statesmen in Canada still protest that their Dominion shall not be drawn into the mad vortex of European politics. But, whether we wish it or not, America is now, and must forever remain, a factor in affairs affecting the whole world, and more and more both the United States and Canada must take account of world conditions.

This very occasion illustrates the fact of internationalism on this continent. A Canadian speaker on the platform of the Christian Endeavor Convention in Los Angeles is as much at home as he would be in Toronto. The dividing line between the two countries and their two governments is by no means imaginary, but the two peoples are not so

Rev. Robert E. Preflow

Rev. George E. Burlingame, D.D.

Rev. Claude E. Hill

Percy S. Foster

Arthur J. Gatter

Rev. Robert F. Coyle, D.D., LL.D.

divided. Sovereignty meets sovereignty and flag meets flag along the four thousand miles of transcontinental boundary. The two peoples have their interests and ideals and purposes all interwoven. The people cross and recross until from the Rio Grande to Hudson Bay and from Cape Breton to California there is being erected a vast community of interests, of opportunities, and of obligations, which makes America unique among the continents, one in its life, one in its responsibility, and one in its message to the world.

The American Situation.

The singular situation on this continent is significant of a process embracing the world and involving more and more all continents and every nation. Here in North America we have two sovereign governments, administering each by itself the affairs of two national units. But their two peoples reach out far beyond the sovereignty of either government, and interlock their sentiments and sympathies, their commercial and financial undertakings, and their social and industrial developments, until in their intercivilization the integrity and prosperity of each are the accepted obligations of both. Millions of Canadian-born have found homes under the Stars and Stripes. Millions from the United States are setting their faces northward to the Canadian land of promise. By these vital threads the United States and Canada are woven together, the warp and woof of the English-speaking fraternity of the western world. Between these two nations war is forever out of the question. It would be civil war. It would be fratricidal war. Against the very thought of it every commercial interest and all the highest instincts of both our people would rise up in irresistible protest.

Men have said, sometimes on one side, sometimes on the other, that this or that trade policy would work for political union on this continent. They think only on the surface who so speak. Tariff or no tariff, the United States and Canada are two national units, and two in their distinctive forms of government they shall remain. But our English-speaking peoples are one people, one in the thousand years of their historic background, one in their inbred passion for liberty, one in the genius of their law, one in the wealth of their literature, one in the foundations of their faith, one in the eternal purpose of the God of nations. What God has joined together, let not the petty politics of man put asunder.

Does some one ask, Why not then unite the two governments in one Parliament or Congress of the continent? Sir, there are wider horizons and more splendid visions even than those of America. In the defence of American civilization and in the mission of America to the world these two nations are more impregnable and more impressive under their two flags than they would be, were but one red, white, and blue to wave from the Gulf to the pole.

The True International Doctrine.

The true doctrine of international relations on this continent was propounded to me by the former ex-secretary of state, Mr. Knox, when he said:

"Instead of desiring the political union of these two nations it is to the advantage of the United States that Canada remain outside this American republic and within the empire of Britain. The power of America to-day is the power of the United States and the power of Canada plus the power of Britain. Were Canada to separate from the British Empire and become either an independent commonwealth or a group of States in this republic, there would be no 'plus the power of Britain.'" To the people of Canada that "plus the power of Britain" counts. It counts not only in matters of security from attack by sea, but much more does it count in national dignity, aspiration, and prestige; to be the half-way house of an empire that sweeps round the world challenges all that is best in the young Dominion of the North.

America Plus Britain.

But that "plus the power of Britain" counts for the United States as well. It counts every time thoughtful Americans reflect on what may some day be involved in the assertion of the Monroe Doctrine. It did count, and count for much, in one memorable crisis on Manila Bay. Not once merely or twice in the story of the Pacific has it been made plain that blood is thicker than water. And in days to come, days which some of us may live to see, it may mean everything for this American republic, as well as for the Canadian Dominion, that under the Southern Cross Australia and New Zealand, at the far gates of the Pacific, rise up in their youthful might "plus the power of Britain."

But, while America and Britain and the British Dominion must mean much to one another in their mutual defence, they have a message of immense importance to all the world. Is not this their message, that what has been done on this continent and what is being done among the English-speaking peoples may also be done on all the continents and among all peoples in the great family of the nations?

The Wider Sweep.

Internationalism takes a wider sweep than the Anglo-Saxon fraternity. America itself is bound by ties of blood and of interest to the great republic of France and the great empire of Germany.

The early history of the United States in colonial days, and most emphatically in the great days of the Revolution, binds this republic to France in bonds of sympathy and gratitude. The reflex of American independence on the history of France multiplied those binding cords, and made them enduring through the years. Such names as "Louisiana" and "Lafayette" awaken memories that America will not willingly let die. Canada on one side boasts that one-third of her population to-day, while they give loyal allegiance to the flag of Britain, pride themselves on the blood and traditions and language of the fair land of France.

Germany, too, out of all her states has given of her best to build up the commerce, the industry, the educational institutions, and the religious life of America, and both the United States and Canada are bound to the German Fatherland by the Teuton blood that in America's veins mixes perfectly with the Saxon and the Celt.

So, too, Britain itself is bound by all the vital ties either of kinship or of association, or of inextricable financial interests with Germany, with France, with Italy, and, indeed, with all Europe. And not America and Europe alone, but the Orient as well, is being swept by the rising tide of internationalism into one great intercivilized and intersocialized fraternity of nations.

What does all this mean? It means that the people of each nation in their abundant life are outgrowing their local governments. The authority of the government stops at the shore, but the people cross and recross the seas, cover the continents with their new works of transportation and trade, weaving and interweaving a wide web of life and of sentiment, and of sympathy and of ideals, and of commercial relations, and of financial interests, until out of all these there shall emerge international ideas, international customs, international conventions, international courts of justice, and a body of international public opinion, which shall become law for the nations

"Till the war-drum throbs no longer, and the battle-flags are furled,
  In the Parliament of man, the Federation of the world."

The Function of the Church.

In this great world-wide movement of internationalism does the Christian church play any worthy part or know any high obligation?

Sir, the church stands in the forefront. Its very genius is international. By its original commission, by its programme and its purposes, and by the immeasurable range of its evangel, it is above all other institutions splendidly international. The glad tidings of Bethlehem were not for Jews alone, but "for all nations." The marching-orders from Olivet, "Go ye into all the world," take no account of political divisions, or local patriotism, or national flags.

Of necessity, the state and its government are confined within the bounds of their own domain; but for the church "the field is the world." Into that world-field the church goes, not with any national flag or any political programme, but with a pregnant idea and with the irrepressible emotion of a new life. This is indeed the glory of the church; this the secret of its world-embracing power, that with its pregnant idea, with its mastering emotion, and with its regenerative life the church goes to every nation and tribe and tongue. Jew to the Jew, Greek to the Greek, Oriental in the far East, monarchist in England, republican in America, that it may win each for Christ, lift each to its highest self, and out of all build up one everlasting kingdom of truth and peace and liberty into which the nations of the world shall come, bringing their glory and honor with them.

It is the duty of the Christian church in all nations to apply without flinching the principles and the motives of Christ, not only to the hearts and consciences of individuals, but with equal directness and emphasis to that public opinion which creates national progress, and controls and directs international policies of peace and of war.

The Church and War.

A leading member of the British House of Commons made this declaration: "The Christian church, if it would rise to the height of its responsibility, and be really true to the message and the legacy of the Prince of peace, has it in its hands to settle the problem of war." The vote of American statesmenship would indorse the declaration. Emphasis would be given to it from Germany. Had the churches of Britain and the churches of Germany and the churches of America, those three great Protestant world-powers—had they been true to themselves and true to their supreme gospel of the Kingdom during the past half-century, Europe to-day would not be an armed camp, and the situation in the world East and West would not be a mockery of Christian civilization and a blasphemy against the gospel of peace on earth and good will to men.

tI is the duty of the church in America to repudiate impious allegafulness of war, its wanton waste of the people's wealth, its crushing burdens on the poor, its poisoning of the nation's life, and its irreparable demoralization of the manhood of the country.

It is the duty of the church in America to repudiate impious allegations like that of the Harvard lecturer who declared that war is God's way of removing the weaklings and securing for the nation the survival of the fittest. In all ages and through the history of all warlike nations the church has witnessed through war the reversal of the laws of evolution, the survival of the unfit, and the awful penalty of war's biological reaction.

Citizens of the World.

It is the inescapable duty of the church to train the children, as Sir Francis Vane so urgently pleads, "to become citizens of the world." That British soldier-hero of the South-African war makes appeal that "the natural democracy of childhood" should be taught this indisputable truth brought home to him amid the ghastly scenes of war, "that the high color of chivalry and nobility in which war has been painted for them is really only a lie and a disguise." And with the enormous and growing financial burdens of armed peace only a little less disastrous than actual war it is the duty of the church to expose and to denounce the selfishness and crime of vested interests and war syndicates, which promote war-scares that they may wax fat on the money taken from education and social reform and expended on their armor-plate and Dreadnoughts and implements of slaughter.

It will make for the power of the church and for the peace of the world if the church recognizes and responds to the international significance of its own missionary effort. The burden of armaments will not be relieved, or the menace of war taken away, until the weaker nations— weak, because divided, ignorant, and in bonds—are made strong, compact, and free. China, for instance, creates the storm-centre in the Far East because China has no national unity, and as a prize to the strong is exposed to the cupidity and aggression of the exploiting powers. Make China a national unit, with a national ideal and a well-regulated national life, and the possibility of partition is gone, and the war-cloud lifted forever.

For more than sixty years the missionaries of the churches of Britain and of America have been sowing the seed all over the Chinese Empire, which, unexpectedly to themselves, perhaps, is now yielding the abundant harvest of new ideas, not in religion alone, but in politics as well. The Christian slogan of the New China is, "All China for Christ; all Christian Chinese, a united church of China, and all China itself a united Chinese republic in promoting the redemption and transformation of mighty China." The Christian church widens the bounds of internationalism, solves the problem of the Pacific, and brings within sight the permanent peace of the world.

The Prophecy of Peace.

And in these last days, when among the nations in the Temple of Peace at The Hague, as among the tribes of Israel in the house of the Lord at Jerusalem, there is being set up the court of international law and international justice, it is the duty of the Christian church the world over, with Isaiah's arbitration manifesto in its hand, to call to all nations and to their governments with them:

"Come ye, and let us go up to the mountain of the Lord; and he will teach us of his ways, and we will walk in his paths; and he shall judge among the nations, and shall rebuke many people; and they shall beat their swords into ploughshares, and their spears into pruning-hooks; nation shall not lift up sword against nation, neither shall they learn war any more."

O house of Britain, magnifying law and order through your thousand years of struggle and blood; O house of Germany, holding high the flaming torch of science and truth; O house of America, first and greatest among the republics of freedom, three inheritors of a common blood, a common faith, and a common mission, come ye, and let us walk in the light of the Lord.

OUR OPPORTUNITIES IN THE COLORED CHURCHES.

By Rev. Julian C. Caldwell, Secretary of the Allen Christian Endeavor League, Nashville, Tenn.

It is indeed a rare privilege to stand before an audience so high in intellect, splendid in quality, vast in numbers, and earnest in its animating

Rev. W. T. Johnson, D.D.

Rev. Benjamin W. Arnett, D.D.

Bishop Walters

Prof. Aaron Brown
Secretary of the Varick Christian Endeavor Union

Rev. Julian C. Caldwell, D.D.
General Secretary of the Allen
Christian Endeavor League

influence to discuss "Our Opportunity at Home and Especially in the Colored Churches."

It is very fitting that such a subject should be discussed at this time, since we are this year celebrating our fiftieth anniversary as an emancipated people. The progress we have attained has challenged the admiration and wonder of the world. In all the annals of the world's history there is no parallel to it; and this progress, remarkable as it is, has been in all lines and in all departments of life and activity.

To secure some adequate conception of what the negro is to-day, we must compare him with what he was yesterday. A generation ago he had practically nothing. He started out with scarcely a name, poor, ignorant, degraded, demoralized, without a home, without a foot of land, ragged and destitute. That poor, ignorant man of yesterday owns to-day one hundred and seventy-five thousand farms and homes worth seven hundred and fifty million dollars. He has personal property to the value of two hundred million dollars, and has raised nearly twenty million dollars for his own education.

Starting out fifty years ago from the home of American bondage through a wilderness bristling with nettles and fiery serpents and Alpine heights of ignorance defying our progress at every step, our journey has been steady and onward. Where once stood the slave-pen we have built lighthouses in the shape of churches and schools, and whereas the nightmare of wide-spread illiteracy once held us down, now the ratio of knowledge among us is so great as to seem incredible.

Beginning with the reduction of illiteracy ten per cent during the first decade of freedom, the stupendous pall has been wiped away so that only forty per cent of ignorance remains; 1,500,000 negro children fill the common schools, while 25,000 graduates from American and foreign colleges are abroad in the land. Some 2,000 are engaged in the practice of law and 3,000 in the medical profession; there are 6,000 trained ministers, 35,000 teachers, 659 authors of books, 650 newspapers, 51 colleges, and 56 banks.

Our greatest asset, thank God, has been our religious development. We were brought to this country as heathen, worshippers of the unknown God, whom we ignorantly worshipped; Him declared you unto us. We imbibed your religion, studied your Bible, sang your songs; and, if the religion we have is not what it ought to be, it is what you gave us, though I confess we have improved somewhat upon it.

We have to-day twelve denominations controlled and supported wholly by the negro himself, with 20,859 organizations, 21,007 church edifices valued at $27,626,434, a seating-capacity of 6,892,314, and a membership of 3,591,129. There are nineteen denominations composed of colored people but controlled by white people, with 5,713 organizations, 5,139 churches, with a seating-capacity of 1,008,651 and a membership of 507,826, while the value of the property is $7,236,734. Uniting the two we have thirty-one denominations, 26,572 organizations, 26,146 church edifices, property valued at $34,963,168, and a membership of 4,098,955. This is a bird's-eye view of what the negro himself is doing and what is being done for the moral and religious training of this race.

When in 1881 the Christian Endeavor movement was started by Dr. Clark, it was not long until it was adopted by the negro denominations, namely, the African Methodist Episcopal Church and the African Methodist Episcopal Zion Church, for as early as 1893 these two denominations were represented on the board of trustees of the United Society of Christian Endeavor, Bishop B. W. Arnett of sacred memory representing the African Methodist Episcopal Church and Bishop Alexander Walters, still active, representing the African Methodist Episcopal Zion Church.

More and more was it realized that the church would increase its membership not so much by conquest as by Christian nurture, and the boys and girls in the Sunday-school must be saved for Christ and the church, hence the young people's departments were started and secretaries elected for the purpose of organizing these young people.

What are the results? The Baptist Young People's Union of the Baptist Church, the Epworth League in the Methodist Episcopal Church (colored), the Varick Christian Endeavor Society of the African Methodist Episcopal Zion Church, and the Allen Christian Endeavor League of the African Methodist Episcopal Church, and in other churches of color the Christian Endeavor Society, making a total of Christian Endeavor societies among the colored churches of America 5,667 with a membership of 181,440. Of these societies there are 3,710 in the African Methodist Episcopal Church with a membership of 124,000, 1,204 in the African Methodist Episcopal Zion Church with a membership of 37,150, in other denominations 743 societies with a membership of 20,290. Including the young people of the Epworth League and the Baptist Young People's Union there are more than a quarter of a million negro young people being trained for service for Christ and the church.

But there is a great work to be done and especially in the South-land. We have just begun the stupendous task of reaching the unreached and training the untrained. Upon us God and the age have cast the task of the times.

"He is sounding forth the trumpet that shall never call retreat."

It is all right to send our missionaries and field workers to the foreign field and carry there the bread of life, but open your eyes and behold the field ripe to the harvest right at our door. Thousands of young men and women charged only with the crime of being black, without God and without his Christ, are appealing to you. Will you heed the appeal?

"Behold I have set before thee an open door," the open door of opportunity.

THE SPIRITUAL DYNAMIC THE ESSENTIAL OF PROGRESS.

By Rev. J. Percival Huget, D.D., Detroit, Mich.

The truth herein stated is doubly important. Its importance and value lie in part in the principles thus stated and in part in the programme thus suggested. The principle is stated in the topic. It declares that progress in the realm of the spiritual, in the life of the church and the field of religion, in the lofty concerns of the kingdom of God, is conditioned upon power, upon the quickening, enabling, guiding spiritual power which becomes the cause of achievement and of progress.

It is also immediately evident that in the same statement is contained the wisest of programmes. Progress is secured when the conditions are met, when power is secured and utilized.

Progress, for our present purpose, can hardly be better defined than "the continual advance toward higher and more perfect forms of life." It involves a goal and a continued approach to that goal. It is not only in going somewhere, but in finally getting there. It is not alone in proceeding, but in arriving. And just this has been the record of the long centuries. Benjamin Kidd says, "There is no phenomenon so stupendous, so bewildering, and withal so interesting to man, as that of his own evolution in society."

In modern times there has been a great quickening of the pace. Progress has become exceedingly rapid, especially along material and scientific lines. We lag behind somewhat in some of the finer things, in social adjustments and in moral and spiritual values. Yet even here the central fact is this fact of continued advance.

And it is the peculiar glory of Christianity that it has ever occasioned and guided this upward endeavor along moral and ethical lines. Christianity believes in the establishment of the kingdom of God, and labors for it. Its great words are not war and conquest, but righteousness and service. Progress, to the Christian, then, becomes the majestic outworking of the will of God, the achievement in individual lives and in society of the ideals of Jesus.

If we attempt to define the phrase "spiritual dynamic," we shall find that religion has been and is one of the ever present and ever powerful factors in human life. In the aspirations and ideals of humanity there has ever been an effective force originating in and emerging from the spiritual realm. It is the power that comes from God, from the author of life, the inspirer of progress, the soul of the universe.

The connection is at once clear. Progress and power are linked in the laws of life. The first great condition of progress is struggle. But the condition within this condition is that of power, and a third condition essential to them both is that of continued resources and reserves of power, of help, of guidance from an exhaustless source.

These are some of the principles of power. The applications are evident. The theme offers a programme for the religious life. The challenging endeavor for religion in our day is to learn how to use God, how to get into vital communication and contact with him as the source of power. This is the heart of a spiritual programme. God is life and light and power. If we but fulfil the conditions of faith and obedience, he will work in and through us. The result will fill the world with light, with power, and with glory.

This may be made very definite and practical. The programme for personal progress is the programme of power received and used. The programme for the church is the same. The church without spiritual power is like a lighthouse without light, an engine without steam, a body without life. But the church of the Spirit is the church of the divine dynamic. Before such a church nothing shall stand. It shall go from victory unto victory.

And this also is the programme for this day of social service. Age-long evils and ancient wrongs are being challenged by the new conscience and the new humanity. For these great endeavors nothing is adequate but the vision and devotion, the passion and sacrifice, of the Christ-filled life. Let no one miss the connection between faith and progress. Faith is vision, but faith is also high endeavor. And yet more, faith becomes co-working with the infinite and eternal.

The spiritual dynamic, then, as the source of progress in soul and in kingdom, furnishes us both principle and programme for life. In scientific phraseology it declares that progress comes from life's grim and unescapable struggle. In the realm of religion it also declares that progress is through faith and high endeavor under the guidance of and in the power of God.

ENLARGEMENT FOR EFFICIENCY
By President E. A. Watkins, D.D., Albany, Mo.

These two words in the relations indicated loom up big with meaning if we contemplate their content and significance. The first suggests the real genius of the gospel; the second, the final goal of all its activities. "Enlargement" means freedom, liberty, and opportunity in new fields of endeavor, new worlds of conquest, new realms of service, and new enrichment of life and soul, while "efficiency" prophesies the end, or the means to an end, and declares that the hungry world, crying for the bread of life, will never cease its pitiful wail, nor be satisfied until the goal has been reached.

But why emphasize the importance of enlargement of the field of our operations? Why this expansion policy? Are we to enlarge our activities and the scope of our work simply for the sake of bigness and the sake of the thing in itself? If efficiency is to be the end and enlargement simply the means to that end, it is worthy the effort. The Christian world

has been praying for three definite things : a world-wide revival; reform
of social, economic, and political life, and the evangelization of the whole
world. These three movements will realize a victory whenever the forces
of righteousness begin to meet the necessary conditions and render an
adequate and efficient service.

I find myself unable to appreciate any programme for the salvation
of the whole man that does not place the emphasis upon the importance
of the individual. A living contact of the individual with Jesus Christ
means the solution of the problems of to-day when that programme has
been extended.

Thus what I say to-night has significance largely for the individual
life, and that in turn must make its contribution toward the solution of
the whole problem.

There are many lines along which the soul needs a larger field for
rendering service, but I can indicate but three or four.

An enlargement of our fellowship will continue to bear considerable
emphasis. Christian Endeavor has played a large part in enlarging this
circle, but the end is not yet. The dove of universal fellowship has
hovered over the troubled waters for centuries, but now "hope sees a star,
and hears the rustle of a wing." But there is room for vast improvement as long as more than a hundred denominations battle for the mastery and an unsaved world looks on and chants,

> "O wad some power the giftie gie us,
> To see oursel's as others see us !"

Love must finally conquer; but it cannot be caged, but must have the
whole heaven in which to sing.

Our faith and vision needs expansion and enlargement. This is an
age of doubt. I shudder when I think of the masses of young men and
women going out of our colleges and universities, many of them having
thrown overboard their standards and now facing life's issues without
the necessary anchorage. Christian Endeavor at home has been one of
the conservators of faith, but the vision of the past is too circumscribed
for the needs of to-morrow. It must yet comprehend and grasp the solution of the live problems of the future. Why should it not include in its
programme the labor question, the social problem, and the world's peace?

If the foregoing programme has been worked out, a larger service
will follow. Anything less than this belittles Christian Endeavor, and
is unworthy the strength of its manhood and womanhood; for no cause
ever succeeds without a big job on hand. Like the iron monster on the
steel rails, Christian Endeavor must have a heavy load to give her balance, poise, and dignity.

The future cannot be replete with an efficient service unless there is
added an enlargement of soul life. I am sure many of us have never
touched the hem of the garment of possibility and that there is an enrichment of life that would bring us a fruitage far beyond the largest
stretch of the imagination.

This generation cannot be adequately served with the same measure
of spiritual power answering the needs of the day just past any more than
could the old type of steam-engine draw the heavy-loaded overland express to-day. A higher type of life is demanded for to-morrow. This
age of forty-story buildings, with its increase of structural steel and deeper
foundations, must have men and women living forty-story lives. To-
morrow's problems demand that the horizon of our soul life be enlarged
if we would be efficient servants.

WANTED—AN OPPORTUNITY TO RISE.

By Rev. W. T. Johnson, D.D., Pastor of the First Baptist Church, Richmond, Va.

It can be truly said that we are living in a wonderful age, an age of thought and progress along many lines.

No sane man can deny the fact that a great awakening among Christians has taken place in this twentieth century. Men and women are manifesting more sincere interest in one another's welfare.

The subject, "Wanted—An Opportunity to Rise," is capable of several interpretations; but for present use I prefer that interpretation which presents the negro appealing to his more highly favored neighbor for an opportunity or a favorable chance to rise.

About 294 years ago the negro was brought to this country from his native home in Africa. He was enslaved and held in bondage for more than 250 years, being used as goods and chattels.

When the days of bitter struggle between the contending forces of the North and the South had ended, the result was liberty for four million negroes. We can see the negro coming out of such a chaotic condition, with his eyes just opened to freedom and responsibilities, making an earnest plea for an opportunity to rise.

The opportunity of the negro in this country has not always been what it is to-day. The rising or elevation of the negro is the science of all that relates to his social, intellectual, moral, material, and religious conditions, which are involved in his existence and his well-being as a member of an organized community.

Let us look at the American negro when he was transformed from the likeness of former things and placed in the ranks of citizens. A dark and ominous cloud of illiteracy was overhanging him; he had no home, no church, and no other institution which would make for the social development of a race. He came out of the hard school of slavery just as unlettered as the very cattle upon the hills. He had lived in this condition for many generations.

He knew nothing of the higher life from his own experience. Since that time, we know, there has been a wonderful change and improvement; and yet he has not had so much aid, encouragement, and opportunity as has been given to the other races. And I think that it is hardly fair to measure the social status of the negro by the standard that centuries of civilization would set. But it is fair to estimate the negro's social condition by the depth from which he has come beneath the common level rather than by the heights to which he has gone above it.

Since the race that stands highest has attained to that height gradually, the same opportunity must be given the negro.

The things that have contributed to the development of other races must contribute to the development of the negro race. The negro has worked steadily and humbly to reach the heights attained by others, and by so doing has developed into what he is to-day.

His appeal for an opportunity to rise in the educational world was heard by an army of Christian workers of the North and a number of consecrated workers in the South, and with combined forces the negro's illiteracy has been reduced 66 per cent in the past forty-eight years.

His appeal for an opportunity to rise as a home-builder was also heard, and a chance was given him by his Creator to play his part in the great drama of life. Home-making by a people is always an earnest of permanency, self-respect, and moral responsibility.

His appeal for an opportunity to rise as an economic factor was also heard, and we see the negro following his own appeal a short while after emancipation. The negro was quick to see that he had been ushered into a high state of society, where wealth is both the cause and the effect of progress and power, and poverty is the fruitful parent of misery, vice, and crime; and thus he decided to lay a foundation in the accumulation of property, and hence to become an economic factor in a civilized country. As an evidence of his thrift along this line the last census gives the negro credit for paying taxes on seven hundred million dollars' worth of property in this country.

His appeal for an opportunity to rise in the moral and religious worlds shows his good sense and sound judgment.

For the true valuation of a race's activity is measured by its moral and religious worth. The true worth of a race does not consist in what it owns, nor in the facts that it knows, but in what it really is.

Hence character is the measure of the real value of the race. It is character that builds empires, founds kingdoms, and reforms institutions. Where character holds sway, there is less disease, poverty, and crime.

The Christian Endeavor Society answers the negro's appeal for a moral and religious uplift by laying great emphasis upon personal religion and work for others. It also impresses the idea that in a home there should be liberty without license, time for a family's intercourse, space for personal solitude, and room for increased happiness; and it further teaches that there should be over all a tender, trustful, daily atmosphere of true devotion to one another and sweet communion with God.

The negro of to-day is also anxious for an opportunity to rise in the scale of good citizenship, because he realizes the value of a good citizen to a community and to the world.

The Christian Endeavor organization comes in answer to this appeal by placing before him civic studies, the faithful study of which will prepare one to rise to the highest heights in civic life and civic righteousness. Thus prepared, the negro cries for an opportunity to rise by having the chance to put into practice the knowledge that he has gained in the ways that we have herein mentioned. The question comes to you, my fellow Christian Endeavorers,

First, Will you aid us to rise to the end that God may be glorified?

Second, Will you aid us to rise to the end that the church may be benefited by our Christian activity?

Third, Will you aid us to rise to the end that we may measure up to the obligations of the liberty that we have received, and that fallen humanity may be helped by our endeavors, whether in this land or in foreign countries?

Fourth, Will you aid us to rise to the end that we may recognize in every man our brother, and thus be led on to see the great beauty and intrinsic worth of the great doctrines of the fatherhood of God and the brotherhood of man?

THE SPIRITUAL MESSAGE OF JESUS.

By Rev. George E. Burlingame, Pastor of the First Baptist Church of San Francisco, California.

Jesus is pre-eminently the advocate of spiritual values. In a world whose standards of value and whose media of intercourse are tangible and ponderable he declares that a man's life consisteth not in the abundance of the things which he possesseth. His presence in the world, his sacrifice for the world, his message to the world, are one persistent and insistent assertion of the reality and permanence of spiritual values.

I. Spiritual values involve spiritual ends as the goal of life, and the spiritual message of Jesus is an apologetic for these spiritual ends. In the realm of ideals the end to be sought is the will of God. In the realm of personal experience the end is holiness. In the realm of social relations the end is the kingdom of heaven. In the realm of ultimate attainment the end is eternal glory.

II. Spiritual values involve spiritual means for the attainment of spiritual ends. "My kingdom is not of this world," said Jesus in a crisis of his own life and of his cause; "if my kingdom were of this world, then would my servants fight, that I should not be delivered to the Jews; but now is my kingdom not from hence."

The spiritual means which Jesus commends for the attainment of spiritual ends are

1. "I am solemnly convinced," says Dr. J. H. Jowett, "that the lapse of private prayer accounts more than anything else for the forcelessness of the modern church." Prayer is the characteristic of the people of God, and only through prayer will the spiritual ends be attained.

2. The word of God. The whole missionary movement falls naturally into two distinct phases, that which includes and that which excludes or ignores the word of God as a means of evangelization and moral transformation.

3. Testimony. The mere perfunctory testimony sometimes heard in modern prayer meetings may only serve to bore the devout and to harden the unbeliever; but a real New Testament type of testimony, telling of a personal experience of redemption through Christ, is a potent means for the attainment of spiritual ends.

III. Spiritual means involve spiritual forces for the energizing of spiritual means, and these spiritual forces Jesus discovers to us in his spiritual message. He discloses the Gulf Stream of divine grace flowing through the sea of the moral universe, to which we may with confidence commit our interests and our enterprises and our dreams and hopes.

1. The eternal counsel of the Father is a spiritual force working through spiritual means for spiritual ends. In Paul's words in Rom. 8:29, 30, we have the bud of the present life of the Christian, now justified, and the perfected flower of his glorification; but back of flower and bud are stem and root and seed; and the seed is the eternal foreknowledge of the Father, who purposed our redemption in Christ before times eternal.

2. The eternal sacrifice of the Son is a spiritual force working through spiritual means for spiritual ends. The cross of Christ is more than a fact of history; it is a perpetual dynamic of redemption. "The word of the cross is to us who are being saved the power of God." The atonement of our Lord is a spiritual force of infinite and eternal quality, energizing our prayers and our testimony and the word of God for the attainment of spiritual ends.

3. The ministry of the Holy Spirit. Richard Baxter, near the end of his life, in a careful review of his ministry, regrets that he had not magnified more largely the ministry of the Holy Spirit in the church of Christ. "I now see that the Holy Ghost is the witness of Christ, and his agent in the world. The Spirit in the prophets was his first witness, and the Spirit by miracles was the second; and the Spirit by renovation, sanctification, illumination, and consolation, assimilating the soul to Christ and heaven, is the continued witness to all true believers."

This is the spiritual message of Jesus: a plea for spiritual ends as the goal of life; a proffer of spiritual means for the attainment of these ends; and a revelation of the spiritual forces available for the effective use of these spiritual means for spiritual ends. His spiritual message indicates for the believer and for the church the conditions of moral and spiritual victory.

THE INFLUENCE OF THE SCHOOL IN CHARACTER-BUILDING.

By President John Baer, LL.D., of Occidental College. Los Angeles.

After making his memorable commencement address Horace Mann, when asked whether he had not exaggerated decidedly when he said that "no possible amount of time, thought, and treasure could be too much to expend if it would save one boy from ignorance and evil, and train him for life," answered, "Not if it were my boy!"

There you have my conception of the ministry of education, and let the answer of Horace Mann make a dent in your memory, "Not if it were my boy!" Men and women, education is so important. But what is education, after all? Let's define it. Turning away from many profound and academic definitions of the word "education," I select as the highest the plain, simple, honest statement of Edward Thring, the old head master of Uppingham. "Education," said he, "is the transmission of life from the living through the living to the living." And so the heart of the conception of my subject emerges. "Character is caught, not taught." There are many banners in these days, but from the flagstaff of every school, college, and university I should like figuratively to unfurl this trifolium; "Culture. Citizenship. Christianity."

First, Culture. We must stand for sound teaching. More important than bricks and mortar are books and brains. We need more teachers of the right kind, and none of the wrong. Mr. Roosevelt once said, "The one thing supremely worth having is the opportunity coupled with the capacity to do a thing well and worthily the doing of which in its vital importance touches all humankind." That paragraph, pregnant with potentialities of the right kind, is most carefully selected as the best one to remind all who teach of their important place and part in the world's civilization. The teacher's job is a big one. We have that kind of opportunity. May God make us increasingly capable.

Teachers, you are here to-day in large numbers proportionately. I offer you three watchwords, Opportunity. Efficiency. Personality. And the greatest of these is personality. Pouring out knowledge is not advancing culture. Hearing classes recite is not teaching. Lecturing clearly is not the final word in teaching. "Precept freezes; example warms." Teachers, by your life and not your wisdom you will be known. Remember, "Character is caught, and not taught." What we need now in our classrooms is more, plain, honest men, who will not trim and who will not blur the lines between good and evil, men who will give their best and not cheat God. And what shall I say of our women teachers? Take this for your motto; it is not mine, but I borrow it for you: "Honor the school, and the school will honor you. Exercise these womanly graces, strength, simplicity, and sincerity; and all mankind will be your debtor." Teachers, you do not have the opportunity to teach some of the parents of your pupils, however much a school for parents is needed; upon your shoulders is rolled the heavy burden of the home, which ought not to be. But do not be recreant to your trust, but thank God for your chance.

Frivolity, irreverence, and dishonesty are the common sins of some homes. Some parents are unmindful of their own sons and daughters in their mad swirl to lead in business and society. Deceit is practised daily. Some mothers are losing their fine, sensitive, discriminating touch; and our streets are filled with girls and women too immodestly dressed, the result being that some men and boys are finding it increasingly hard to keep their lives pure. Fathers and mothers, let me stop right here to ask, Are you among the number who are shifting your responsibilities in the home upon the school and the college? Let me draw the curtain right here with the sad words, show, sham, shame. Again I say, teachers beware. Remember, character is caught, not taught.

Citizenship! Our graduates are the trustees of posterity and the prosperity of the country. Education is a tool, not a toy. Democracy must be natural. Honesty in business and purity in the home desired;

we want more young people who are bravely good. Life is more than a living. What we need is "not more men, but more man." Sound teaching is good. Pure living is better; sound teaching and pure living is best. Unless our ethical and social life keep abreast of the ever-rising tide of commercial prosperity it will be the rift within the lute that slowly widening will make the music mute. Our schools must be more than culturing institutions. The school must be an influence for God, and citizenship of the right kind must be inculcated, political independence fostered, class hatred demolished. In schools of the right kind young men and women will be taught to cast their ballots in the fear of God; and their standards of life will forever be a menace to the brothel, the gambling-den, the saloon, and every cesspool of iniquity private and public.

Christianity! Now abideth culture, citizenship, and Christianity; but the greatest of these is Christianity. The first advertisement of Columbia University in 1754 was this: "The chief thing that is aimed at in this college is to teach and engage the children to know God in Jesus Christ, and to love and serve him in all sobriety, godliness, and righteousness of life." Would to God that all the schools of the land had the courage and the desire to advertise to-day as Columbia University did more than a century ago. Alas! in our advance in culture and citizenship we have not constantly kept pace in our religious teaching. O, I know that in our public institutions, supported by enforced taxation, we must be mindful of the reasonable need for non-sectarian teaching. But there is not a school, public or private, where under the right kind of teachers religion in its best sense may not be taught. It is not necessary that we should all worship God alike, but it is well for all alike to worship God. One need not wear his religion on his sleeve to be religious. Were I a member of a school board, I would not select a teacher to control any school of any grade whose life was not God-controlled.

My hat is off to many teachers who are asking a large contribution to the community wherein they live by passing on to those under their influence character of the right kind. What we need in the country to-day more than ever is teachers that are "enthusiastically alive, divinely inspired, and God-intoxicated." May I be permitted to say that I believe the day is coming again when the English Bible will be taught in the classroom of State schools of every grade from primary to university? Why should that day be long deferred? At present, the Christian schools and colleges as a rule have a monoply of Bible instruction, but they earnestly desire to share it with the State schools. Until that time comes the responsibility of the Christian school and college is only the more important, and our provision in these schools must be correspondingly wise and adequate. I appeal for a stronger religious life in our schools. It need not be obtrusive; it must not be sectarian; it will not be offensive; it can and must be vitalizing.

I do not apologize for closing this address with an enthusiastic approval of the Christian school and college, and urge Christian parents to support them and adequately equip them. Many a church, school, and college is struggling in the midst of Christian parents who send their boys and girls away from their homes into State universities where positive religious teaching is entirely omitted from the curriculum, and where frequently the instructors have little if any religious convictions, and their influence has a tendency to create doubt in the mind of the young, which often undermines the faith that children from Christian homes have when they enter. Christian fathers and mothers, you do well to stick by the Christian school, and your boy and girl will be more apt to stick to God and his word. The small Christian academy and college are fast coming to their own, and we are only beginning to appreciate what God has in store for the Christian school if we are true to him. We want more education transmitted by men and women who believe in God and practise the principles of the religion of Jesus Christ.

THE QUIET HOUR IN A NOISY AGE.

By Rev. H. F. Shupe, D.D., Editor of *The Watchword*, Dayton, Ohio.

A noisy age needs the Quiet Hour. The unrest of the world is wearying it. The raucous noises of life are distracting.

We need the Quiet Hour to get acquainted with God. Acquaintance-ship and love are the results of companionship and harmony in tastes.

We need the Quiet Hour to learn the language of God. During the flood in Dayton, O., a man was frantic through fear. He was advised to pray. Not having learned the language of God he cried out, "God, you know I'm a son of a gun, but help me if you can." Those who knew God spent the days and nights of horror in attics and on housetops, strengthened by the presence of Him whom they knew.

We need the Quiet Hour to keep us in harmony with God. McCheyne, Scotland's holy man, wrote to Bonar that in this country he found his watch going wrong, out of time with others and with the sun, because there was no reliable clock at hand with which to compare his watch. I often see men stop at the jeweller's window to compare their watches with the officially correct time. The Quiet Hour serves to keep us in time with God by pausing to compare our life with the perfect life.

We need the Quiet Hour to keep the body in tone. A woman, weary, fretful, sick, went to her doctor. After listening to the recital of her complaints he said, "What you need is to read your Bible more." She was inclined to resist the suggestion, but the doctor said, "Go home; read your Bible one hour each day; and in a month come back."

At the end of the month she returned. Looking into her face, he said, "You have been an obedient patient; do you think you need any other medicine?"

"No; but how did you know that was what I needed?" she replied.

Taking up his well-worn Bible, the doctor said, "If I were to omit my daily readings in this book, I should lose my greatest source of strength and skill."

The Quiet Hour is good for the body.

We need the Quiet Hour to deepen the spiritual life. Mr. Trumbull tells of a business man who occasionally spends a whole day alone with God.

The Quiet Hour should be carried into the work of the whole day by "practising the presence of God."

THE SOCIAL MESSAGE OF JESUS.

By Rev. Arthur B. Patten, D.D., Sacramento, Cal.

The social message and the individual message of Jesus are one. There are not two gospels. But there is a whole gospel for the whole man and for the whole world. The evangel is as broad as it is deep. It saves souls in society, and not souls in suspension. Christ says in effect that he who seeks to save his soul for its own sake, shall lose it, while he who gives his soul for society's sake shall save it eternally. The ideal of Jesus is socialized souls and a federated humanity. Only society can give the soul a career, while only the soul can give society a character.

Christianity seeks a reconciled world. The human constitution has always been reconciled; from the beginning human nature has been in the divine image; but human character and human citizenship have been out of harmony. On the foundation of the human constitution Jesus builds human characters into citizenship.

"Go ye into all the world and preach the gospel" means not only, "Go into every land," but also, "Go into every institution and industry and art"; for every deed in the home, the school, the shop, and the state is to become an errand of the Christian chivalry. That sounds much like the words of a familiar pledge, "Throughout my whole life I will endeavor to lead a Christian life."

Jesus believed that his socializing gospel would conquer the world; for he declared that the gates of death should not prevail against his church, which held the keys of the living kingdom of God. He saw the coming generations of children streaming in through the gates of life to inherit the earth. When in old Jerusalem the boys and girls took up the cry of their elders, and shouted, "Hosanna!" Christ declared that out of the mouth of babes and sucklings God was perfecting praise. He seemed to say, "With every new-born generation that praise shall find a larger and richer expression until it shall ring around the world in the sympathy of the new humanity. And then in the child—in his loving trust, in his sublime audacity of faith, and in his democratic spirit—Jesus saw the symbol and secret of his insurgent kingdom.

We find a fitting prologue to the social message of Jesus in the angelic song, "Glory to God; on earth peace." Christ translated this promise and passion into a deathless prayer, "Our Father, thy kingdom come in earth." He preached it as a message of divine-human affection, "God so loved the world"; "Thou shalt love thy neighbor as thyself." He pledged his own imperial love to the fulfilment of his vision, "One is your teacher, even the Christ, and all ye are brothers." He knew that these brothers were to become the light of the world, the salt of the earth; and the leaven of the whole lump of the socialized humanity. Surely he had an imperial social message, comparable to his august social passion and befitting the pre-eminence of his imperial personality.

While Christ declared, "All authority hath been given unto me in heaven and on earth," he also declared, "The Spirit of truth shall lead you into all truth." So, while in his person and in his spoken gospel he gave us all the principles of the social message, he points us to the gospel of the Holy Ghost to learn all the applications. The progressive programme of Christian civilization is revealed and realized only as Christian men will to do God's will, only as they take the yoke of Christ and learn the better social adjustments in loyalty to the world's work. It is at the point of brotherly service that we receive the final illuminations of the spirit for social reconstruction.

I believe that Jesus saw Christian history fulfilling itself in cycles, and that in the parable of the wheat and the tares he gave us the picture of one masterful ideal after another struggling to victory over some colossal wrong. At length the tares were to reach the consummation of their age and be harvested to their consuming judgment and burned. The cycle of black slavery has run its course; the cycle of white slavery is hastening to its completion; and the cycle of wage slavery is nearing its finish, while the cycle of drink slavery sees the beginning of its end. It is the immemorial contest of the right against the wrong. As Jesus closes the parable of the wheat and the tares, he gives us as the climax of his social message for every cycle of reform and for every full campaign of insurgent holiness the glowing words of triumph, "Then shall the righteous shine forth as the sun in the kingdom of their Father."

TWO THOUSAND YEARS OF SERVICE.

A Greeting from Armenia.

By Mr. J. S. Pashgian, Los Angeles, Cal.

I come to greet you in the name of our common Lord and Master, and also in behalf of thousands of young Armenian Endeavorers, some of them here to-day, but most of them far away in other lands.

But some of you will ask: "Who are these Armenians? Are they really a remnant of a civilized nation? Or are they simply a tribe of Asiatics? And, if they have a religion, pray, what is it? Are they really Christians, or what?"

Yes, my friends, Armenia, the cradle of humanity, the land of Eden, has been a civilized country almost from times immemorial. Before the Britons, Franks, and Germans had any villages or towns to dwell in (as far back as one thousand years before Christ) the Armenians (who are true Caucasians) had regular cities and large armies to protect their homes and liberty.

Xenophon tells us that the right arm of Cyrus the Great was that gallant young Armenian prince, Tigranes, and that by his help great Babylon was conquered and the Jews liberated from their seventy years' captivity.

And in the time of our Lord there lived not far from Judea an Armenian King, Abkar by name, who sent ambassadors to Christ, earnestly asking him to come and share the kingdom and heal Abkar's sickly body, though the apostle John in speaking of them calls them Greeks because they spoke the Greek language.

But are the Armenians *now* Christians? Bless your soul, yes, if you can conscientiously call any nation Christian. And, more than this, my friends, the Armenians were the very first nation in all history to accept Christianity as their national faith; for it was in the third century that almost the whole Armenian nation was Christianized and accepted Christ as their Saviour and Christianity as their holy religion as a result of one of the grandest revivals ever recorded in history, under the leadership of Gregory the Illuminator.

And does some one still ask, "But what of it?" Why, simply this: that as a natural result of that ever-memorable event a new and stronger nation was born, with Christ for its only teacher, and his ever-blessed principles for its supreme motive of life and activity. And in the following one or two centuries there flourished in Armenia a literature morally so pure and so rich in love and truth, and with so perfect a translation of the Bible, so true to the original Greek and Hebrew, that it has been affirmed by learned Biblical scholars that, if the original of all Greek and Hebrew Bibles were lost to-day, we could go back to this ancient Armenian version, and translate it into any language without the slightest hesitation, as a trusty substitute.

And Armenia was also one of the earliest of the nations to send out missionaries to other lands, and all down through the centuries some of her children have worn the bloody crown of martyrdom for the love of Christ and humanity, of which one of the last and saddest chapters was the awful massacre of 1895 and 1896, which you probably remember.

"What of it?" Why, simply this: All through the Dark Ages, and ever since, Christian Armenia has been the only standard-bearer of a true and practical Christianity in dark and barbarous Asia—Asia, so cruel and ignorant, whose wild children were roaming here and there, devastating and ruining so much that was good and sacred. And Armenia, standing on the meeting-point of darkened Asia and Christian Europe, has bravely borne the greatest hardships, while holding back the darkness and keeping alive the light of a true Christianity in those benighted lands.

Go and travel through the Near and Far East; eat, play, and sleep in the huts or palaces of every nation in Asia, and then come back to that downtrodden land, Armenia. Enter her homes; dwell for a few days with her people; then will you see a difference. For in a true Armenian home you will find safety and sincere love of home and parents and of wife and children; and also more love of country and of one's neighbors, and more love of decency and of chastity, and a more Christ-like love for humanity in general, than anywhere else.

So I am proud to bring to you the greetings of my fatherland, Armenia, and I should like to leave with you this message: Be sincere. Be strong and steadfast in the love of Christ, even as you are brave and numerous and prosperous and victorious. And, even if there does not fall to your lot the exceptional honor of martyrdom, the good Lord is sure to give to you, his followers, the selfsame crown of glory which he has given to many a martyred saint, in far-away Armenia.

FELLOWSHIP WITH CHRIST.

By Rev. Edwin F. Hallenbeck, D.D., San Diego, Cal.

My theme is one that lies close to our hearts. Let us forget everything else but the Master's presence. I wish to call your attention to the remarkable words written of Jesus in Mark 3:14.

I used to think that they were chosen to blaze a trail for Jesus, but these words prove something else. They were to be *with him*. Fellowship precedes service. Without it we cannot succeed.

Let us discover what this fellowship will mean to Christ. In Psalm 149 we find this: "The Lord taketh pleasure in his people." Let us let him know that there is nothing to cut our fellowship with him. God needs his people, and we can be far more to our Master than we have been.

Let us see what his fellowship means to us.

1. Security, safety. You will know that you are safe. The picture in the ninety-first Psalm is an ideal one of safety. It is the superlative of confidence—"ten thousand at thy right hand, but it shall not come nigh thee"—to whom? Go back to the first verse. "He that dwelleth in the secret place"; that is to be with him.

2. Peace. We often think of peace as something put in a package and delivered at our door, or left there if we are not at home. No, peace is himself. In Ephesians it says, "He is our peace." (Mark Guy Pearse's story of the sea and the cloud.) Just so with us. If you will fix your heart on Jesus Christ, just as silently he will lift you above the world, and you will rest like a child in its mother's arms.

3. Zeal. We need to have burning hearts. After Calvary the disciples went back to their work, and you remember how the stranger caused them to say, "Didn't our hearts burn within us when he spake?" and you recall the change in their lives. They were now alive for Him.

4. Transformation. We shall be transformed into Christ-likeness. I remember once having stood on the bank of a river in Italy and looked at a most beautiful sunset. As I stood there, I thought of the river, and glanced down. Behold! The sun had changed that muddy river into a stream of glory. If the sun can do that with a river, it is only a suggestion of what Christ can do with a soiled life. We must let him take us, and let him throw the light of his face into every movement.

You and I know what this restless, dissatisfied old world needs. It is Jesus. He says, "Ye are the light, salt, shall be witnesses;" and we have let the lights burn low, have lost our savor, and have failed to witness because of the lack of fellowship. We have no glad songs to sing because we have failed to listen at heaven's gates. Let us live the life of fellowship, and we shall walk in the sunshine and have a life of victory.

ONE CITY'S PURITY CAMPAIGN.

By Rev. E. A. King, President of the Washington Christian Endeavor
Union, North Yakima, Wash.

We are all familiar with educational and reform movements that
originate in private societies and are promulgated through the agency of
public institutions, but it is not customary to think of a municipality as
engaging in a purity campaign on its own account. But the city of North
Yakima, Washington, with a population of fifteen to eighteen thousand,
has become officially interested in such an educational reform.

A little less than one year ago the city commission abolished the
so-called "red-light" district, and thus opened the whole question of sex
hygiene. Advantage was taken of this opportunity by the local Society
of Social and Moral Hygiene, and the city commission was requested to
publish at the people's expense a series of five educational pamphlets to
be distributed free of charge to the general public.

The request was granted, and a special committee consisting of five
prominent citizens was appointed with instructions to prepare the literature and publish and distribute it. This has all been carried out successfully without any serious criticism on the part of any one. The literature
was put out as health-department matter in neat, attractive envelopes
printed in two colors and arranged for sending through the mail.

These pamphlets are written to five distinct classes of people, namely,
parents, boys, girls, young women, and young men. The first three in
the order named are enclosed in one envelope, while the other two are
separately wrapped. The five pamphlets may be sent through the mail
for two cents, the first three in one package for one cent. Thus the
mailing-cost is reduced to a minimum.

The distribution of such literature is always difficult, but the plan
devised by the committee has, so far as it has gone, been successful. The
board of education was called upon to assist, and willingly gave its co-
operation. As a result the principals of all the city school buildings were
called together in a conference, and the following plan was agreed upon.

Each principal prepared a list of families from which children were
sent to school, and saw that none were duplicated. After selecting a small
group of dependable pupils to distribute the literature the parents were
consulted as to their willingness to have their children engage in such
work. When all was ready, and the number of pamphlets needed for each
school was known, the health department delivered the literature to the
school buildings.

As the object has been to reach the homes first, only the first three
pamphlets were delivered by the school children. In this way two thousand of these circulars were placed in as many families. In connection
with this distribution the newspapers published numerous articles, and
brought the matter favorably to the attention of the people. Without the
aid of the newspapers the work would have been much more difficult;
but, as it was, the public was prepared to welcome the new departure.

In addition to this method of distribution the committee had the
hearty co-operation of the Presidents' Council of Women's Clubs, and
thus access to all the women's organizations of the city. The Young
Men's Christian Association and Young Women's Christian Association
gave valuable assistance, and one of the Sunday-schools in the city distributed the pamphlets to all its pupils. Pastors have distributed them
at church services. Hundreds of them have been mailed to people in the
country districts, and have also been distributed in connection with public
meetings in schoolhouses and churches in the outlying communities.

One very interesting feature of the campaign has been the publicity
which it has gained throughout the United States. Newspapers and
magazines have printed extended notices of the undertaking, and as a

result hundreds of requests have come to the city for sample sets of the little books. They have aroused wide-spread interest, and have been the means of helping materially many local reform movements and educational campaigns. One minister in the East sent for seventy-five copies to distribute at his church service on "Mother's Day."

We are sure that a great deal of good is being accomplished by this city campaign. One incident will show the advantage of having the city itself engage in this kind of work.

An advertising agent representing some medical company in the East came to the city not long ago, requesting permission of the mayor to distribute a large number of medical booklets on the subject of men's private diseases. Upon examination the city commission concluded that the little books were nothing more nor less than quack literature, and the mayor told the agent that the city published its own sex-hygiene literature, and the man could not distribute any of his. In fact, the mayor told the man that, if any of his circulars were found in the city, he would be arrested and fined. This action on the part of the city officials shows a high standard of efficiency in respect to morals.

Our work is still going on, and next season there will be held many parents' meetings and public gatherings in connection with the purity campaign. Already the public library is furnished with a supply of good books on the subject of sex. In all the work we have endeavored to impress upon the people that the literature is their own, the books are free, and that it is a people's movement throughout. Such work can be carried on in many communities, and we urge upon citizens everywhere to undertake something of the sort. In response to a request addressed to the North Yakima Health Department and enclosing a two-cent stamp a sample set of the pamphlets will gladly be forwarded to any one interested in such educational reform.

CHRISTIAN ENDEAVOR AS A TRAINING-SCHOOL FOR MINISTERS AND MISSIONARIES.

By Rev. S. Z. Batten, Philadelphia, Penn.

We are living in a great and fateful time. The signs of change are all about us. One age is passing, and a new time is coming. Old leases are running out, and new leases are being framed. An age, some one has said, is a time when God does new things. In our day the signs of God's presence and activity are all about. The promise of Scripture is being fulfilled, and the Eternal is indeed making all things new.

There have been several such epochs in the past, and we may therefore expect that another such epoch will dawn. The eighth century before Christ was a fateful time, one that saw the beginning of some great movements and some great nations. The first century of our era was another, the age of the Son of man, the time when Christianity arose to change dates and turn the course of history. The sixteenth century was another, the time of the Protestant Reformation, when the soul of man was emancipated and modern democracy was born. And now once more in our time a change is coming, and a new age is struggling to the birth. In our day a great movement is gaining direction and momentum, that is full of significance to the human race and one that is destined to change the face of the world. We are standing in the dawning light of a new day. Whether it will be a better day it is for us to determine; that it will be different from yesterday is certain.

It is a strange, troubled age, this in which we find ourselves. Society is full of unrest and agitation. The world is full of rumors of change and upheaval. The barometer indicates unsettled weather. Stormy days are ahead of us. Our institutions and our methods are going into the melting-pot, and no one is wise enough to foresee the outcome.

But all these things are signs of promise. As in the days of old, so now; when the sky is full of clouds and changes are in the air, we may lift up our heads, for we know that our redemption is nigh. When I was a boy, it sometimes happened that I had pains in my knees at night. My father used to comfort me by saying that these were good signs, as they were growing-pains. Society is full of aches and pains to-day, but I believe that they are growing-pains.

When Charles Sumner went to Washington to take the place in the Senate left vacant by the passing of Daniel Webster, he was met on the streets of the capital by Thomas H. Benton. The aged statesman greeted the newcomer very cordially; then, looking upon him in a pitying way, he said, "But, young man, you have come too late; all the great questions are settled."

Young people, it is a great day in which to live and to serve. You have come to the kingdom for a great time. There are more fateful questions before us to-day than have ever faced the men of any other generation. But every problem is an opportunity, and so this is an age of great opportunities. It is not a time for the coward, for men without faith and hope; but it is a great time for men of courage and men of vision. I congratulate you that you are called to live and to serve in such a time as this.

It is not easy to characterize this age in a word or a sentence. Some would say that this is the age of young people, and that is the case. This movement of the young people is full of significance and promise. Some would tell us that it is the age of the social gospel, and that is the case. We are beginning to interpret the gospel in new terms; we are coming to see that Christianity is essentially social; that, as John Wesley said, "the Bible knows nothing of a solitary religion." Still others would say that it is the age of practical religion, and it is all this. We are hearing much about pragmatism, and this means that ideas and systems are judged by their results and fruits. A doctrine, an idea, an institution, a system, that does not function does not receive much consideration. We see now that religion has to do with practical things, and is to be judged by its fruits. Still others declare that this is the age of democracy, and this is gloriously true. There is a great movement going on in our world, the steady, world-wide coming up of the people out of the place of obscurity into the place of authority. The foremost nations of earth are growing a determination to have the essential principles of Christianity, liberty, equality, fraternity, realized in all the realms and relations of life.

In a sense all of these things I have named are but parts and aspects of one great time, and that is the new search for the kingdom of God, the determination to build a more Christian type of human society. This is the goal of all effort; this interprets all other movements; this calls us all to the great divine enterprise of our time and of all time.

There are two or three things implied in this which we must consider, for they are related most vitally to our subject.

1. The young people's movement is a movement toward essential Christianity. It was a sad day for the cause of religion when the church came to mean the clergy and a distinction was made between the sacred and the secular. According to the great apostle, the Christ has given to his church all kinds of workers, with all sorts of talent, apostles, prophets, teachers, gifts of healing, helps, governments, tongues. Every gift is a work of the Spirit, and every worker has his place. Every disciple has a mission and a commission. Every disciple should be a trained worker. All this is a part of the pledge which each member accepts. There are no blanks in the church of Christ. There are no idlers in the kingdom of God. There are no exemptions in the army of the King. This, it is needless to say, does not mean a levelling down but a levelling

up. Every disciple is a man under authority. Each has an important work to do.

2. Along with this there has come a new conception of the work of the ministry. The work of the ministry is a great work,—the highest and noblest ever given to the sons of men. Preaching is one of the means that God has ordained for the extension of his kingdom; to the end of the chapter there will be a place for the preacher of the word. The world has not known its best preaching yet. Instead of believing that preaching will be outgrown I believe that it will be more highly honored in the days to come. But preaching the gospel, however necessary, is only a part of the minister's work. It may be that some men will be called to devote themselves to the work of preaching alone. But for the average minister this cannot be the case. He must be a teacher and leader as well as a preacher and prophet.

This means that a new type of ministry is demanded in the days to come. It will be less scholastic and more practical. It will not be less scholarly, but it will be more human. The time has gone by when the minister can be invisible all of the week and incomprehensible on Sunday. He is called to be a man among men, a leader of the people, a shepherd of the sheep, the teacher of the young, the friend of all. He is to live in close touch with life, to be interested in everything that concerns man, to be a neighbor, a citizen, a man among men. It is often said that men have lost interest in the work of the ministry, and that the ministry itself no longer appeals to the most virile and vigorous young men. There is a basis of fact here, for some types of ministry no longer appeal to men. But a new conception of the ministry is growing to-day—that great apostolic, human, all-around service of men, that great, divine work of leadership in the kingdom of God. And this new type of ministry will appeal to the best manhood of the church; it will bring into the service of the Kingdom the most virile and consecrated of the churches' sons.

And in large part this new conception of the ministry is the direct product and result of the young people's movement. In the Christian Endeavor Society we honor the church, and pledge to it our allegiance. In the Endeavor Society we consider the work of the Kingdom, and realize that life is a service. In the Endeavor Society the claims of God and the nobility of service are pressed home upon the heart and conscience. The young people's society is giving us an enlarged conception of the church and its work. The young people's society is ever showing us the opportunities for service. The young people's society is doing several things. It is showing us the glory of the life of service. It is the proving-ground for gifts and talents. It is a training-school for the ministry that is to be.

3. One other thing falls to me at this time. I must consider the relation of Christian Endeavor to the calling and work of the missionary.

The missionary idea is part and parcel of the gospel of Christ. Christianity by its very nature is missionary. It is a gospel for all the world. Every man in the world needs the gospel. The man who has no interest in missions either does not know what missions mean or he does not know Jesus Christ as he ought to know him.

The cause of missions, like all great causes, has passed through three stages. First of all there is the stage of indifference. It is hard for us to understand the indifference and apathy of men on this great question. It is only a little more than a hundred years since a young man, one William Carey, proposed that the ministers, having considered all the questions before them, should now consider the question of their obligation to give the gospel to the benighted peoples of earth. Then the moderator, good Dr. Ryland, thundered out, "Young man, sit down; when God wants the heathen converted, he will do it without you."

Later Andrew Fuller volunteered to go up to London to seek to interest Christian people in this blessed work. But everywhere he met indifference, rebuffs, scorn. It is not a pleasant sight to see this great, strong man, so often finding the door closed in his face, turning aside into some alley to weep over the indifference and apathy of Christian men.

This period of indifference has slowly passed, and more and more the church has come to a new mind. Now missions is a part of the regular and recognized work of the church.

Then came the period of criticism. In course of time missions grew into favor as the story of missionary successes became known. But soon men began to ask questions about the missionary and his work. In the first flush of success men had expected that the gospel would sweep the world and nations would be converted in a day. But men discovered that it was a long, slow process. They found that the number of converts was distressingly small. Calculations were made, showing that after all our efforts for a hundred years there were more heathen people in the world now than before the missionary movement began. From another side criticisms were brought against the missionary and his work. Every people, we are told, has its own religion. Our religion may be adapted to us, but it is not adapted to the other nations of earth. Keep your religion to yourselves, and leave the peoples of the earth to enjoy their own.

And once more we have all read accounts of the failure of the missionary in the letters of some globe-trotters. The missionaries are a lot of weak and incompetent men, we are told; they have no influence among the intelligent people; they are meddlers and disturbers of the peace; they are doing as much harm as good, and had better be called home. And so the story runs through all the gamut. These globe-trotters as a rule have never seen a real live missionary at work; they picked up all of their information in the lobby of hotels or the smoking-room of steamers; they listened to the tales of dealers in rum and other abominations, who were obliged to leave these heathen lands for the good of the people. But these criticisms, true and false, have had some influence upon the people at home, and for a while missionary interest flagged.

But now comes the third stage, the stage of conviction; and this we are just entering. To-day we are beginning to have a larger and truer understanding of the work that lies before us. To-day we are beginning to realize the meaning and magnitude of the missionary enterprise. We have begun to see that the cause of missions means the extension of the Redeemer's kingdom throughout the globe. We have begun to realize that we are called to give the whole blessing of the Kingdom to the last man of the race.

The time has gone by when we can accept any small conception of missions. In the days past we have been regaled with figures showing how long it will take to have the gospel preached in the hearing of every soul in the world. We have been edified with calculations showing how many people one missionary can reach with the gospel in the course of a year.

But in the new and larger conception of missions there is growing in our hearts a new conception of the work of the missionary. We see now that we are enlisted for a long campaign. We see that we are to carry the whole blessing of the Kingdom to the lives of men. We see now that there is a place in the mission field for all kinds of workers. We see that men and women are needed as missionary preachers, as missionary doctors, as missionary farmers, as missionary mechanics, as missionary social-service workers.

This great, new Christian conception of missions is growing in the minds and hearts of our young people. And from our young people's societies is coming a host of consecrated disciples who will dedicate their lives to the work of extending the Redeemer's kingdom. The young people's society is in large part responsible for this new interest in missions. The young people's society is the training-school for missionary workers. From the young people's societies will come a new generation of workers filled with the vision of the Kingdom and dedicated to the great work of establishing that kingdom among men.

And now let me gather up the threads of this discourse and notice the relation of all this to Christian Endeavor and the relation of Christian Endeavor to the ministry and to missions. The Christian Endeavor Society is a training-school for the study of the Kingdom. The young people come together to study the Scriptures that they may know the will and purpose of God; they study the condition and needs of men in the light of the Scriptures; they study the works of God in his world to-day. They study the church and its work; they study society and its problems; they study missionary history and missionary triumphs. They run the gamut of human life; nothing common to man can be alien to them. This means that a new and better understanding of the Kingdom and its work is growing in the minds of our people.

The young people's society is developing a new conception of the church and its work. We see more clearly than ever before that the church is a divine institution, that it has a great work to do, and that it furnishes us the agency through which men can co-operate in this search for the Kingdom. "The true and good idea of a church," said Thomas Arnold. "is that of a society for making men like Christ, earth like heaven, and the kingdoms of this world the kingdom of our God." To be a member of the church is a great honor. To be the pastor and leader of a church is a divine privilege.

The young people's movement is turning the attention of young men toward the gospel ministry. Figures are not available showing the number of young men who have been led into the ministry through the young people's society. And, after all, figures in this realm can tell very little; for in the inner life of the soul, the throne-room of the life, where decisions are made, it is not possible to weigh and measure influences. The tide of life in our churches is turning. In the days to come many of our best, most virile and capable young men will dedicate themselves to the work of the gospel ministry. But, as I have said, it will be a new type of the ministry that is to come. In the long future it will appear that the Christian Endeavor movement was a potent agency in giving the church this larger and better type of ministry. May I suggest here that a more determined and concerted effort be made to present the claims of the ministry to the young men, and then to train a larger number for service in the Kingdom?

The same is true with respect to the work of missions. These are great days in which we are living. But greater days are ahead of us. The doors of the nations are open, and the missionary is welcomed. The nations are ready for the gospel; and we have a gospel for the nations. To-day we need recruits for mission work in a score of lands. We need missionaries as preachers, teachers, physicians, farmers, mechanics. I see the day when from the ranks of our young people will come a host of consecrated lives to dedicate themselves to the work of extending the kingdom of God among men.

THE INFLUENCE OF THE HOME ON PRESENT-DAY LIFE.

By Rev. Robert F. Coyle, D.D., LL.D., Denver, Col.

The home life of its people is the unwritten history of a nation. A country goes up or down according as its homes are godly or ungodly. The statement is supported by all we know of the past and the present. The decay of governments begins at the fireside. No wonder it should be so emphasized in the Holy Scriptures. The development of Israel is the history of a family. There is no place like home to make or unmake a nation. If it be good, it is the greatest blessing out of heaven; if bad, it has more possibilities for mischief than anything else out of hell.

The stuff out of which homes are made is not brick and mortar; it is intangible; it is an atmosphere whose essence is love purified and glorified by religion. Without these there may be boarding-houses, but no homes.

Nothing is doing more to diminish the beneficent influence of the home than the lack of Christian instruction on the part of the parents. They turn the children over to the Sunday-school for a half-hour a week, and great multitudes do not even do that. There is no family altar or family pew. The lowered standards are far too apparent.

The home is threatened by the terrible pressure of competitive industry. In the intense struggle for existence large numbers of women are driven into offices, mills, and factories and thus made unfit for parenthood. In many cases the wages of the father are too small to maintain the family; and, where the wages are large, the stress of business is so great that the amenities of the home are neglected.

Then there is the divorce-mill. The number of marriages in proportion to the population grows smaller; the number of separations increases. Since 1870 two million divorces have been granted in the United States. One hundred thousand of these were obtained in 1912, which deprived 70,000 children of one or both parents last year.

The causes for the overthrow of the home are manifold, and among them are low wages, the rum devil, the craze for pleasure, and the over-organization of the church.

I believe something can be done to stop the downward drift, and I now proceed to indicate the remedy. It is a compound of various elements. There must be the inculcation of higher ideals everywhere. We must lift the people to Scriptural levels as to the home and the family. More sanctity must be thrown around the marriage relation. The stain of easy divorce must be wiped out. Trial marriages should be put in the same catagory with polygamy. As between a man's having all his wives at once and having them in quick succession I see little to choose from the point of view of morals and the effect upon the home. Then we must have better legislation against bad housing and bad physical environment. Overcrowding should be made a crime. Let the city furnish the poor with better homes and cheaper transportation instead of parks and boulevards and civic centres. The great thing is people, not property.

All this more than suggests where our suffragettes can be of immense service. If woman's place is in the home, let them demand it with their votes. Let them ballot the liquor traffic into the bottomless pit. Let them see that the altar is set up and kept up beside the hearthstone.

I am no pessimist, and this is not a note of despair, but simply a call to aroused interest. The home is still mighty, still the hope of the nation, still the saving ballast of our ship of state; but there is danger.

Our young men and women can help mightily. The to-morrow of the home is mostly in their keeping. Let them pledge themselves to the purity and preservation of the family if they would serve God and their generation before they fall on sleep. To defend the home, to protect it against all foes, whether they approach through channels of irreligion or through impurity or industrialism or drink or lust, should command all that is best and most heroic in the manhood and womanhood of our times.

THE RESPONSIBILITY OF THE CHURCH FOR THE TRAINING OF ITS FUTURE MEMBERS.

By Rev. J. T. McCrory, D.D., Pittsburg, Penn.

The more I consider this subject, the more deeply it impresses me. A generation of real church-members fully trained would mean the salvation of humanity.

What is a church-member? A real church-member is a person joined by a living bond to the living, glorified Saviour, a member of his body. For what is a church-member to be trained? To respond to the "Head," the will of Jesus Christ who is the head of the living body. What is the will of Jesus Christ? World-conquest, to bring back this rebellious, alienated race to allegiance to his Father.

What things specifically should future church-members be trained to do? These four things:

1. They should be trained to *testify*. What this alienated world is waiting for is testimony. To testify, one must have knowledge. What do you know? Hearsay does not go on the witness-stand. Not, What does Paul say, or Isaiah? but, What do you know? What do you know about Jesus Christ as a Saviour? You must have an experience to be able to testify. If you can tell of a changed heart, forgiven sin, power to live an upright, honest, joyful life, you will do for a witness, not otherwise.

2. They should be trained to *pray*. It is not in foreign missions alone that the church must make progress on her knees. That is the only way to make progress in any enterprise. A prayerless church-member is a dead soul. A prayerless church is a dead church. The great Christian Endeavor movement has done a good work in teaching multitudes to lead in public prayer; to give intelligent expression to the desires, longings, and aspirations of the soul. But that is not to be trained to pray. One must be moved by the conviction of the omnipotence of prayer to be trained to pray. Prayer has removed mountains of hoary prejudice, superstition, hatred, out of the path of the missionary church. But the full power of a praying church is yet to be tested. The church that teaches a generation to pray will inaugurate the movement that will transform the world.

3. The church must train her future members to *give*. The teaching of Jesus Christ as to the relation of the saved man to his own life and his possessions is revolutionary. The church must be trained, however, to appreciate and apply the Bible doctrine of *stewardship* before it will be able to meet its Heaven-ordained work of world-salvation. We say the reason our churches are not able to do one-fourth of the work that lies at their hand is lack of money. And yet there are individual believers who, if they gave but a tithe of what they hold as stewards, could make the whole contributions of a denomination for a whole year look like thirty cents. There are a million church-members in this country who could give, if they responded to the spirit and claims of stewardship, a thousand million dollars a year and would be the better off for it.

4. The church must train her future members to *live*. Now the only life that really tells is the life filled with the Holy Spirit. Every church-member is expected to be the channel for the forth-putting of the power of God by the Spirit on an unsaved world. We complain that the world has lost the God-sense. That is true. The masses of this age are living as if there were no God. The only way to awaken in them the God-sense is to bring them into contact with men and women filled with God. Church-members must be trained to communicate as well as possess the Spirit of the Almighty.

THE COLLEGE MAN AND THE CHURCH.

By President Henry Churchill King, LL.D., Oberlin, Ohio.

The college man belongs to a peculiarly privileged class. As such he owes a correspondingly great service to the community in which he lives and to the nation of which he is a citizen. College education ought certainly to produce the thoughtful man, and we may be better prepared to measure the peculiar obligations of the college man by thinking of what may be rightfully asked from the thoughtful man.

First of all, the college man ought to be worthy of Emerson's old definition of the scholar as "man thinking." He should be able to grapple thoroughly with the pressing problems of our time, and think them through in masterly fashion. The need is both a personal and a national one. The danger is, on the part of us all, on the one hand, that there will not be even thinking enough to know ourselves or our own task, to keep clear of becoming a mere echo or imitation of another. On the other hand there is the danger that we shall not do thinking enough as a nation to see what democracy means, and the solution of its problems, thinking enough to feel and to purpose a true democracy, and not merely theoretically to discuss it.

The college man should be the thoughtful man also in the sense of discerning the laws of life. It is the very secret and business of scientific mastery to discern the laws of nature and human nature. And in developing such insight into the fundamental laws of life the colleges and universities ought to be natural leaders.

The college man should be a thoughtful man, in the third place, as one who sees things in true proportion, for whom the great is really great, and the little, little. The community and the national life both greatly need men, not of convictionless indifference, but of discriminating breadth and of tolerance that roots in great convictions.

The college man should be the thoughtful man, in the fourth place, as considerate. College students seem often inclined to try to combine the freedom of men and the irresponsibility of boys. The two are not consistent, and the man who would be truly free must have a like delicate respect for the freedom of other men. It ought to be expected of college men that they should be trained to stand squarely against the marked selfish lawlessness of our time.

And, finally, the college man should be the thoughtful man as one who is determined to profit by his great historical inheritance, determined to enter into the great spiritual achievements of the race, the scientific spirit, the historical spirit, the philosophical spirit, æsthetic appreciation, the social consciousness, the religious ideal.

For every element in this historical inheritance has preparation to give for community service. The scientific spirit means the determination to see straight, to report exactly, to give an absolutely honest reaction upon the situation. And this is often the first step in community as well as individual improvement. The historical spirit involves the ability to put one's self at the point of view of the other man and race and time. The philosophical spirit is the endeavor to see things whole and to grasp their meaning. Æsthetic appreciation opens great sources of permanent satisfaction. The social consciousness underlies some of the most ideal aims and accomplishments of our age, and is perhaps its highest glory. And religious faith is required that permanent meaning may be given to all the rest. At all these points the college man should be able to render a genuine service to the community and the nation.

THE GREATEST SOCIAL PERIL AND HOW TO MEET IT.

By Rev. E. A. King, North Yakima, Wash.

The Black Plague and the White Plague.

Everybody is acquainted with the phrase, "the great white plague," and all understand that it refers to the rapid spread of the disease of tuberculosis. So awakened are the citizens of every city and State over the fact that it is a preventable disease that they willingly submit to a tax in order that proper efforts may be made to eliminate the causes, prevent the spread, and prosecute the cure of the disease. The gains made in these directions are wonderful, and we expect the time to come when the serious aspects of the disease will entirely disappear.

It has been comparatively easy to carry on successful campaigns against tuberculosis because no serious personal moral questions have been involved, but it is altogether different with the "great black plague," of which I am about to speak.

The "great black plague" is so called because it is a plague very much worse than tuberculosis, which is called "the great white plague." It is more difficult to describe and discuss because it has to do with the great problem of sex, and has been a subject of profound study and experiment from the beginning of time.

It all grows out of sexual immorality, and is, therefore, one of the hardest problems with which to deal. Any adequate study of the theme plunges the student immediately into a study of the personal and social sins of others; and such delving is thoroughly unpleasant, though to the scientific investigator it is an interesting process.

The Subject Has To Do With Venereal Disease.

We are dealing here, then, with sex-diseases such as gonorrhea, syphilis, etc. Not until comparatively recent years have sufficient figures been compiled to acquaint us properly with the terrible ravages of these diseases. Of course, informed people have always known that venereal diseases were intimately connected with prostitution, but not every one realized the full significance of the fact. When we are told, however, that the majority of men, 75 or 80 per cent, in our great cities have gonorrhea once or several times, that 40 to 60 per cent, some say 75 per cent, of all operations upon women for diseases of the womb and ovaries are caused by clap or gonorrhea, that 20 per cent of all blindness is due to germs of gonorrhea or clap getting into the eyes of children at birth, that most men who have had these diseases think they are cured, and yet may not be so, one begins to wake up to the seriousness of the situation.

This is only a part of the sad story, however. Men who are diseased often marry pure girls, and communicate these diseases to their innocent wives, who in turn convey the virus to their children; and thus the stream of life is polluted at its very source.

Perhaps a good way to bring the facts to our minds is to contemplate the statements made relative to the prevalence of the disease in the army and navy; for here is congregated a vast concourse of men, mostly unmarried and away from home. The figures are as follows:

The average strength of the United States navy in 1903 was 37,248; there were in the hospital for venereal diseases 4,560, a loss of service to the navy of 114,571 days, equivalent in fighting strength to the loss of a second-class battleship yearly.

The cost of venereal diseases in the British army during 1896, 1897, and 1898 was $2,244,750 yearly, with a total loss of 1,738,688 days' service a year. The average strength for the three years was 201,200 men; the average yearly admissions to hospital for these diseases was 54,334 (more than 25 per cent during one year), an explanation as to army inefficiency of interest to the tax-payers.

One-eighth of the total of the United States army was in hospitals for venereal diseases in 1903. In this and previous statements those suffering from the disease are not included where disease did not necessitate confinement to hospital.

Prostitution the Cause of the Black Plague.

The chief source of these diseases is prostitution. In almost every city there have been developed centres called segregated or "red-light" districts, where prostitution has been carried on as a business under the protection of the police department as a so-called necessary evil.

This question of what to do with prostitution has been and is to-day one of the most serious of municipal problems. Every kind of safeguard has been thrown around the business, including medical inspection; but nothing has yet been devised by which the business is made safe from disease. It is the confession of nearly all municipal authorities that this sort of protection does not materially reduce the spread of venereal disease. It is a well-known fact that every prostitute, public or private, acquires venereal disease sooner or later; hence all of them are diseased some of the time and some of them practically all of the time. The man who patronizes them risks his health at every exposure. In some cities the system of segregated vice has been abolished with good results; but even the abolition of protected, segregated vice-resorts will not alone solve the problem, though it will help materially.

Victims of the Diseases Hard to Distinguish.

Another dreadful aspect of the "black plague" is that no ordinary person can tell surely who the victims are. Of course there are hospital and asylum cases that are painfully clear to those who have them in charge, and occasionally one sees a man or woman with unmistakable evidences of venereal disease. For the most part, however, it is a hidden disease because of the nature of the malady and because most of the victims shun polite society. This is due partly to the fact that no public records of these diseases are kept, no man or woman is quarantined.

Venereal disease is a virulent corruption, from which germs are carried. From the standpoint of epidemiology these diseases belong in the same class with smallpox, diphtheria, and scarlet fever. The health department puts up danger cards on houses even where measles are found, and quarantines the victims of smallpox, diphtheria, etc.; but, as the late Dr. Prince A. Morrow said, venereal diseases are completely ignored. In an extended article on syphilis by Dr. Gottheil, written for practising physicians, he says, "The patient must be segregated from regular life, from home and family, for at least eighteen months." What shall we say, in the face of this expert testimony, to the 80 per cent or more cases in great cities that are not segregated?

Innocent Persons May Be Infected By Accident.

In all this discussion there is one very vital fact that must ever be kept in mind, and that is this: venereal infection may result from contact with articles once used by the diseased, such as toilet or table articles, tooth-brushes, drinking-glasses, sponges, forks, pipes, penholders, the public telephone, etc. This means that many causes of infection are extra-genital, and thoroughly innocent people may contract the disease. This is one reason why the present status of the venereal infection is so serious.

These diseases are increasing, and many, supposing gonorrhea (or clap) no worse than a bad cold, are not at all careful or sanitary; and thus the health of the general public is jeoparded. To counteract this danger, public drinking-cups are being removed, public towels are becoming less used, and public toilets are being made more sanitary. No human being is absolutely safe from the ravages of this plague, but with proper care and thoughtfulness any one may protect himself from the ordinary channels of infection.

Why Prostitution Exists.

This paper would be incomplete if it did not undertake to explain why prostitution exists and continues to hold so large a place in community life everywhere. I will, therefore, enumerate eleven contributory causes that have helped to perpetuate the evil.

1. The first and most fundamental cause is the sex instinct itself. There is no instinct so strong, and it is so for the purpose of making the propagation of the race a constant and dominating factor in life. A lamentable mistake was made, we think, early in the development of ethical religion, when sex as such was considered as an evil thing in itself. The sex instinct is not an evil, unholy thing; it is God-given, and in human beings it should be always under the control of the will. This has not been the case, however. As far back as one can penetrate the pages of history he finds the common mind possessed with the belief that the exercise of the sexual organs is necessary for the maintenance of perfect health, and this conviction has led countless millions of men to excuse their sexual excesses and irregularities. The belief in sex as essentially evil has prevented the spread of proper knowledge and understanding of the subject, and all considerations with regard to it have been driven to cover and secrecy, and mystery has ever since surrounded the sex question. In all discussions concerning this subject these two facts must never be forgotten, namely, that the sex instinct is natural, strong, and as intrinsically clean as any other department of human physiology. Whatever of evil there may be at present associated with it is due to man's fault and his unholy imaginings.

2. The following are merely contributing causes of the social evil; and, though they are worthy of much more elaborate consideration, I can take time merely to mention them in passing. They are as follows: the changing conditions of city life, making the sense of the need of home less forceful; woman's increasing economic importance; the unwillingness of young people to begin home-building on humble lines; easy divorce; immodesty in dress on the part of girls and young women; unwholesome and questionable amusements; low wages paid to working women; feeblemindedness; sex perversion; the saloon; and last, but not least, ignorance of parents and children as to the meaning and hygiene of sex. There are other contributory causes of sexual irregularities, but these are perhaps the most important.

How to Meet the Black Plague.

We are now in possession of the essential facts that make up what we call the greatest social peril. While there are many interesting phases of this great problem, we must for brevity confine ourselves to the question of practical remedy.

First and foremost in the list of agencies for the eradication of impurity and all its attending train of evils I would place education in all matters pertaining to the sex life. It has been the custom for so many years not to mention the subject of sex in polite society that a lamentable ignorance has grown up among us. This is due largely to false modesty on the part of parents and teachers, but there is no satisfactory excuse for attempting to keep the knowledge of sex from the young. They are bound to discover the facts for themselves by blundering, or they are instructed from impure sources to their physical and moral undoing.

Perhaps this reticence is due to lack of knowledge on the part of parents, but this silence leaves the child without the fortification of proper safeguarding knowledge. For this lack young people grow up in ignorance of one of the most important and vital human functions; and the results are frequently seen in wrecked men and women, unhappy homes, diseased children, and both physical and moral wretchedness.

To meet this condition, there must be undertaken in every community some kind of education as to the hygiene of sex. It may well begin by inviting to the community a lecturer who can set before the public the facts and present the need for education. Perhaps there are capable people already there who can be utilized for such work. One of the best agencies to accomplish the desired end is a Society of Social and Moral Hygiene similar to those in New York City, Chicago, Spokane, Seattle, and Portland. Through such an organization all the people in the community interested in these subjects could be co-ordinated and utilized for practical reform. Through such a society literature on the subject of sex could be secured and distributed, parents' meetings held, and authoritative information conveyed to the entire community. The city health department may undertake the task of popular education on sex as in North Yakima, Wash.

The Importance of Home Instruction.

One guiding principle may well be kept in mind; namely, the home is the most desirable place for instruction of the young on the subject of sex, and every effort should be made to reach the parents of little children, and those who may reasonably expect to become parents. But it is not always possible to accomplish this; so instruction as to sex must be carried on by the lecture method and by the dissemination of literature to men and women generally.

Create a Sex-Hygiene Department.

Good work may be done by creating sex-hygiene or purity departments in Sunday-school associations and Christian Endeavor unions. The Ohio Christian Endeavor Union has had for some years an efficient purity department under the direction of Mrs. Mabel Hester of Norwalk. Some Sunday-school associations have carried on this work for years; of course the Woman's Christian Temperance Union, the Young Men's Christian Association, etc., have done and are doing splendid work along these lines. The latest plan of this kind has just been adopted by the Inland Empire Sunday-School Association, consisting of eastern Washington and northern Idaho, reaching a constituency of nearly 100,000 persons.

Teach Sex Hygiene in the Public Schools.

Sooner or later instruction on sex will be given in the public schools, but not until the normal schools have trained the teachers. It is still an open question whether the subject should be taught by the regular instructors or by special teachers trained for the work.

The Need of a Moral Motive.

In discussing the subject of sex-education it is worth remembering that knowledge is not safety, though it is power. Information concerning sex alone will not solve our great problem. There must be a moral motive running through all our endeavors, and for this reason we must be careful as to the choice of persons who are to impart information as to sex, and we must also use the same judgment in selecting the books on sex-enlightenment that we place in the hands of young people. Many a boy or girl knows more than his or her parents and some of his or her teachers about the facts of sex. What such young people need, then, is not so much information as the creation of new moral ideals. We cannot count much on the help of formal religion; but real personal religion, the kind that is linked with ethics, the sort that feels moral responsibility, is and has always been the best antiseptic against vice and passion. Any system of sex-instruction that ignores this element will fail to produce the much-desired result.

The Single Standard of Morals.

In connection with the ethical side of the subject it should be taught that there is an unwritten but authoritative moral law binding upon every intelligent human being. This is the single standard of morals that holds both men and women equally responsible for sexual immoralities. Hitherto, and even at the present time, the woman who has gone wrong usually suffers the more, frequently carrying all the ignominy, suffering, ostracism from society, while the man in the case often goes scot-free. This should not be true in a Christian civilization, but unfortunately it is true in most communities. We should exert our influence to secure legislation that will erase this double standard from our statute-books.

The Need of Cleaning Up the Community.

There are other things that should be done in order to complete the great plan of reform. For example, we suggest that every community have attractive, free public parks and playgrounds for children where outdoor life may be enjoyed to the full. Besides this it would help materially if the community authorities would clean up everything that savors of obscenity or impurity so that sexual temptation, so far as possible, may be removed from the sight of the young. This should include not only reforms in the public dance, censorship of the moving-picture shows and the vaudeville stage, but bill-boards on the streets, posters, post-cards, and pictures of immoral suggestion everywhere.

The Influence of the Saloon.

One of the most prolific contributory causes of prostitution is the saloon. While I could say a great many things against this institution, I will confine my remarks to two or three suggestions. If the saloon could be wholly abolished, this would be the ideal solution of a difficult problem; but, where it still remains by the will of the majority, it is possible to institute some reforms. Saloons should be prohibited in houses of prostitution, and all minors and women should be prevented from entering.

Prostitution an Economic and Social Question.

Another and exceedingly important corrective reform should be undertaken; namely, the industrial conditions of the community should be studied in order to see what is the relation between low wages paid to women workers and the prevalence of prostitution. It is said that, where women's wages are high, prostitution among them is at a minimum. Any one who wishes to aid in this reform can do no better thing than to work for the minimum-wage law for all working women.

The Variety of Reform Agencies.

In all that I have so far said relative to methods of reform it will be noted that many different kinds of effort are needed, and all of these are essential to produce a satisfactory result. It is no slight or simple task that we have set before us. It cannot all be accomplished in a year or in one generation; but, if we seek to reach the source of life itself and clarify the environment into which our children are born, we may reasonably hope that sometime in the future prostitution may be reduced to the minimum and the consequent plague of venereal disease practically stamped out. This condition greatly to be desired will result because young men and young women will learn how to control their sexual natures, will practise the laws of eugenics, will teach their children what they need to know about the subject, and will thus contribute to the building up of a healthy and vigorous race thoroughly clean and strong. Meanwhile, you and I must do all we can for the good of the cause and the purification of the coming race.

CHRISTIAN ENDEAVORERS AIM TO BE EFFICIENT IN SERVICE.

By Mrs. J. S. Norvell, Los Angeles.

I. A Well Body.

It would seem to be almost a crime for any one to grow up deformed, crippled, or physically defective in these days of medical skill, with hospitals and scientific surgery at our command, with dispensaries and free clinics, organizations for physical welfare, physical-culture classes, the open gymnasium, the outdoor sports, athletics, etc. With all this attention given to the promotion of the "gospel of good health" it would seem something criminal to allow any one to grow up with physical defects or deformities.

However, you and I have only to look about us to-day to find much sorrow and suffering caused by physical wreckage all about us. To illustrate, here is a man with a splendid inheritance of good physique, organically strong, cultured, educated, trained, of upright character, noble in sentiment, full of integrity, successful in business. He becomes absorbed, consumed, infatuated, yea, intoxicated, by his profession. He fails to eat and sleep and exercise properly, and in a few short years is absolutely incapacitated by a nervous breakdown. Surely he is as guilty as one who "wasted his substance with riotous living."

But as Christian Endeavorers we stand on a higher plane than simply the recognition of the value of a well body symmetrically developed, properly cared for, and enjoyed as a personal asset or blessing. We have come to know that our bodies are very precious to God, that they are loved by Jesus Christ, his Son, who redeemed them and watches over the physical man as well as the spiritual.

The children of Israel were led, fed, clothed, made and kept well by observance of the laws of health and hygiene, also by miraculous healings and deliverances. Though we are claimed by death, yet God's guardian angels will watch over and carefully guard the sacred dust, and we are promised that it shall be brought forth in resurrection power and glory, and dwell eternally in the presence of the Great King, even as our redeemed spirits are to dwell with him. How careful, then, ought we to be of this body of clay in which we live, when we recognize the truth that this body is the dwelling-place (the temple) of God, that he has chosen it! God had myriads of higher, holier, available places; yet he chooses to dwell in your body and mine. This brings a sacredness, a dignity, a self-appreciation, that nothing else could give. Not that I am anything of myself, but I am chosen as the clothing, the habitation, the temple of God. Then I will keep my body clean. Nothing shall defile it. Nothing shall degrade it. No indulgences, no intemperance, no habits, shall be allowed that would interfere with the best and highest service I may render my God by keeping my body clean, whole, and holy.

My spiritual and moral self are dependent largely on the physical. Experience in juvenile courts shows that physical defects and weaknesses precede and are responsible for a large percentage of moral delinquencies and crime.

Let us go away from this twenty-sixth International Convention of

Christian Endeavor to think more highly of these bodies in which we dwell and to regard them more sacredly. Let them be the avenue through which our spirits (God's Spirit) shall speak and minister. Jesus came in the flesh; the Holy Spirit comes without a body, that he may have yours and mine.

"I beseech you therefore, brethren, by the mercies of God, that ye present your bodies a living sacrifice, holy, acceptable unto God, which is your reasonable service."

2. A Clean Mind.

Human intelligence was the highest gift of the Creator to man, the head of the animal creation, in order that he might have dominion over the animals; also through this avenue of man's intelligence the Creator sought to reach the sons of men, that man might commune with him.

This mind is to be kept clean and wholesome, and is to be developed and made active in useful service for my Lord. Anything that would blur or make cloudy the sensitive cells of the brain, anything that would incite to undue stimulation or imagination, I am to beware of, as of deadly poisons. This means that I am to exercise special care in the selection of the food (reading) which shall be allowed, and which furnishes the material of which the brain cells are built or upon which they feed.

This principle guides to the amusements which we shall choose. That which gives superficial ideas of life, that which inculcates false estimates or values of life, that which sets a premium on vice and immorality, that which inflames one with dreams of things unreal, and unfits one for the more rugged or enduring realities of our every-day life, should no more be allowed to flow through my mind with its contamination than I would allow the unclean sewer to pour its filth and germs of disease and poisons of death through my body or my home.

The Scriptures give us much valuable instruction concerning the need of a clean mind. In Rom. 12:2 we are urged to be transformed by the renewing of our minds, that we may prove the will of God. Then in Phil. 2:5 we are lifted higher, and the thought is made clearer by these words: "Let this mind be in you which was also in Christ Jesus."

The mind that led him to robe himself in humanity's garment; the mind that said, "I must be about my Father's business"; the mind that enabled him to gird himself with the towel and from the basin wash the disciples' feet; the mind that kept before him always the dignity and purpose and possibilities of his life; the mind which held him to the highest service when tempted to accept, as in the temptation in the wilderness, a lower place, as also when taunted by those who gazed at him at the crucifixion-hour, saying, "If thou be the Son of God, come down from the cross"; the mind that kept him steadfast, loyal, faithful, joyful, true, patient, kind, tender, sympathetic—let this mind be in you.

Let us leave this convention place with a prayer upon our lips that our minds may be kept clear, clean, unobstructed avenues through which his life and grace are to flow, first for our own enrichment and fruitage, and for the enlarged blessing which shall come to those who may come under the shadow of our lives and be helped into more efficient service.

3. A Pure Heart.

"Blessed are the pure in heart, for they shall see God."

The Christianity that Christian Endeavorers possess deals most largely with the heart. That which this needy, suffering, sorrowing world needs is heart power, not so much head power. The most efficient service is rendered when these two, heart power and head power, are brought together in perfect and harmonious relation to each other. The one who goes forth with well-stored mind, clean and wholesome though it be, minus heart power will do only half what he might have accomplished had he taken the "whole armor." The one who goes forth with only heart power will find his zeal running away with his knowledge and will need often to rectify the mistakes of his judgment; but, if one must be weak and the other strong, let the heart overpower the head.

Heart power comes by way of heart purpose. Paul received his divine unction for his splendid and fruitful service because he had decided, determined, chosen, by a definite act of his will to know Christ and to live Christ. You and I will have efficiency in service by the application of a life force, a great passion, a definite choice of the heart, a definite dedication of our life to the Master.

The natural heart, we are told, cannot see God. He is spiritually revealed to those whose hearts are renewed. The stony heart must be removed, and the heart of flesh must take its place. Upon that God writes his statutes and his commandments. I like the story concerning Saul. When Samuel went to anoint him, the prophet said, "The spirit of the Lord will come upon thee, and thou shalt be turned into another man."

In the recognition of the call of God upon us, facing the need of the world as it calls to us, endeavoring to render our largest and best service and bear the fruitage that will honor our Lord, we need to have our hearts made pure by his indwelling grace. We need the incoming of his divine spirit, purifying our hearts, and flowing through us in "living waters" to bless and save other lives.

With this trinity of power, a well, strong, holy body, presented to God for his service; a clean, renewed, transformed mind, leading us to live and to serve as did our Master; and with a pure heart, in which dwell God's presence and spirit and power, we go forth equipped for valiant and efficient service.

AMERICA A FIELD FOR HEROIC ENDEAVOR.

By Rev. Robert E. Pretlow, Seattle, Wash.

The heroic has a perennial appeal to youth. Youth's swelling muscles, its enlarging vision, its keen, constructive mind, all cry out for something big to do. We would not have it otherwise. That way lie growth and progress. Human powers actually stretch to meet the task imposed. The soul expands to compass the field of larger vision. The whole being grows big in the process of doing big things. So youth properly looks for fields for heroic endeavor.

In that search the commonest tendency is to look to the far fields. Familiarity seems to dwarf the things at hand. Always the persimmons are mighty big away over yonder, and the pot of gold lies at the foot of the rainbow. Too often because we cannot reach the rainbow's foot we despair of large service, cripple our ambitions, cramp our souls, and try to be content with the little and the trivial.

There are big and heroic tasks afar. With Japan on tiptoe, China wide-awake, India stirring, and Africa beginning to rub its eyes, there are tremendous tasks and magnificent opportunities for service. All honor to those who are called to service there, and in the Master's name go out to meet the mighty needs.

But to most of you those special calls and particular opportunities will not come. To you who are not called to far fields, who cannot go, who ought not to go, is my message to-day. It is not a message of consolation, but of congratulation. For the biggest tasks of all the world to-day, requiring the highest heroism, the broadest intelligence, and the deepest consecration, the most of "grace, grit, and gumption," are right here under your hands in America. Tasks large enough to test courage and ability to the final limit. This half-hour would not suffice for a mere catalogue of them. But may we glance briefly at some of the foremost?

There is the problem of the foreigner. And this problem is a two-fold one. First, he is to be considered as an element of American life. I need not deal in figures to make you realize the size of the unceasing stream of people who pour in through our gates into the United States and Canada. We are beginning to realize that this stream is so great that we must assimilate it or be assimilated by it. America has been called the melting-pot, and in a melting-pot the predominant element gives character to the mass. Are we content to have a resultant mass with all the dross left in? Or shall we in love and loyalty to Christ make the melting-pot a refining crucible? If American ideals are to be kept high and clean, and American practice is to accord with those ideals, there is need of the most earnest, unremitting, and intelligent effort that our incoming guests may learn to know not merely the freedom that there is in America, but also that larger and higher liberty that is in Christ Jesus.

Not merely for self-protection is this labor needed, but as a service to the world. Multitudes of these foreigners return and carry back with them the evil or the good which they acquire while on our shores. The obligation is upon us as citizens of the world to see that this returning stream be made to carry with it tc the far places of the earth the best of our religion and of our civilization. The results will be manifest afar, but the work that produces them must be done here.

One of the greatest and most effective contributions which we can make to the cause of the evangelization of the world is to inspire and instruct the adventurous souls who come to us, so that, when they return to their own, equipped as they are with the language, with kinship, with complete familiarity with customs and methods of thought, they may become the most effective of missionaries.

Closely associated with the problem of the foreigner is the industrial problem. Fundamentally this is a problem of justice and of values. It is a challenge as to whether we really believe that a man *is* much better than a sheep. Upon both sides of the question we meet all the embattled hosts of selfishness and greed in their most unattractive guise. It is a problem which only the spirit of the church can ever solve. We are often told that the working men are estranged from the church. If it be true, it is because the church is too much estranged from their problems. They may properly demand that a religion which promises to make everything all right throughout eternity should demonstrate its claim upon our faith by beginning to eliminate injustice and to remove too heavy burdens here and now. The only solution of the industrial problem is its Christianization. This problem flings its challenge to most heroic endeavor.

To the Endeavorer remote from cities some of these problems seem almost as distant as the far mission fields. To such the great problems of rural life and the rural church are close at hand. The country was once America's stronghold of religion and of sane and clean citizenship. Such it must become again for the health and welfare of the nation. The cause of the declining' rural church must be discovered and sources of new life and vigor found. Inadequate methods must be discarded and efficient ones substituted. The church must be wedded to the vital problems of the country. Its energies must not be directed solely to the saving of *souls*, but to saving and filling the whole life of boys and girls, of families and communities. The problem of church-federation is a vital and integral part of the rural problem, and perhaps your own church may find that in losing its life it may find its highest service. Few tasks press upon us with more urgent need than the tasks of the rural problem, and few require more perfect self-abnegation and more heroic courage.

In this presence why should I even mention the liquor problem? Every Endeavorer is already enlisted in that fight. One who is not whole-heartedly and consistently in active opposition to the saloon is not worthy to wear the Christian Endeavor emblem. There has been and is good fighting all along the line. And yet perhaps in no other field of our efforts has there been more lost motion or more fighting at cross-purposes. We have made progress, but the battle is by no means over. The enemy is alive and alert and desperate. In the fight to realize our vision of a saloonless nation by 1920 we shall have need of courageous service and wise generalship. This is the paramount problem of our generation just as slavery was that of our fathers.

But already its successor in the primacy of problems is at the door. God is sounding his reveille for the awakening of a new conscience against militarism, and for the abolition of war as the next great step in human progress.

We are beginning to realize the fact that militarism and Christianity are fundamentally and unalterably opposed to each other. One inculcates love; the other, hatred. One teaches to save; the other, to kill. One seeks to serve; the other, to subjugate or to destroy. One strives to lighten human loads; the other imposes the heaviest burdens which human society is compelled to bear. One lifts man's ideals toward those of the Son of God; the other debases them to the place of the tiger and the jackal.

Militarism poisons the very springs of life spiritual and life physical. In teaching the disobedience of one commandment it brings all into contempt, and by its anti-social practices and lowered moral standards it pours into the social body a stream of physical disease that blights the lives of pure women, and damns generations yet unborn. It is a relic of heathen barbarism lingering beyond its time, and its continued presence is a loud call to the endeavor of every young follower of the Prince of peace to send it to the limbo where its kindred, cannibalism and slavery, have already gone.

America, of all the nations, is best fitted to lead in freeing the world from the barbaric blight of war and substituting for it a reign of righteousness and justice according with the teachings of Jesus, and in harmony with his Spirit.

And what body is better fitted to lead America in this new crusade than the brave and loyal hosts of Christian Endeavor?

I can mention but one other of the great opportunities open before us here at home—the opportunity of the Christian ministry. The highest courage is not always that which does the unusual and spectacular thing. Oftentimes more is required to perform the more inconspicuous round of necessary service, the results of which are not so immediately apparent. The ministry is such a service. The minister must in his own inner life get so close to God that he may become a man of vision. Then he must show to men the vision of enlarging life. In proportion as his work is deep and permanent it is likely to be slow and inconspicuous. But none the less is it vital and fundamental.

Just now the church is stationary in respect to population. It must win America if America is to win the world. Sometimes in the face of adverse currents it is a victory to hold our own. But more than this is necessary. If the church is to win she must have men of brains and character and courage and consecration to be her ministers and lead her on to victory.

The world to-day is looking to this continent for leadership in Christian advancement. To make good our right to leadership we must solve our own problems. No generation of men at any time or place since our first parents fled from the flashing sword at the gate of Eden has been confronted with greater or more important problems. Their difficulty and significance are none the less because they are chiefly moral rather than material, constructive rather than destructive. And because the weapons of our warfare are not carnal the call upon our heroism is heightened rather than diminished.

Let nobody make you think you are weaklings or shirkers because your place is at home rather than abroad. Let no one delude you into the thought that you have no great place in the world's progress because you are here. If America retrogrades, the world slips backward. If America does not advance, the march of humanity is halted. Believe in God and in the future. In the place where he has placed you do your part in the Kingdom, and your service shall not be in vain.

CHAPTER XVII.

A WORLD-WIDE NIGHT.

Auditorium Endeavor, Sunday Evening, July 13.

EVERY nook and cranny of Auditorium Endeavor was packed on Sunday evening for a meeting the theme of which was "The World for Christ." Ten thousand people were there. Yet this was only one of half a dozen Convention gatherings from several of which hundreds were turned away. At least 22,000 people were at the various meetings this evening alone. Every meeting-place was packed to the doors.

The first greeting was from Hawaii, a song by three native Endeavorers.

Rev. Edgar E. Strother, field secretary for China, and his wife were interesting figures at the Convention. For some years these Endeavorers have labored up and down the length and breadth of the Chinese empire, explaining the principles of Christian Endeavor and in apostolic fashion establishing the hearts of native Endeavorers. They know China through and through, and Mr. Strother therefore fittingly spoke on "Christian Endeavor in a New Republic."

"When some one asked when the present revolution began," said Mr. Strother, "the reply was, 'When Robert Morrison landed in China.' During China's dark days Christian Endeavorers prayed long and earnestly for a pure government and a free country." Mr. Strother's address was very convincing and follows:

CHRISTIAN ENDEAVOR IN A NEW REPUBLIC.

BY REV. EDGAR E. STROTHER, General Secretary of the China Christian Endeavor Union.

It is indeed a privilege to bring to this great convention the greetings of your twenty-three thousand Chinese fellow Christian Endeavorers.

I have been asked to speak of Christian Endeavor in the new republic of China, and I desire first of all to say something of

I. *The Influence of Christian Endeavor in the Formation of the New Republic.* A prominent Chinese official, when asked, "When did this revolutionary or reform movement begin?" replied, "When Morrison landed in China."

Although Christian Endeavor has been going along quietly, without any great blare of trumpets, it has had no small share in the development of the spirit of democracy and the training of Christian men who have helped in the establishment of the new government.

THE ORCHESTRA AND CHORUS

The hundreds of noble Christian Endeavor martyrs, who laid down their lives for Christ rather than deny him during the Boxer trouble in 1900, powerfully influenced the whole nation. The remarkable growth of the church since 1900 proves that the blood of the martyrs is indeed the seed of the church. The faithfulness of those Chinese Endeavorers, even unto death, was in large measure the reason for the change in the attitude of the people towards the gospel.

The Chinese Endeavorers have prayed continously for years on behalf of their nation, praying that the old Manchu dynasty, which was so corrupt and so bitterly opposed to Christianity, might be overthrown, and a new and purer government established. Who can estimate the influence of these prayers with reference· to the formation of the new republic of China?

A great many of the Chinese Christian Endeavorers had some part in the revolution. Some went bravely to the battle front, joining "the dare-to-die corps"; others did noble relief work in the hospitals and on the battlefields in connection with the Red Cross; some engaged in evangelistic work among the soldiers, giving Scripture portions and preaching to them; but the most notable connection of Christian Endeavor with the revolution was the part which Mr. E. S. Little, one of the officers of the China Christian Endeavor Union, had in the peace conference, which was held in his residence in Shanghai, at his suggestion.

It is gratifying to know that the new government is favorable to Christianity, two-thirds of the new officials being either Christians or favorably inclined toward Christianity. When we remember that under the old régime every official was required to participate in idol-worship as a part of his official duties, we realize how great a change has taken place.

A number of Chinese Christian Endeavorers are now in government positions, and some have refused to accept high-salaried offices, that they might continue in Christian work.

II. *The Origin of Christian Endeavor in China.*

It is interesting for us as Endeavorers to note the fact that China was the second country in the world to have Christian Endeavor, the first Christian Endeavor society in China having been organized at Foochow in 1885.

III. *The Growth of the Christian Endeavor Movement in China* was steady from the beginning. At the close of the first quarter of a century of the history of Christian Endeavor in China there were about four hundred Christian Endeavor societies, most of them in the eastern provinces. During the past three or four years the blessing of God has been upon the work in a remarkable way, and about four hundred more societies have been organized, many of them in the far inland provinces; so we have now about eight hundred Christian Endeavor societies in China, with some twenty-three thousand members. Some of these societies are found in each of the provinces. There are forty-three denominational mission boards represented in our Christian Endeavor fellowship in China, which proves the thoroughly interdenominational character of the work.

IV. *Our Estimate of the Value of Christian Endeavor in China.*

During the past three and one-half years, Mrs. Strother and I, as general secretaries of the China Christian Endeavor Union, have had an unusual opportunity to observe conditions on the mission field, having travelled many thousands of miles in all sorts of Chinese conveyances, in more than half of the provinces, and having come into contact with the missionaries of the various missions working in those provinces; we have also corresponded extensively with the missionaries in the provinces we have been unable to visit; and after our consultation with the missionaries and our observation of conditions we are glad to say to you as Christian Endeavorers that we are firmly convinced that Christian Endeavor is one of the most effective evangelistic agencies at work on the mission field to-day. We say this for two reasons: first, because Christian Endeavor stands for a deep spiritual life among the Chinese Christians; second, because Christian Endeavor stands for aggressive evangelistic work by the Chinese Christians.

Various agencies are bringing Western education, Western commerce, and other elements of our Western civilization to China, some of which are good, others alas! being of doubtful benefit to that land; but what China needs more than anything else is the gospel of Jesus Christ, and the most effective way of bringing that gospel to the 426,-000,000 of people in that great land is by the verbal testimonies of Chinese Christians, backed up by consistent Christian lives. If China is to be evangelized, the work must be done largely by the Chinese Christians. It is because Christian Endeavor stands for this very thing that we say it is so important an evangelizing agency.

V. *The Helpfulness of Christian Endeavor in China.*

1. *The Christian Endeavor Society in China has been a great help to overburdened missionaries.* Usually a missionary has to attend to an amount of work that would be shared by half a dozen workers in the home land; therefore it is most desirable that the native Christians should be trained as rapidly as possible to share in the responsibility of the work.

As an illustration of the way in which Christian Endeavor does this I will tell you a little about the Christian Endeavor work in the Wenchow district. That is a large district of some five thousand or six thousand square miles, with the great walled city of Wenchow and hundreds of villages in the district surrounding the city, with about two million inhabitants. In that large district, with that vast population, there are less than a dozen missionaries working. These few missionaries have to go from place to place, preaching and teaching, establishing schools and churches, overseeing the building of chapels, translating and writing books and tracts, and doing a multitude of other things. It is evident that with so much work to do, and the amount of it increasing as the churches increase in number, it is impossible for those few missionaries to do the amount of evangelistic work among the heathen and pastoral work among the Christians that they would like to do.

During the past eight or nine years, since Christian Endeavor was introduced in that district, some sixty-three Christian Endeavor societies have been organized in the churches and chapels, and hundreds of the Christians have become good Bible students and efficient Christian workers. These Chinese Christian Endeavorers are now assisting the missionaries in teaching the inquirers and preaching the gospel to the heathen. The missionaries say that it would be impossible for them to carry on the great work which is being done in that district without the help of those Chinese Christians who have been trained in the Christian Endeavor society.

2. *The Christian Endeavor Society has been a great help to Chinese Christians who have been left without a missionary to shepherd them.* There are many places in China where missionaries have worked for a time and gathered companies of Christians; and then because of sickness, or for some other reason, they have had to leave, and there have been no other missionaries available to take their places. There are also hundreds of villages all over China where there are little isolated groups of Christians, with no missionary or Chinese pastor to preach to them or to conduct regular services. In such cases the Christian Endeavor society has

proved very helpful to these lonely Christians, for they have found that they could follow out the suggestions in "The Christian Endeavor Manual," having simple meetings for Bible-study, testimony, and prayer, and carrying on aggressive soul-winning work. We have heard of several districts which are being thoroughly evangelized by Chinese Endeavorers. where there is no missionary.

3. *The Christian Endeavor Society in China has been a great help in training leaders for the Chinese church.* When visiting in Fukien province, where Christian Endeavor was started in China, it was gratifying to find that many of the leading pastors and evangelists and church officials in the churches of that province were men who had been trained in the Christian Endeavor societies during the past twenty-five years. The missionaries say that the talents of many of these men would never have been known, had it not been for the opportunity afforded by the Christian Endeavor Society for discovering and developing them.

The following extract from a letter from one of the oldest and most conservative missionaries in China is a testimony as to the helpfulness of the Christian Endeavor Society in training leaders for the church:

"In my seven country churches there is only one pastor, and the Sunday services must be conducted largely by the laymen. The Christian Endeavor Society training has developed their talents for this work, and the laymen always conduct the preaching-services when the pastor is not present; and, as he has seven congregations, this means practically all the time."

4. *The Christian Endeavor Society has been a great help in China in enlisting the rank and file of the members in service for Christ.*

The following is an extract from the letter of a missionary writing about a Christian Endeavor society only a year old:

"You will be pleased to hear that the Christian Endeavor society goes forward, and I would like to add my testimony as to the help it has been to the work all around. We find that those who were workers have been stirred up to greater earnestness and zeal, while those who did little have moved forward, and those who did nothing heretofore have become real workers, which means that at present we have not one really idle member in the church."

It is such testimonies as these, coming from missionaries in all parts of China, which greatly cheer our hearts and encourage us to go forward in the extension of this blessed movement throughout the length and breadth of the land.

VI. *Just a word, in conclusion, regarding the Future Outlook for Christian Endeavor in China.* We believe there are great possibilities for the multiplication of the number of socieies many-fold if the work can only be properly organized and pushed at this crucial time.

The Efficiency Campaign literature is being translated and published in Chinese, and we hope soon to have many Chinese Christian Endeavor Experts.

We are sure that the Chinese Endeavorers will heartily adopt Dr. Clark's suggestion regarding the observance of a Christian Endeavor self-denial week, and enthusiastically take up the slogan "Increase and Efficiency" for the coming years.

Another surprise! A delegation of seventy-five Chinese Juniors, boys and girls, bright as buttons, who sang, accompanied by their own Junior orchestra, the stirring song, "The Banner of the Cross." This captured the audience.

Then Dr. Clark unfurled the new Chinese flag,—five bars of different colors, which the Chinese call the beautiful rainbow flag. The red bar stands for China proper, the yellow for Manchuria, the blue for Mongolia, the white for Tibet, and the black for Chinese Turkestan.

Rev. T. Sawaya, former field secretary of Japan, received, as he deserved, an ovation when he brought this greeting: "The land of the sunrise to the land of the sunset, greeting! Three thousand Endeavorers of the far East send their message of peace across the sea to their brethren in the far West. They stand with you pledged to maintain fraternal relations and to keep faith with those great principles of Christ's kingdom, truth and justice, love and loyalty, which know no bounds of age or sex, of clime or race."

He told of Christian Endeavor among the Japanese. He pleaded for fraternity and love. Moreover, he invited the Endeavorers to visit Japan. "We'll not bite you nor dynamite you," he said. Indeed, there is no fear. Every heart was with Mr. Sawaya and with his people, who have given to American missionaries the best of soil for sowing the gospel seed. His address follows:

CHRISTIAN ENDEAVOR IN A NEW OLD EMPIRE.

By Rev. T. Sawaya, Field Secretary of the Japan Union of Christian Endeavor, Okayama, Japan.

Christian Endeavorers in the land of the cherry and the chrysanthemums wanted specially to send their greeting to this Convention which is opened in the Golden State of the American continent. So at their request I have come upon that errand. Here is the greeting I bring from Japan.

GREETING FROM JAPAN.

The land of the sunrise to the land of the sunset, greeting!

Three thousand Endeavorers of the far East send their message of peace across the sea to their brethren of the far West. They stand with you pledged to maintain fraternal relations and to keep the faith with those great principles of Christ's kingdom, truth and justice, love and loyalty, which know no bounds of age or sex, of clime or race.

Tokiyuki Osada, President.

James H. Pettee, Treasurer.

For the Japan Union of Christian Endeavor, Osaka, Japan, June 4, 1913.

The number of Christian Endeavorers in Japan is not very large. But I can safely tell you that most of them occupy quite important positions in the church. More than half of the senior members are helping the Sunday-school either as teachers or as officers. Many have become local Y. M. C. A. secretaries or temperance workers. Most of the Christian activities in Japan you will find largely indebted to the loyal service of Endeavorers. We decided at the convention held in Tokyo last April that we will centralize all our activities for the coming year in helping the church service Sunday morning and also the midweek meeting of the church. I am following you American Endeavorers in the Efficiency Campaign idea now, and am doing my very best in helping the church with those three thousands of loyal Endeavorers in Japan.

Now, my friends, America is a name that sounds most friendly and familiarly to the ear of every Japanese, specially to that of Japanese

Christians. It is America that has sent us the largest number of missionaries and is still aiding many of the largest and most influential institutions of education and philanthropy in Japan. It is America that educated most of our Christian veterans who have done or are still doing splendid work in our nation.

You say that you discovered Japan half a century ago by the brave voyage and generous action of Commodore Perry, and we Japanese, in turn, say that we Japanese discovered America, for Japan has proved the best soil in which you Americans have sown the seeds of Christian truth and up-to-date civilization. Japan has tested many excellent citizens of America, and shown their good works to the world. We appreciate and are ever thankful to America on account of Drs. Verbeck, Hepburn, Davis, DeForest, Harris, and many others. Those great missionaries have truly done much toward making new Japan. You educated Dr. Neesima, Bishop Honda, Paul Sawayama, Dr. Harada, and others, and sent them back again to Japan to mould the character of our youth as theirs was shaped in this country. So long as the names of these Christian heroes are remembered, and the works they left exist among us, America will ever be remembered most appreciatively by our nation.

Although Christianity has done great work and has many excellent people as its members in Japan, it has not been treated by the government and nation at large as other old religions such as Buddhism and Shintoism were treated. But recently both the government and the people have begun to realize that those old religions are not good enough to rely on, specially in building up the character of our young people. Christianity is now genuinely welcomed by many government schools and by society at large.

I desire to say to you American brethren that it is a very important time now for us Christian workers in Japan. Just one more effort is necessary for building a strong foundation for the Christian civilization in Japan. And so it is a very important time for you Americans too who are helping Japan. Just one more effort! Push it once more! Be patient! Don't get discouraged! Just one more effort, I say to you again. I am afraid that some of you are getting tired of Japan. Don't burn up with the fire of impatience or temporary ill feeling the crops of drying grain which you have patiently gathered together through many thousand days. We are moving into a hopeful time now in Japan. Be patient and earnest a little longer and then you will be able to reap a great harvest in newest Japan.

Now, my dear friends, allow me a word about the friendship between America and Japan. What is the essential thing in bringing two nations into truly friendly and fraternal relation? Is it not an acceptance of the Christian religion? Is not the love of Christ, is not the principle of our Lord's teaching, the only thing that can make nations forget their difference and remember their oneness in the sight of God? Have not you first given this precious thing to us Japanese? I stand here representing many thousands of Christ's followers in Japan. We are doing our best to instruct our nation in the principles of Christ's gospel. Brethren, I beseech you to trust us and help us. And I trust you American brethren to do all in your power to evangelize, to Christianize, those Japanese who are in this country already. Make them Christians and then they will be your helpful partners, true friends and loyal servants. I want to appeal to American Christian Endeavorers specially. Will you not redouble your interest and unite your forces for the evangelization of all Japanese in this empire State of California? To Christianize as many of them as soon as possible is, I believe, the best way to maintain and to improve that fraternal relation that has existed for threescore years between America and Japan.

One more thing, my friends. I desire to extend to you an invitation from our Japan Union to cross the water which separates America from my country, to visit Japan. Nothing is better than seeing with one's own eyes to understand the real nature of things. Japan excluding Korea, Formosa, and southern Manchuria is not so large as your State of California. But there is plenty of room in it to entertain you all as guests. We can show you some beautiful scenery, some old paintings and interesting temples, many of them more than ten centuries old. We can introduce you to people who have done some things worth your hearing about. We will not bite you, nor dynamite you. On the contrary, you may find that the Japanese are quite a courteous people who love peace and good order.

I congratulate you over this great and successful Convention. I hope the time may soon come when we can welcome you to our capital city, Tokyo, to hold a World's Convention there. I had a hard time to come to America this time. Your steamship company would not sell me a ticket until I had passed a very severe examination, medical and otherwise. But we believe that you Americans are all right. We will not bother you with a strict examination. Come to Japan. Don't be afraid of that narrow strip of water called the Pacific Ocean. If you don't like boating, why, come in your flying-machine. We will shout at you.

Again I congratulate you over this large Convention and thank you for your patient attention to my imperfect speech.

A surprise was given the audience in short addresses by Chief Odoche and Harry Hays, both full-blooded Indians. Chief Odoche asked for fair play for his people and sang an Indian war-song, although he said that his war-days were over in the long ago. Mr. Hays represented the Nez Percés Indians of Idaho.

Then came India, represented by Mr. Stanley A. Hunter, who has spent two years in college work among the young people of that land. His topic was "Christian Endeavor in India." He told of Christian Endeavor in the mission schools, and how it has penetrated even to leper asylums with their hundreds of wretched inmates. In one of those asylums sixteen untainted children of lepers are banded together in Junior Christian Endeavor. In another asylum there is a "sign-post" society of lepers. A sign-post, they say, is fixed, and cannot move around, *but it can show the way.*

It was a very strong and a very helpful address. It follows.

CHRISTIAN ENDEAVOR IN INDIA.

By STANLEY A. HUNTER, of the Arthur Ewing Christian College, Allahabad.

California's irrigation projects have impressed us all. We have seen gardens where there was waste, and we have witnessed the wonderful effects of water on sandy soil.

After two years' work among young people in India I come tonight to tell of the vast reclamation projects of the missionary enterprise there. One of the great channels for the water of life is Christian Endeavor, bringing blessing to the fields of forty missionary societies. For workers it has forty-five thousand members. In all India, Pentecost is duplicated every two weeks, but numerical additions to the church can never show the great change. Endeavorers have a prominent part in the ingathering. From what different walks of life they come!

I think of our own Allahabad schoolboys meeting this Sunday night in the old building on the Jumna banks. Fifty-six years ago it was pillaged in the Indian Mutiny. Missionary and Christians fled for their lives. Now the mutiny and its martyrs are only a memory, and India is wide open for the preaching of the gospel.

Across that river is the mission leper asylum. Christian Endeavor has penetrated even there. Sixteen untainted children of its inmates join in the singing of our hymns. In the leper asylum at Sholapur to the Christian Endeavor society was given the name of the Sign-Post Society. A sign-post, said they, is fixed, but it can point the way. Christian lepers can not go out to preach, but they can point the way to faith and hope.

I think of another society. You could not forget the sight of 125 Christian orphan girls of Fatehgarh marching in white to the old church. Thirteen years ago, in famine time, most of them were brought by dying mothers.

Near by in Etah is a model Junior Christian Endeavor society. Its enthusiasm is as warm as the weather. These boys in their villages darkened by centuries of oppression are despised, yes, cursed by their overlords, for are they not outcasts?

The thirteen hundred societies of Endeavor in India are all different, yet all one. More can be organized if the Agra Convention plan for additional Indian secretaries is carried through to its completion. Your genial Secretary Halliwell could find the men.

India has seen some great conventions. In the south the Syrian Christians gather twenty thousand strong, young and old. Their auditorium is a dry river-bed. A few months ago was held in the north the Mainpuri convention.

One Indian speaker there divided Christians into three classes according to their supply of the water of life, the water-bag Christian (the water-bag is the village water-works system); the well Christian; the fountain Christian. I recall the happy faces of Indian friends who belong to this third type, whose love and trust always overflowed. One was a student, soon to be a doctor, who would come to my room at nine o'clock after the day's work, to study "In Memoriam"; another, a Brahman convert who was beloved by Hindoo and Moslem students alike, although he was always telling them of Christ, his Master; a third, a Mohammedan three years ago, whose name in the Arabic means "a seeker after truth," and who, like Saul of Tarsus, beheld the Lord in a vision. Now he is a member of the little band of Christians whom our Indian professor of chemistry used to meet on Sunday evenings in his home to study President H. C. King's latest book. Last Christmas was organized the Student Volunteer Movement.

The national missionary society is eight years old, and now has its thirty workers. The spirit of such service as that of those two friends of our movement who have passed to their reward within the year, Dr. Ewing and President Huntly, is contagious.

Young women are not behind. Even in America we sing the hymn which a daughter of India wrote, "In the secret of His presence how my soul delights to hide!" That hymn tells the experience of many of her comrades. I know of homes they are making bright as oases in the desert. India needs the lesson of the dignity of woman which Christianity has brought.

Remember India, her vast population of 315,000,000, ninety-nine out of a hundred still out of the fold; her illiteracy; her idolatry and priestcraft. Superstition is still intrenched, poverty and hunger are everywhere. The land of social tyranny with caste, child marriage and its awful sequel, child widowhood, needs Christ.

Remember India's potentialities. She gave Buddhism to China and Japan. Remember her religious aspirations. All through the centuries she has been climbing with her burdens up the world's great altar-stairs. Two million pilgrims we saw on one day in Allahabad. They had to bathe in the sacred river, the goddess Ganges, and to carry back in little flasks over the weary, dusty miles the precious water.

Kipling closes the history of England with a poem called "The Glory of the Garden." The garden is the British Empire; the appeal to young people is to make it more beautiful. The empire of Christ is the true garden. God has given to us the water of life. Dry and thirsty lands await its transforming power. Some by going, more by giving, but all by praying, can make this ever-growing garden more glorious.

Paul Cowey, a Hindoo medical student who is doing missionary work among his people on the Pacific coast, made a five-minute address in which he said that he longed for the vocabulary of a "Billy" Sunday to interest the people of California, especially in the Hindoo men at their door.

"They are in a Christian land, yet the only time they hear the name of our Lord Jesus Christ is in blasphemy in saloons," declared Mr. Cowey, "and unless you reach them with the gospel when they return they will be a menace in India. They are outcasts here, and it behooves every Christian Endeavorer to help evangelize, for I believe that when India is Christianized we will have the United States of India." Miss Ethel Foster, with violin accompaniment by Sydney A. Clark, rendered a beautiful solo. Dr. Lapsley A. McAfee lifted the congregation to the heights in a searching decision-service.

It was the most impressive moment of the Convention and one that will mean much to many hundreds of people in heathen lands as well as in the home land, and followed the programme theme dedicated to "The World for Christ."

The days of Christian chivalry with the spirit of the early crusades were revived when the flower of young manhood and young womanhood, too, volunteered to go forth as a little band of individual workers, missionaries to the foreign lands of all the world and the islands of the sea. Singing the great missionary hymn, "Where He Leads I Will Follow," with ten thousand people looking on the consecration of their young lives, youths and maidens rose in all parts of the great auditorium to volunteer for Christian service.

In the great auditorium packed to its fullest seating-capacity there was a potential calm as in reverence the spectacle of the crisis of young manhood and womanhood was being manifested; and, joining with those volunteering for foreign service, there arose another group to volunteer for home-mission work, also singing "Where He Leads I Will Follow," and then still another group to the more active work in individual churches, and yet again, another group, to do the best in individual environment for the Christ and His kingdom.

THE THEATRE BEAUTIFUL.

Sunday Evening, July 13.

More than four thousand persons were turned away from the doors of the Theatre Beautiful on Sunday evening, unable to get in. Fully a thousand of them, however, found admission to another hall where the addresses given in the theatre were repeated.

Rev. Hugh K. Walker, D.D., of Atlanta, Ga., presided. Rev. Charles M. Sheldon, D.D., had for his subject the title of his famous story, "In His Steps." His address was direct and of crystal clearness. "Jesus Christ would be the greatest optimist on earth," said he. "He would be the happiest man alive. He would believe that the world is growing better all the time." The full address follows:

"WHAT WOULD JESUS DO?"

By Rev. Charles M. Sheldon, D.D., Topeka, Kan.

For hereunto were ye called: because Christ also suffered for you, leaving you an example, that ye should follow his steps.—*1 Peter 2: 21.*

The greatest example in the way of character or conduct the world has ever seen is Jesus Christ. We must have some standard by which to act. What shall it be? A rule of conduct is not enough. We need a person, and we have one in Jesus. He lived a normal life exactly like any human being, with the one exception that he was sinless. His example is the only safe one to follow *because* he was sinless. And the only safe example because what he did was always done from the very highest motives.

We cannot tell what Jesus would do in details of dress or living, or in many matters of expediency or every-day habits.

But we do know what the general principles are upon which all his conduct would be based, and we can state them as follows:

1. Jesus would act in any age of the world always for the highest interests of the kingdom of God, regardless of the personal results to himself.

2. Jesus would not make money or pleasure or power his first object in life, but the will of God.

3. Jesus would love all mankind. Race prejudice would be impossible with him.

4. He would have one supreme passion in life, to save humanity from its sin and bring it to God.

On those four basic principles every act of Jesus would proceed. Judging from what he did do when he was on earth, we may safely assume that he would probably do the following things if he were on the earth to-day:

1. He would be a part of the age into which he was born, and not be afraid to face its problems or try to answer its questions.

2. He would engage in some honest work of head or hand, and live a simple, happy life.

3. He would probably speak on the great questions of this age—temperance, child labor, selfish capital or labor organizations, social vice, marriage, education, race prejudice, war, wrong newspaper ideals; in short, his spoken word would enter into all the current phases of men's real struggles as we know them to-day.

4 Jesus would probably emphasize the great need of church federation, and give counsel for its practical working out.

5. He would not do many miracles, but would encourage all human efforts towards the elimination of disease and the common health of mankind.

6. He would emphasize the brotherhood of men, and show how it may be realized.

7. He would be the greatest living optimist and declare the fact that the world is getting better every century.

8. He would love his church, and instead of criticising it he would praise and encourage it.

9. He would assert the same everlasting need of forgiveness of sins and the glad fact of eternal life.

The different action of Christians is a stumbling-block in politics, business, amusements, and in general.

Christians should study their great Example more closely and follow him more unselfishly. Jesus' example is the eternal hope of the world. It is practical and feasible, and if followed would revolutionize the world.

"Religion; the Heart of Reforms," was the subject to which Rev. William Patterson, D.D., of Belfast, Ireland, addressed himself. It was one of those heart-searching sermons that grip. It follows:

RELIGION THE HEART OF REFORMS.

By Rev. William Patterson, D.D., Belfast, Ireland.

I take it for granted that those who selected this subject intended the word "religion" to mean regeneration, for in our world there are religions many as there are gods many, but only one of them is true and undefiled before God the Father, the religion which purifies the lives of individuals and through them cares for suffering humanity. This religion is the very core of all true reform. It is difficult to overestimate the effect a man's surroundings will have on his physical, moral, and spiritual nature, the house he lives in, the air he breathes, the food he eats, and the people with whom he associates. Yet all these things are without the man and his life; his real life consists not in them. His environments may be as favorable as those of Judas, while he may remain a traitor at heart, or they may be as unfavorable as those of Enoch, while he may be walking with God. A great statesman is reported to have said, "It is the nation's duty to make it easy for men to do right and difficult for them to do wrong." This is surely an ideal condition, for in so many cases the reverse is true, but it is our duty to do all in our power to bring about this state of affairs, to crush out the white-slave traffic, to kill the drink demon, to break the rod of oppression, to lift the masses into a purer and more comfortable atmosphere, and to make smooth the path for those who are running life's race. But let us never forget that, while we may have reformation without regeneration, we cannot have regeneration without reformation. We may filter the water in the stream, but when we stop the process it goes back to its original state; but the great Teacher said, "Purify the fountain and you purify the stream," or, to change the figure, make the tree good and the fruit will be good. Art galleries, beautiful parks, and commodious houses have an uplifting tendency, and nature in her glory should lift man's thoughts to nature's God, to the One who paints the lilies and beautifies the hills and the vales. But we so often find that where every prospect pleases only man is vile. From the historian and the traveller we learn that frequently when art and nature have touched the highest point, sin and misery have sounded the greatest depth.

The Book of books has done more to lift humanity and to better the conditions of mankind than all the pictures that have ever been painted and all the human laws which have ever been enacted. We frequently speak of the great Reformation that revolutionized all Europe and lifted such a large section of it out of the darkness of ignorance and the misery of sin. But when and how did it begin? Was it not through the truth of God touching the hearts of men like Luther, Calvin, and Knox, the mighty angel flying with the everlasting gospel which reached the hearts of men, changing their lives and through them lifting and reforming nations? Let us do all we can to help men socially, to lighten their burdens, and to make their paths more pleasant. But let us begin at the right end, for out of the heart are the issues of life. We must get men right with God if we are ever to get them right with one another. The secret of Britain's power and of America's greatness is the old Book which speaks of the new heart, the necessity and possibility of the new birth. John Knox hit the nail on the head when he cried out, "A Bible in every home, a church and a school in every village." The carrying out of this motto lifted Scotland out of her degradation and made her the mightiest nation of her size the world has ever known, great in the physical, intellectual, and spiritual world. If we can say this of the Scot, what shall we say of the Ulster Scot who helped to cut down your forests and build your cities? They led in the struggle for independence, while the Grants, the M'Kinleys, and the Wilsons have dwelt in the White House, lending dignity and power to the presidential chair. Follow this great river of civilization and prosperity back to its source and you will find that its fountain was pure religion. That which started the Reformation in Europe centuries ago is now working in China, and please God this leaven of true religion will keep on working until the whole is leavened, and then will the isles be glad and the nations rejoice, for peace shall reign from the river to the ends of the earth.

The third speech was by Rev. Claude E. Hill, of Valparaiso, Ind. He spoke of theatres' being open to minister to man's desire for pleasure, and of restaurants' being open to feed the body, while only too often the church closes down. One good point about Christian Endeavor, however, is that it goes right on attending to its business, no matter what closes.

The text was Christ's transfiguration, or rather the prayer meeting that accompanied it. On the mount the disciples were being trained to know their Master; and this is the business of Christian Endeavor, to train young folks to know Christ. And thus the place of prayer will become a place of vision.

CHAPTER XVIII.

THE LAST DAY.

Auditorium Endeavor.

Monday Morning, July 14.

CHRISTIAN ENDEAVOR BEYOND THE SEA.

OUR SHARE IN HUMAN UPLIFT.

THE World-wide Work of Christian Endeavor" was the theme of Monday forenoon's meeting. Rev. Julian C. Caldwell, D.D., superintendent of the Allen Christian Endeavor League, stirred the gathering by an eloquent address on "Our Opportunities at Home." He traced the progress of the black man from slavery and ignorance up toward the light. Material advancement has been great, but not greater than the negro's religious development. Not very long after the Christian Endeavor movement was organized two negro denominations, the African Methodist Episcopal Church and the African Methodist Episcopal Zion Church, accepted Christian Endeavor as their young people's society. To-day in colored denominations there are 5,667 societies with 181,440 members. Adding to these the Baptist Young People's Unions and the Epworth Leagues, there are nearly half a million colored members of young people's societies. The door is open; let us enter in.

General Secretary Shaw's topic was "The Undeveloped Fields." He outlined the need in some of our great States which are weak in Christian Endeavor, yet anxious to be strengthened and helped. They need not only the inspiration of our fellowship, but the practical aid of Christian Endeavor methods and plans. Where field workers have been able to pay even brief visits, they discover scores of societies absolutely out of touch with our movement yet anxious to come in.

In a series of vivid word-pictures he brought before us the need of the heathen world—India; China, Japan, Korea, Africa, and some parts of Europe. The need of these lands comes to us as a challenge. What shall we do to send to them the story of Christian Endeavor and instruct them in its principles?

Brief greetings were brought from Mexico by Rev. James D. Eaton, D.D., of the American Board, a pioneer Endeavorer in that country. At Dr. Clark's suggestion a good-will greeting was sent to the Endeavorers of Mexico.

A LOS ANGELES ENDEAVORER
By the kindness of the Los Angeles
"Examiner"

PART OF THE REGISTRATION COMMITTEE
By the kindness of the Los Angeles "Examiner"

A Hawaiian representative brought greetings from his beautiful isles; and following him, an Armenian, John S. Pashgian, spoke for thousands of Armenian Endeavorers.

Dr. Clark told the story of the World's Convention in Australia, 1914, and then launched into a strong, brief speech on "Our Obligations Abroad."

But inspiration without expression is worthless. It fell to Field Secretary Lehmann's lot to give the Endeavorers a chance to show how deep is their belief in the movement. Christian Endeavor is a missionary proposition. Money given to it is missionary money. The promotion of Christian Endeavor means the addition of active workers to the missionary forces on the field through the training of natives in church-work.

Then followed a period of hilarious giving, with snap and ginger in every minute. Harrisburg, Texas, a society with only twenty members, led off with a pledge of $100 a year for two years for Christian Endeavor extension. The Chicago union came up with the largest pledge of the day, $1,000. Then came a number of State and local unions with $100 pledges, others with $50 pledges, others with $25, and so on until $8,000 had been pledged for Christ and His church in lands beyond the sea.

Monday Afternoon.

THREE BULWARKS OF CIVILIZATION.

The Home, the School, the Church.

The auditorium tent during these Convention days has been a busy scene, but never busier than on Monday, "the last day of the feast." A great meeting in the morning was followed by an even greater in the afternoon, when the subject was, "The Field of Christian Endeavor: the Home, the School, the Church."

The first address, strong and virile, was by Rev. Samuel Z. Batten, D.D., secretary of the department of social service of the Northern Baptist Convention. He dealt with Christian Endeavor as a training-school for ministers and missionaries. The young people's movement is a movement toward essential Christianity, which at bottom is the service of man. A new conception of Christian work in which all may participate has arisen, and this conception is largely the result of the Christian Endeavor movement.

The young people's societies are largely responsible for increased interest in missions. The Society has proved to be a training-school for missionary workers, because it leads them to study the things that advance the kingdom of God in the world.

Rev. Robert F. Coyle, D.D., of Denver, ex-moderator of the Presbyterian General Assembly, is one of our greatest living pulpit orators. His theme was, "The Influence of the Home on Present-Day Life," a topic of tremendous importance, since the decay of nations begins in the home. The history of Israel, he said, is the history of a family, and the thought of home was so woven into their thinking that they spoke of God as "our dwelling-place in all generations."

Dr. Coyle depicted in flaming language the downward drift of the modern home. For home life is slipping away from us. The hard condition of modern industry is endangering the home. The divorce-court mill is grinding the home to powder. Last year seventy thousand children were deprived of one of their parents from this cause alone.

What, then, he asked, can be done to turn back the tide? We must wipe the stain of easy divorce from our national escutcheon. Trial marriages, ex-wife and ex-husband going around looking for other victims, should be put into the same unclean category as polygamy. These things are progressive polygamy, which is as bad as the kind that is stationary. Then we must have legislation to throw safeguards around our hearths. If woman's place is the home, she must demand by her vote that home be made worth having; and she must help to legislate the drink traffic, the great home-destroyer, into the pit.

"The Influence of the School in Character-Building" was the subject on which President John Willis Baer spoke. Before he became a college president Mr. Baer was for years an educator as general secretary of the United Society of Christian Endeavor. He held up in the light the great principle that lies behind all true education, the principle of personality. "Education is the transmission of life from the living, through the living, to the living." Character is not taught, but *caught*, transmitted from heart to heart, from life to life. Precept freezes; example warms.

We need culture, more of it, clean and pure. We need more noble citizenship. Pure living is more than sound teaching. Our schools must be more than culture-institutions; they must be an influence for God.

We need more Christianity, greatest of all. It is not necessary that all should worship God alike, but it is necessary that all alike worship God. Were I a member of a school board, I would not select a teacher whose life is not God-controlled. I believe that the day will come when the English Bible will be read in every State school from the lowest grades to the gates of the university. One-fifth of the entire population of the United States are enrolled in some kind of school or other, and eighteen million young people are in State schools. The teaching in all schools must be vitalized. To get that we must have teachers that live out the principles of the gospel of Christ.

The subject, "The Responsibility of the Church for Training Its Future Members," was taken up by the United Presbyterian trustee of the United Society, Rev. J. T. McCrory, D.D., of Pittsburg, whose address was vibrant with power.

He showed that the object of the training of church-members is to make them responsive to the will of Christ, just as we train the members of our bodies to obey our human wills. Then he laid strong emphasis upon three directions which training should take. Church-members should be taught, first, to witness for Christ; second, to pray to God; and, third, to give to the work of God. With apt incident and illustration Dr. McCrory clinched every point. His speech prepared the way for what followed as hardly anything else could have done.

One of the unique things in this Convention was Dr. L. A. McAfee's searching decision-services. Never before at any International Convention have we had anything like them. They gathered up the spiritual impulses liberated during the speaking, and focused them in definite resolves.

This closing service capped all the rest. Cards were ready, the "Christian Endeavor Covenanters' Life-Work Covenant," and those who desired to make a decision for the service of Christ were asked to come to the platform and sign them.

It was an experience never to be forgotten to see this great crowd of one hundred and ninety-one Endeavorers file down the long aisles of the tent and mount the platform to render their decision and their testimony before men while they sang, glorified, "Where He leads me, I will follow."

Then pastors and other Christian workers were asked to come forward, and sixty-eight responded.

Then Dr. McAfee asked the Comrades of the Quiet Hour to rise. Half the audience stood up, and many more pledged themselves to become Comrades. Here, surely, lies the secret of California's power: the Endeavorers are a praying band.

When Dr. McAfee called for those that give one-tenth of their income to the Lord, a great number arose to their feet.

And, finally, when the leader asked those to stand who surrendered themselves wholly to God, practically the whole audience got up. This means that in many churches there are groups of young men and women who have given themselves to the Lord for the service of His church.

Monday Evening, The Climax.

THE GREAT PURPOSE MEETING.

Long before the hour of opening for the last meeting of the Convention, the great "Purpose Meeting" with which International Christian Endeavor Conventions usually close, delegations of Endeavorers had begun to assemble in the auditorium. It was a magnificent scene—ten thousand young people, the flower of the land, East and West, gathered in the King's name around their banners of many colors.

After the consecration and decision-service of the afternoon the congregation was in a mood for singing praises, for it was, exultant. That is doubtless why Endeavorers and choir—nearly a thousand voices—responded to every touch of Percy Foster's hand as he led.

The men sang, and then a group of a hundred and fifty young men and women in beautiful white uniforms. They were some of the pages and guides off duty for this meeting.

And right here it deserves to be said that nothing superior to the service of these pages and guides has ever been seen at any International Convention. Never was service more willing and courteous, or help more generously rendered. These boys and girls gave most efficient help to thousands of visitors everywhere and all the time. For they were everywhere all the time. Their organization was superb.

May pages and guides become an institution at all future Conventions. Mr. Harold Cross's pages and guides have set a high standard.

And what has been said of them applies with equal force to the ushers. They were organized in every detail and drilled in their duties. Never a hitch occurred. It was wonderful.

But the singing is over now. It has lifted us to the heights, melted us, thrilled us, translated us, and prepared us for the devotional exercise led by President John Willis Baer.

He touched upon a fact that all have felt, namely, that there has been an indefinable, intangible something about this Convention that has made it different from others, something that has been quiet and stable, and has given to the testimonies the ring of certainty.

This young man with that huge bouquet of beautiful hydrangeas is one of the pages, and the flowers are for Dr. Clark from the pages' and guides' committee.

A closing message was brought by a Los Angeles Baptist pastor, Rev. J. Whitcomb Brougher, D.D., the newest trustee of the United Society and one of the most popular pastors on the Pacific coast. He took his life-motto as the basis of his thought, "For to me to live is Christ," and, "As the Father hath sent me, even so send I you." "The only true life," said Dr. Brougher, "is not the joining of pleasure and man, or money and man, but Christ and man. 'Christ . . . me.'

"So the young people who join their lives with Christ may become a force for good in the world.

"That life manifests itself in seven C's. First, it comes to light in our conflict. Then in conversation, for this world must be won largely by talk and example. Third, in conduct. Again, let your courage be worthy of Christ. Once more, we need concentration; 'be of one mind.' Further, let character be worthy of Christ. And finally, the thing that the church most needs to-day is absolute, whole-hearted consecration."

The committee on resolutions proposed the thanks of the Convention to the Convention committee, the chorus, the city, Dr. Clark, and a host of others.

The Convention registered its approbation of the appointment of Daniel A. Poling as national superintendent of temperance and citizenship, and pledged to him its support.

There was hearty enthusiasm in the Convention's reception and approval of Dr. Clark's proposed Increase and Efficiency Campaign.

Mr. Charles G. Stewart, of Winnipeg, was thanked for his generous offer of $5,000 wherewith to start a campaign for securing needful funds for the extension of Christian Endeavor.

"We believe," read the resolution, "that our International Conventions should be held more frequently in Canada than heretofore, and we approve the wish of the trustees that the Convention of 1917 be held there."

The resolutions denounced child labor, lawlessness, intemperance, gambling, and graft, and favored arbitration of labor disputes, the Bible in schools, evangelization of immigrants, help in extending Christian Endeavor among negro churches, Floating Endeavor, the peace programme, non-intervention in Mexico, a saloonless nation in 1920, national prohibition by an amendment to the federal Constitution, a national convention in November, at Columbus, Ohio, of all the temperance organizations in the country, good-citizenship day, the red-light abatement law in California, and a pledge-signing temperance campaign—"that in all things He might have the pre-eminence."

The registration committee reported that delegates had registered from forty-seven States and Territories; Canada had seven Provinces represented, and delegates were present from seven foreign countries. The total registration was exactly 10,001.

The 1913 Committee, which directed all the arrangements for the Convention, were one by one called to the platform and introduced to the audience.

Seven of these men are ex-presidents of the State union. They were all dressed alike in white suits, sixteen of them; and a finer group never stood on any platform. With these men before us we no longer wondered that the arrangements were perfect and that the Convention was a success.

Dr. John Willis Baer was the last on the list; and, as he mounted the platform with Dr. Clark and Mr. Shaw on either side, he fairly brought down the house. Californians love mightily.

But what shall we say of the purpose-service that followed, when the delegations stood together, expressed their purpose, and sang a verse of hymn or song?

Canada's Provinces were first called upon.

QUEBEC expressed her purpose as "Forward, march."

ONTARIO found her purpose in the hymn, "Blessed assurance, Jesus is mine."

MANITOBA expects to take up evangelistic and temperance work and the extension of local-union work.

SASKATCHEWAN'S slogan calls for a society in every one of the two thousand churches of the Province.

ALBERTA'S watchword is Livingstone's motto, "Anywhere, provided it be forward."

When Dr. Clark called to the platform the Christian Endeavor Experts present, nearly four hundred responded. The hall seemed alive with them as they arose and marched down the aisles; yet they were only representatives of 1,200 others. La Rue Watson, a California boy now residing in Hawaii, the first to take the examination, made a real expert speech for the crowd. "The question," he said, "is not who is the first or the second or the third, but who shall be next."

Then came to the platform Master Wallace Weirick, of Pomona, Cal., a thirteen-year-old boy, the first Junior Christian Endeavor Expert in the world, who passed an examination in "The Junior Text-Book," answering every question in the book correctly.

What is this? Eight white-capped nurses! They are the nurses that have been in attendance throughout the Convention. Besides them two doctors have given their services, and two stretcher-bearers, who are there, stretcher and all. These doctors and nurses treated 131 cases in the Convention hospital, and sent six cases to the city hospital.

And now we are again in the midst of responses from delegations. Let us listen to their purposes.

NEW JERSEY wishes to emphasize spiritual responsibility: "I'll go where He wants me to go."

NEW YORK will make positive and persistent efforts to turn this country into a saloonless nation by 1920.

ALABAMA wants to increase the efficiency of every society in the State so that she may be able to go to Chicago in 1915 and take the next Convention to Birmingham.

ARIZONA, one of the baby States of the Union, has only ten societies now, but wants to increase them to one hundred. Her testimony ended with a real snap when she promised $25 a year for two years for the extension of Christian Endeavor work.

ARKANSAS desired to make a great increase in numbers and efficiency, and her motto is, "Arkansas for Christ."

PENNSYLVANIA had a big delegation present, and they expressed their purpose in a motto, "Pray and Work."

MARYLAND promised to be in the Efficiency Campaign of the future.

COLORADO'S purpose is to be in the front in the Increase and

Efficiency Campaign, to advance good citizenship and temperance, and to attain State-wide prohibition by 1915.

CONNECTICUT is determined to make real and vital the mission of Christian Endeavor.

FLORIDA, through "Secretary Grace," who works with all and is loved by all, expressed her will in the song, "I'll go where He wants me to go."

INDIANA's wish is found in the prophet's words, "Not by might, nor by power, but by my Spirit."

ILLINOIS was a mighty host led by the State president, Walter R. Mee. "Illinois to the front" is their motto, and their purpose is to make it good.

IDAHO is going in for more Christian Endeavor Experts (knowing their value), and will make a feature of the Tenth Legion.

IOWA gave a practical sample of her purpose by pledging $200 toward the world-wide work of Christian Endeavor.

KENTUCKY proposed to continue to give especial attention to prison Christian Endeavor, heeding the words of Jesus, "I was in prison, and ye visited me."

KANSAS hopes to raise $3,000 according to her budget, and promised to add another $100 to a similar sum pledged earlier in the day in order to send Christian Endeavor abroad. Mr. Gilbert Fenton takes up field work in Kansas on September 1.

LOUISIANA, which has only twenty-three Christian Endeavor societies, ten of them new, will work for the increase of the Endeavor hosts.

MASSACHUSETTS, which accompanied Dr. Clark across the continent to Los Angeles, will continue to follow him in all his plans for the advancement of the Christian Endeavor cause.

MICHIGAN is determined to do her part in carrying out the suggestions that Dr. Clark has made for increase and efficiency.

MAINE appropriately expressed her purpose in Paul's words, "I can do all things through Christ which strengtheneth me."

MISSOURI seeks to rise to a higher plane of efficiency, and hopes to secure $2,000 this year for China.

MINNESOTA will push for efficiency and for twelve months of field work instead of six. Her delegates pledged $50 for world-wide work.

MONTANA's programme embraces temperance and good citizenship, missions, the Tenth Legion, the Quiet Hour, the Headquarters-Building fund, the sanctity of the home, and personal purity for both sexes.

NEBRASKA's motto is, "Pushers Pushing." The Endeavorers of the State will work for efficiency and a saloonless nation.

NEW HAMPSHIRE will seek to get more young men to work for Christ and the church.

NEVADA showed her spirit when her president, Mr. J. M.

Ellis, pledged $50 for the work of the World's Christian Endeavor Union.

NORTH DAKOTA expects every Endeavorer to be a committee of one to spread the gospel and fight evil in every form.

NEW MEXICO, the second baby State of the Union, hopes to perfect its union and carry the gospel message everywhere within its borders.

OHIO introduced its purpose with a song, "We're from Ohio." The purpose is expressed in the words on the State banner, "That in all things He might have the pre-eminence." Judging from the great crowd of Endeavorers present, it takes more than floods to put Ohio out of business.

OKLAHOMA promises to push an Increase and Efficiency Campaign and Intermediate work. The motto on her banner is the pledge, "We do."

OREGON, with a fine delegation, is determined to make it impossible to get liquor anywhere in the United States. The aim of the union is "Efficiency."

RHODE ISLAND'S motto is "Hope," and in this spirit the State will take up the campaign for more efficiency.

SOUTH DAKOTA had only a small delegation, but the members gave one of the best responses of the evening, "We are not speakers nor singers, but we're on the firing line."

TENNESSEE, the State that had the first society to attain one hundred per cent in the Efficiency Campaign, is going to try for one hundred more Young People's societies, one hundred new Intermediate societies, and one hundred new Junior societies. In addition, the last State convention resolved that every State officer shall be a Christian Endeavor Expert and every society shall be in the Efficiency Campaign.

TEXAS, standing under the Lone Star flag, promised to put the saloon out of business in the State. It has done it before, and will do it again, permanently. The State will also do special Junior field work.

UTAH, represented by her president, Hon. C. E. Marks, is deeply interested in increase and efficiency. The delegation present was five hundred per cent larger than ever before attended an International Convention from this State.

VERMONT has one expressive word for its motto, "Others."

WASHINGTON wants more efficiency. The Seattle union and Orange County union, Cal., have arranged a contest in Experts. The union that wins will get a banner from the losers.

WEST VIRGINIA, too, desires efficiency. She will work for prohibition laws that have teeth, and for better social life and recreation among the young people.

WISCONSIN has a new vision and a new message that spell a new forward movement. This State has several societies that have reached one hundred per cent in the Efficiency Campaign, but have not reported to the United Society.

THE DISTRICT OF COLUMBIA responded by singing, "My country, 'tis of thee."

HAWAII made her response in a song by half a dozen native Endeavorers.

ALASKA sent her greeting from the far north with this text: "Be strong in the Lord."

Beyond the Border.

CHINA will be faithful to the Chinese name for the society, "The Strive-with-All-Your-Might Society."

JAPAN has decided to put its strength into efforts to increase church-attendance and thus make the letters C. E. stand for "Church Extension."

INDIA takes the far look, and wishes to make the glory of Christian Endeavor the fact that its heart throbs throughout the entire world.

MEXICO's representative was a native who said that through Christian Endeavor he had been raised out of ignorance and superstition.

Special letters of greeting were received from Germany, England, and South Africa, the saintly Rev. Andrew Murray, D.D., the honorary president of the union, being the writer of South Africa's greeting.

One Armenian asked for prayer for Armenia.

Then a group of Mexican Endeavorers, holding the flag of their country, arose and brought another greeting. They asked that the only intervention that comes to Mexico may be Christian Endeavor intervention that will lay a sound foundation for the building up of their national life.

Some Stirring Scenes.

FLOATING CHRISTIAN ENDEAVOR was represented by a large delegation. The motto was, "More Sailors for Christ." These Endeavorers stood under the only flag that is permitted to wave above the Stars and Stripes, the white flag with a cross in the centre.

Dr. Clark then called on the PAGES AND GUIDES for a greeting. They made a pretty sight in their white uniforms as they stood on the benches, the boys holding the chairman, Mr. Cross, shoulder-high. They propose to form a permanent organization and continue their career of helpful service.

"THE USHERS," called Dr. Clark. Then something happened. From every part of the hall they came running, all uniformed in red—a great throng of a hundred and fifty of the finest young men in the State. They had served with unfailing courtesy, each one at his post, through trying Convention days, and had made things easy for speakers and audience alike. We understood the reason when we heard their motto, "Let all things be done decently and in order." These splendid young fellows pledged $50 toward the foreign work of Christian Endeavor before they left the platform.

Then came the RECEPTION COMMITTEE. They had been attending to their duties all the time. They had their work so organized under the leadership of the chairman, Mr. J. G. Warren, that members of the committee met trains not only as they entered Los Angeles, but also when they stopped at various points outside the city. This committee left no doubt in any mind about the heartiness of California's reception. Every delegate received gifts of flowers and fruit as soon as he or she set foot on California soil. The committee's finely appropriate motto was, "Salute every saint in Christ Jesus."

THE REGISTRATION COMMITTEE, whose work was hard and trying, gave away the secret of success when they quoted their text, "Not slothful in business, fervent in spirit, serving the Lord."

Then the CHORUS received a deserved ovation, together with its leader, Professor L. F. Peckham.

Finally, Dr. Clark called on CALIFORNIA to give her greeting and express her purpose. It is this: To extend Junior work and to push Intermediate work and missions. "First Things First," is the State's motto; and this explains much to those that wish to understand why the Los Angeles Convention has really been the best yet.

THE CANADIAN HEADQUARTERS BOOTH AT THE LOS ANGELES CONVENTION.
NOTICE THE SHEAVES OF GRAIN.

CHAPTER XIX

REPORT OF THE COMMITTEE ON RESOLUTIONS.

A GENERATION old as an agency of the church for the evangelization and religious education of the children and youth, Christian Endeavor has more than justified the faith of its friends that it came into the kingdom of Christ not only for such a time as this, but for all time.

Every year a company of untrained young people is ready to take the places in the local society of a similar company of trained young people going out into the varied activities of the church after five, six, seven, or even more years of active membership in Christian Endeavor. As long as there is such supply and need there will be imperative demand for a comprehensive training agency, and nothing nearly so efficient as Christian Endeavor has been suggested; nothing better is anticipated. Most ambitious local substitutes for Christian Endeavor are now but dismal memories of the foredoomed failure of poor counterfeits and weak imitations. Interdenominational young people's movements soon discover that there is no need of another such agency as Christian Endeavor.

Even the very worthy denominational young people's societies, whose right to be is conceded by very virtue of the fact that Christian Endeavor has been committed from the first to loyalty to the rules and decrees of one's own church, are finding and are frankly admitting that a local society of Christian Endeavor is as intensely denominational as any church society could be, and that it is as amenable to ecclesiastical control, and as free from outside control, as would be the most exclusive society of the strictest sect. Having reached this conclusion, the leaders of some of the churches that formerly exercised their right to organize denominational young people's societies are beginning to urge their young people, for the sake of the good they may get and give in the larger fellowship, to affiliate their societies with Christian Endeavor.

In accordance with the co-operative Christian spirit of the age it is our judgment and our hope that such federation and union of young people's work in all the churches may go on until, still true to their own churches, "they all may be one" in name and fraternity, an irresistible power for the salvation of the youth and an unconquerable antagonist of the enemies of youth.

INCREASE AND EFFICIENCY WEEK.

Rejoicing in the blessings which God has bestowed upon the movement since the last Convention, we hereby indorse the prayerful and, we believe, the prophetic plans and suggestions of the founder and President of the United Society of Christian Endeavor, as outlined in his annual message to this Convention. That the Increase Campaign proposed by Dr. Clark four years ago, and the Efficiency Campaign inaugurated by him two years ago, have both been divinely favored is too plain to encourage our hesitating now to accept with zeal this definite proposal from the President's message to us:

"That we henceforth make the week in which occurs the second of February, our Christian Endeavor anniversary, an Increase and Efficiency Week, when we shall take stock of our activities, see whether we are in any good measure living up to our ideals, and go forward in the Master's name to new and larger endeavors."

We also recommend that all our societies and unions adopt, and adapt to their needs, the programme outlined in this message for making Increase and Efficiency Week duly fruitful and permanently valuable to our work.

MR. STEWART'S OFFER AND CHALLENGE TO OUR FAITH.

We have heard with profound appreciation the generous offer of Mr. Charles G. Stewart, of Winnipeg, to contribute the sum of five thousand dollars to the United Society as a fund with which to develop a permanent financial constituency, and so to organize and relate the general work of Christian Endeavor to proper sources of religious-extension income as that henceforth the growth and usefulness of Christian Endeavor need not be hindered by poverty and the church be denied the blessing of Christian Endeavor activity.

Almost unaided by contributions from the church this organization has grown to its present proportions as an exclusive and potent agency of the church. It has trained five generations of its active members in the grace of giving of time, talent, and treasure to their own churches; and a new era of Christian benevolence has thus been ushered in, to the tremendous increase of the supply of denominational workers and funds.

But the very immense proportions of the movement, and the corresponding demand which is coming for its further extension and modern development, compel the United Society to ask that its own offering of the entire profits of its publishing department be supplemented annually by many other thousands of dollars, no penny of which will be spent except for the organization of new societies and for the promotion of young people's work in destitute fields where the churches so sorely need the movement, in Canada and the United States and to the uttermost parts of the earth. As John Willis Baer tersely and truly says: "Christian Endeavor has always been loyal to the church. Let the church now be loyal to Christian Endeavor"; and surely a grateful church will not be ungenerous.

OUR INTERNATIONAL ORGANIZATION

We rejoice increasingly in the blessed fellowship, which as Christian Endeavorers from both Canada and the United States we have ever had in our International Conventions, a fellowship which has served to merge the young Christian citizenship of the two great neighbor nations in a fraternal unity that at once gives rich promise of the triumphs of the cross, and renders any political getting-together both unnecessary and undesirable, since brothers and sisters who love one another may often best serve the world by dwelling apart, while such separation only makes genuine kindred hearts grow fonder.

But for the sake of Christian Endeavor in particular and of the rest of the cause of Christ in general we believe that our International Conventions ought to have opportunity to meet much more frquently in Canada than has been done in the past, and we heartily approve the decision of the Board of Trustees that the Convention of 1917 shall be held there.

QUESTIONS OF THE DAY

Because of the widely representative character of our Conventions, and because the voice of such a gathering must of necessity carry afar, we cannot afford to be silent when our opinion is asked on any moral question upon which the judgment of a great religious gathering of young people may be appropriately expressed.

In response to communications, therefore, we desire to record our protest against those labor abuses by which nearly two millions of children in America are being ground to physical, mental, and often moral death between the upper millstone of commercial greed and the nether millstone of parental ignorance and popular indifference to child-labor conditions.

We approve the effort of the Alumni Association of the University of Michigan to organize the alumni of all North American universities and colleges against the lawlessness to which some university men have been indifferent if not, alas! in even actual participation. Education inevitably equips men for leadership, and he is of all criminals the vilest who uses the sacred trust of cultured intellect to lead his fellow men into lawlessness and into that public disregard for law which is the chief peril of our generation.

We have been asked to express the convictions of this Convention on such questions as gambling, which we denounce as worse than the crime of robbery; graft, which is often worse than theft, since graft involves bartering for private advantage what is the sacred possession of the people; the political indolence of the upright who habitually absent themselves from the polls, a neglect of the high duty of suffrage, which is chiefly responsible for every recent political triumph of wrong—the otherwise good man, who for personal or financial reasons does not vote becomes in evil fruit-bearing the companion of the bad man whose vote is usually for sale and always cast against the right; party loyalty, for which even some Christian voters have been known on election-day to sacrifice their loyalty to Christ; the necessity for labor strikes, for which present necessity some mutually honorable method of arbitration and amicable settlement should be found, for, whether laborers or capitalists, if we be Christians, we be brethren, and no form of force should be necessary to make brethren act like brothers; the Bible in schools, where certainly there should be no opposition to a reverent reading of such passages of the word of God as could have no sectarian bias and as would lead to the integrity of the citizen and the observance of the Golden Rule; the desecration of the Lord's Day, against which desecration Christian Endeavor stands like Gibraltar always and everywhere; the evangelization of the flood of immigrants breaking annually on both shores of the North American continent, evangelization that is in the nature of self-protection, and that will not await a more convenient season; it must be done now or never; encouragement and help in extending Christian Endeavor among the negro churches in the United States, where the growth of the movement has lately been phenomenal, and where further organization and religious education will meet the heartiest welcome; indorsement of the good work being done for seamen by Floating Endeavor, a work and workers that have been blessed under many skies; commercial greed and the financial and corporate lawlessness, which, so far as they exist, are even more deserving of swift and sure punishment than is the misdemeanor of the poverty-stricken and ignorant lawbreaker who disturbs the peace or purloins a dinner. Wealth, like education, has an inherent power, the misuse of which is doubly a crime because also a violation of stewardship.

A PEACE PROGRAMME.

In response to requests from the Society of Friends and from peace organizations, we refer with pride and emphasis to the consistent stand of Christian Endeavor for individual, intersectional, interracial, and international peace. In order that the unanimous sentiment among us may have practical direction, we recommend that our department of temperance and Christian citizenship próceed as soon as practicable to circulate among local societies such literature, and to encourage such study and discussion, as should be enlightening on the subject of world-peace. We further recommend that wherever possible there be induced the signing of the following pledge, suggested by Rev. R. P. Anderson, in his timely address to this Convention:

"Trusting in the Lord Jesus Christ for strength, I will seek to promote good will among men and peace on earth, and I will work as I have opportunity toward the abolition of war."

It is too evident for argument that the nations are spending so ruinous a share of their revenues in preparation for avoidable warfare that they are sadly crippling the material, social, moral, and spiritual progress of humanity. We commend with all cordiality, therefore, the work of the President and the secretary of state of the United States for the substitution of international arbitration for the brutishness of battle; and while we all deplore the strife in Mexico, and while we regret the losses that Americans engaged in legitimate business in that country are compelled to sustain, we still confidently believe that armed intervention on the part of the United States is unnecessary, that all talk of such intervention is unwise and imprudent, and that the President of the United States and others in authority will do all in their power to discourage such warlike sentiment.

A SALOONLESS NATION BY 1920.

Educate and Exterminate.

In harmony with the Atlantic City resolution of two years ago, "A saloonless nation by 1920, the three hundredth year from the landing of the Pilgrims at Plymouth," and as the next step toward that great consummation, we declare for national prohibition—an amendment to the Constitution of the United States.

Because out of past bitter defeats we have come to realize the vital mistake of intrusting good laws to unfriendly and uncommitted administrations we declare for the election to office everywhere in the nation of political candidates and administrations outspokenly committed, to the enforcement of existing laws and to the destruction of the liquor traffic. We unite for the ushering in of the day when by all political parties the liquor problem shall be recognized and declared the supreme and immediately vital issue before the American people.

A United Temperance Movement.

With enthusiasm we indorse the movement for a national

convention of all the temperance forces of the country, to be held in Columbus, O., November 14, this year. To the council of one hundred temperance leaders soon to make public the call for this epoch-marking convention we pledge our hearty support and unswerving co-operation. We are profoundly convinced that the hour has arrived when, without prejudice to, or interference with, the fundamental principles and policies of any particular temperance organization, all temperance organizations should unite upon a comprehensive, nation-wide programme of education and extermination.

Good-Citizenship Day.

We reaffirm our indorsement of Good-Citizenship Day, the Sunday immediately preceding the Fourth of July. We call upon our young people to make this day truly a national institution. Let it command pulpit, prayer meeting, press, and patriotic and fraternal organizations until the united voice of a free people shall lift to high Heaven a tocsin for peace, brotherhood, Christian citizenship, and freedom from rum. We request the department of temperance and Christian citizenship to prepare a suitable programme for the use of Christian Endeavor societies on Good-Citizenship Day, and to suggest such plans for the observance of the day as will make it an occasion of uplift and practical inspiration.

The Call to Service.

We heartily approve the call to service issued by the Good-Citizenship movement of the United Young People's organizations. We rejoice to co-operate with all the young people of the church in every campaign for civic righteousness.

A Challenge to California.

We congratulate California for her forward steps in temperance and industrial reform. It would be an insult to the Christian citizenship of this great commonwealth to question the outcome of the referendum on the red-light abatement and injunction bill passed by the legislature and signed by the governor. But every right-thinking man and woman, carrying the high responsibility of citizenship, must be thoroughly aroused and unrelentingly active if this eminently desirable law is to be saved from the hands of its saloon and brothel enemies.

The defeat of this law would be regarded as a national invitation for Christian people and decent citizens generally to remain away from the Exposition of 1915.

A Pledge-Signing Crusade.

As the tools of a new pledge-signing crusade we adopt and recommend to the Christian Endeavorers of the nation the following two pledges:

Total-Abstinence Pledge.

Trusting in the Lord Jesus Christ for strength, I promise to abstain from all intoxicating liquors as a beverage and to do my best to get others to sign this pledge.

Name.........................

Address.......................

Date..............

A New Declaration of Independence.

Trusting in the Lord Jesus Christ for strength, no political candidate or party not declaring for the destruction of the liquor traffic can have my support or vote. I will do my best to get others to sign this pledge.

Name.........................

Address.......................

Date..............

We urge all local societies and unions to canvass actively for signatures to one or both of these pledges and thus to join at once the new pledge-signing crusade that promises, in the providence of God, to sweep the nation.

Policy and Programme of the New Department of Temperance and Christian Citizenship.

We recommend the following as the policy and programme of the new department of temperance and Christian citizenship, and call upon all local societies and unions to co-operate actively for its universal adoption.

1. The preparation, for the use of Christian Endeavor societies and unions, of a series of twelve leaflets on the nature of alcohol and the relation of the liquor traffic to industrial, social, and political conditions, these leaflets, with suggestions for their use, to be prepared by the editorial secretary and the temperance superintendent of the United Society of Christian Endeavor.

2. *A publicity and educational campaign;* the distribution of temperance literature; the placing of temperance posters in public places; the attractive presentation everywhere of the known facts concerning alcohol and the organized liquor traffic, along the lines laid down from time to time by the temperance and Christian-citizenship department; the holding of temperance mass-meetings in the great centres of population, addressed by

the recognized Christian-citizenship leaders of the nation; the instruction of the young people in the principles and obligations of Christian citizenship; the creation of libraries of social service and political reform.

3. The co-operation and active participation in local, State, and national campaigns, for temperance and prohibition, with all other organizations uniting in a common forward movement.

4. The institution of campaigns against desecration of the Lord's Day, against law-violation, and for public progress and civic betterment, such as the organization in cities of flower-culture clubs for beautifying waste places; the financing of summer outings for poor children; the institution of campaigns for tuberculosis hospitals and against spitting in public places; anti-cigarette propaganda; movements against prize-fighting and for the elimination of Sunday racing; campaigns for the strict enforcement of Sunday and other liquor laws; investigation of civic and community conditions with a study of the prescribed duties of all public officials and the carrying out in many instances of city and rural surveys; the rendering of assistance to social-settlement centres; hearty co-operation in the national movement for one day of rest in seven for all workers, and for the protection of the American home by uniform laws against easy divorce.

5. A nation-wide pledge-signing crusade—the widest possible use of the two pledges officially indorsed by the United Society of Christian Endeavor.

6. The observance of Good-Citizenship Day.

7. Active participation in campaigns recommended to the united temperance forces of the nation by the national convention to be held in Columbus, O., November 14, 1913.

8. A hearty and unswerving effort to secure the participation of all the young people's societies of the nation in these or similar efforts.

9. Pre-eminent emphasis on national prohibition, an amendment to the Constitution of the United States.

10. The enthronement in the minds and hearts of the Christian Endeavorers of America of the highest spiritual objective for all temperance and Christian-citizenship activities, "that in all things He might have the pre-eminence."

Thanks.

Our debt of gratitude to those who have contributed to the success of this Twenty-Sixth International Convention cannot be paid in resolutions, however cordial and definite. The army of those who deserve the beatitude of the helpers is too large for a roll-call here—we thank all Los Angeles and southern California for generous hospitality, and then would include vast sections of the rest of this State, together with kindly communities all along this coast and in the interior cities we passed through en route hither. For numberless deeds and words of assistance we thank the very efficient chairman and members of the Committee of 1913, and the pastors, churches, and hospitable households of Los Angeles and vicinity. For much of the rare blessedness and joy of the Convention itself we thank the great chorus and orchestra; Professor Peckham, Mr. Percy S. Foster, and the other leaders of music; and the United Society officers, whose quiet power and planning have been felt everywhere, but have been obtrusively evident nowhere.

We thank the mayor and other municipal officers of Los Angeles for their courtesies to the strangers within their gates; and we thank the local press for such sympathetic and generous reports as will certainly project the good influence of the Convention far beyond the city which has been our happy home through these delightful convention days.

The gratitude of the whole Endeavor movement is due and is hereby heartily extended to Dr. F. E. Clark for his priceless world-service of Christian Endeavor during the past two years. to General Secretary Shaw for his wisdom and aggressiveness, to Editorial Secretary Wells and his assistants for the continued consecration of their genius to the building up of the great literature of our cause, to Treasurer Lathrop for valuable volunteer work, to Publication-Manager Shartle for the unprecedented success with which he has directed his department, to Secretary R. P. Anderson, of the Builders' Union, for his good endeavors for a permanent home for the United Society, and to Field Secretary Lehmann for his superb work of Christian Endeavor agitation and education. Faithful servants of Christ and the church are they all.

IRA LANDRITH,
DANIEL A. POLING,
J. T. McCRORY.

Indorsing Superintendent Poling.

Accustomed to expect the President, General Secretary, and Executive Committee of the United Society to meet any great need of leadership by appointing the right man as leader, we were prepared to receive and approve National Superintendent Daniel A. Poling, of the newly organized department of temperance and Christian citizenship. After seeing and hearing him, and after learning about the work he has been called to undertake, we now desire to register our unqualified approbation of both the department and the superintendent, and to pledge to both our constant support and our daily prayers.

IRA LANDRITH.

CHAPTER XX.

WHAT OTHERS SAY.

LOS ANGELES has been greatly impressed during the week as much by the fine character as the great numbers of the Christian Endeavor host. Their faces were stamped with the evidences of clean living and high thinking. They were an inspiration to thousands who realize the country's need in this pleasure-mad age of a steadying force. The composite young man and woman of the Christian Endeavor type is the one America depends upon to find the solution for its growing social problems.

A discriminating follower of the proceedings of the International Convention could not fail to be struck with the practical up-to-dateness of the Christian Endeavor council. Dogma or abstract theology had no place there. The live questions met in Christian work formed the topics. It is very evident that, if the church keeps abreast with the shifting complexities of modern life, it will be because of the movement inaugurated and so ably led by Dr. Clark.

The re-election of the founder to the office of president, and of the long-time general secretary, William Shaw, was a tribute to two men who have richly earned their fame by a wonderful energy and devotion. The Los Angeles churches have been greatly stimulated by the presence of the Christian Endeavor host, and can only regret that the days of their visit sped by so rapidly.—*The Los Angeles Tribune.*

* * * * *

We are glad to have William Shaw in Los Angeles at this time. Shaw has had a grand career as the head of the Young People's Christian Endeavor Society. He is one of the world's ablest religious leaders, and has carried his organization through many a crisis. Above all, he has kept the society imbued with a spirit of youth and of usefulness. He has also preserved it from the radical and from the dead, directing it in the middle course of wisdom. He cannot see Los Angeles and not be its friend, and friends like Shaw are worth while to a city.—*The Los Angeles Times.*

* * * * *

The sun never sets on the field of operations of the Christian Endeavorers.—*The Los Angeles Times.*

Possibly foremost among the characteristics of this invading army, next to its enthusiasm and optimism, is its cosmopolitan character. The Endeavor body originated in a very natural desire for a harmonizing and connecting activity that should form a means of mutual approach among the young people of the various denominations, making possible united inter-denominational effort for practical advancement and uplift.

The protest against futile and wasteful division of sentiment and consequent loss of power and effectiveness found sympathetic support among the young people in nearly all denominations. The interdenominational and international Endeavor organization has arisen to voice a protest, satisfy an impulse, and meet a great need.

Los Angeles welcomes this enthusiastic, earnest, devoted Christian host. Its hospitality is as unbounded and unrestrained as the waters of the great ocean at our doors. This great city of destiny would gather inspiration for its municipal ideals, not from the bigotry and narrowness that is helpless and ineffective while municipalized injustice, immorality, vice, and crime flaunt themselves in the government of cities and States, and even assault the sources of national life and influence, but from the unity, the lofty optimism, and energy of those who represent a great, broad, wholesome idealism that is worth while.

The *Express* welcomes this invading army of young men and young women that stands uniformly for individual rectitude of character and clean, responsible citizenship.—*The Los Angeles Express.*

*   *   *   *   *

The enthusiasm which is manifested by these earnest workers is as inspiring as their philosophy is wholesome. They must succeed because they rely upon organization, combination, mutual helpfulness, instead of rivalry, contention, and self-seeking to attain their ends.

To combine, rather than to compete, is the spirit of the age.

The key-note of Christian Endeavor is *unselfishness.* These co-laborers have learned the true philosophy—that the first condition of happiness is never to seek it for self alone.

The Endeavorers have the right idea. They are young, therefore they have enthusiasms; they are numerous, therefore they are influential; so their cause must grow, their purposes prevail.—*The Los Angeles Herald.*

*   *   *   *   *

The welcome that Pasadena extends these much-to-be-desired guests is one hundred per cent genuine, guaranteed by the hundreds of Endeavorers living here and attested by the many thousands of communicants of Pasadena churches. This city of churches believes strongly in the young people's movement in the churches. The Christian Endeavor Society has numerous representation here, and Pasadena Endeavorers are wide-awake ones.—*The Pasadena Star.*

*   *   *   *   *

The Convention was a success in every particular, and the movement closes its thirty-second year with larger financial resources, a more comprehensive plan of work, and a more enthusiastic constituency than ever before in its history.—*The Congregationalist.*

*   *   *   *   *

Such a great international convention shows plainly that Christian Endeavor is a movement, like the tide, deep and strong. Let its critics assist in utilizing its forces, or be swept aside.—*The Moravian.*

*   *   *   *   *

It was a great gathering of earnest Christian men and women, and for the most part young Christians. Some said it was the best and greatest convention ever held. However this may be, it was certainly great in numbers, in enthusiasm, in devotion to their organization, and above all to Christ and His church. There were also great meetings at which great subjects were presented by noted and notable men, and there was great singing.—*Christian Observer.*

*   *   *   *   *

The Christian Endeavorers are marching on, and they are a great host and power in the church and Kingdom.—*The Presbyterian Banner.*

*   *   *   *   *

The atmosphere of the entire Convention was wholesome and inspiring.—*Rev. W. L. Darby, in The Presbyterian Advance.*

*   *   *   *   *

Among the things that bulk big in a day when only big things seem worthy of mention "Millionaire Endeavor" does not need to feel ashamed. The 10,001 delegates who attended the twenty-sixth International Convention at Los Angeles represented a movement that has drawn into its membership in the last thirty-three years 15,000,000 young men and women, and, if we reckon the number of members in societies that have substantially the Christian Endeavor principles, has now an active membership of 5,000,000 souls.

Evangelistic fervor was not wanting in this great Convention. Personal work for the saving of souls was a topic uppermost in discussion in conference, institute, and upon the platforms of the great mass-meetings. Many street meetings were held by visiting delegations and Christian workers, in which the spiritual influence of the Convention was brought directly to bear upon the pulsating life of the great city.—*The Continent.*

The monster parade of six thousand or seven thousand members of the United Society of Christian Endeavor Friday evening marked the climax of one of the grandest and most successful conventions that ever met in Los Angeles. It was a spirited and impressive demonstration for the cause of causes, and one that rejoiced the hearts of all who saw it.

The Endeavorers have had a great week. Their meetings have been full to the brim, and have been packed with interest. Capital speakers have been heard and live themes have been discussed. The Convention has busied itself with the pressing problems of the day, but, we are glad to note, has kept on the wholesome side of things and has not exploited the "damaged-goods" idea—differing in that respect from some of the convocations of women's clubs.

For almost two scores of years the Christian Endeavor Society has been a potent force for good in the world. The *Times* has watched its progress, and has printed its weekly bulletins from Mr. Ellis. It has had a hearty grip on young people and aroused in them a noble enthusiasm. It can safely be said that no influence has been more effective among our many organized advance movements than that of the Society of Christian Endeavor in fitly shaping the lives of young men and women; none has done more to cultivate the best manhood and the truest womanhood. It has been a veritable fountain of inspiration for thousands, a fountain of living water that has kept their hearts pure and their lives clean.

The *Times* congratulates Los Angeles on the presence here of this admirable body of men and women. The Convention has been a blessing to the city in more ways than one. It is different from many other large and demonstrative gatherings in that it means something. The delegates come here full of vigorous purpose and leave their impress on the community. They are the kind of people we like to have with us. Never has Los Angeles had greater satisfaction in opening her doors and hearts to a convention. God speed ye, brethren!—*The Los Angeles Times.*

* * * * *

From village and city, from foreign state and foreign land, the Christian Endeavorers have trooped to assemble here and lay plans for another year of working for good.

And Los Angeles bids them welcome and is glad to have them here. They make people remember that sordidness and crime haven't a free rein in the world—that there are really more folks arrayed on the side of good than on the side of bad.

The great Christian Endeavor organization is a striking example of how uplift work prospers when operated on an organized basis. A little more than a quarter of a century ago there was no Christian Endeavor. Now it has penetrated to every corner of the world, and with other and similar organizations, is doing humanity incalculable good.

Three decades ago the young folks went to church in the morning with the old folks, and then spent the rest of Sunday being good and probably waiting for Monday to come.

Now, at 6:30 o'clock every Sunday night, the church bells in every town and hamlet literally from Greenland's icy mountains to India's coral strands ring, and at their summons thousands of boys and girls and men and women assemble to hear what progress has been made for good in the week past, and to plan the campaign for the week to come.—*Los Angeles Record.*

*   *   *   *   *

To all that great army of Christian Endeavorers now assembled within the gates of the city—greeting. May great satisfaction and joy attend their convocation and success crown their endeavors.

The enthusiasm which is manifested by these earnest workers is as inspiring as their philosophy is wholesome. They must succeed because they rely upon organization, combination, mutual helpfulness, instead of rivalry, contention and self-seeking to attain their ends.

To combine, rather than to compete, is the spirit of the age.

The keynote of Christian Endeavor is UNSELFISHNESS. These colaborers have learned the true philosophy—that the first condition of happiness is never to seek it for self alone. If we but seek to make others happier, to uplift those who are down and to uphold those who stumble our altruistic efforts return happiness to us as the dividends of our endeavors.

What this old world sadly needs is more of human kindness, man to man, woman to woman; all for one and one for all.

Nothing excites the risibilities of humor more than to see how empty are the hands which have grasped for the bubbles of fame and fortune, titles and estates.

Yet so strong is Youth's impulse for imitation, so feeble are most impulses toward originality, that this race in this age needs concert and organization to direct its endeavors away from the emulation of money-grubbing and office-seeking, and to lend encouragement to efforts for the betterment of humanity.

The Endeavorers have the right idea. They are young, therefore they have enthusiasms; they are numerous, therefore they are influential; so their cause must grow, their purposes prevail.

May they absorb some of the geniality of this Land of Sunshine during their stay, for out of our great plenty we would gladly share with them.—*Los Angeles Herald.*

CHAPTER XXI.

CONVENTION GLEANINGS.

"I'M GOOD for something more than shouting," declared Dr. A. Sterling Barner, pastor of the Memorial Baptist Church, when asked to oversee a number of carpenters who were busily engaged in putting the finishing touches to the lunch-room at Auditorium Endeavor.

To prove his assertion Dr. Barner took off his coat and sailed into the work with great enthusiasm. "I've handled a saw before," he asserted, amid showers of sawdust from his energetic handling of that tool.

The carpenters eyed the Baptist clergyman askance when he first started his enthusiasic onslaught, but finally, carried along by his friendly rivalry, started in earnest to help matters along.

"He knows how to use that thumb o' his'n," admitted one carpenter. "Well, I should say," rejoined another. "I always thought them fellers couldn't do much outside of slingin' a fine line o' talk, but him, why, that feller could take out a card!"

> Chicago, Illinois.
> We want you there,
> We want you there,
> Come with us in 1915,
> We'll show you sights you never have seen
> By dear Lake Michigan waters green.
> In Chicago, in Chicago.

Miss Fannie Sprung at the "information booth" was a mine of information. "They ask me every imaginable sort of questions," she said. "Do I get tired? No, indeed, it's too interesting for that."

What an auditorium that was! It looked as if the committee had roofed in all outdoors, and yet every speaker was heard perfectly by every one of the eleven thousand people that filled all the seats.

Sunday evening there were 22,500 in attendance upon the six simultaneous Convention meetings that were held.

For the second time in the history of Christian Endeavor Conventions the supply of badges and programmes was inadequate. The supply was exhausted the second day, and a simple ribbon badge had to be provided.

"I'll excuse those of you that have no Christian Endeavor pin," said General Secretary Shaw before one meeting, "if you will go to the literature-table and buy a pin. They can be bought at from one cent to a dollar." There was a general exodus, and the business manager thought a cyclone had struck his booth.

How the clinched fists of four thousand men at the great men's meeting must have inspired the heart of our magnetic Christian-citizenship leader, D. A. Poling, for the great task of annihilating the American saloon! No more fellowship and clasped hands, but the knockout blow that will free our civilization from its greatest curse.

How the angels must have rejoiced as they looked down upon those marvellous decision-services led by Dr. McAfee, when hundreds faced the call to the ministry, mission field, or other forms of Christian service, and responded with a joyous consecration of themselves that will mean great things for the extension of the Kingdom.

On Saturday evening the members of the Convention Committee and their wives were entertained at dinner by the trustees in Hotel Alexandria. The chairman, Mr. Leonard Merrill, presented all its members to the trustees in neat little speeches characterizing each one and his work.

If the officers of the Convention and the speakers were not on time, it was not the fault of the pages, who provided automobiles to take them from the hotel to the meeting-place. "Call a page" was the motto seen everywhere.

The State headquarters at Fiesta Park, with the beautifully decorated booths, was a most attractive place and busy as a beehive.

Was there ever a more beautiful sight than the magnificent chorus of nine hundred, and did ever sweeter music come from nine hundred voices than we heard from the Endeavorers of Pasadena, Los Angeles, Glendale, and Long Beach?

What a picture of world-wide Christian Endeavor, a moving picture it surely was, as we heard the inspiring messages and music from representatives of India, China, Japan, and our own American Indians!

Thousands will look back to the sunrise Quiet Hours conducted by President King, which filled the great auditorium of the Immanuel Presbyterian Church, as the most uplifting and inspiring of all the Convention.

In thirty minutes more than $8,000 was pledged, and the "Thousand Associates" was recruited by the addition of hundreds of members.

The first name given to Christian Endeavor in Mexico was literally "Energetic Christianity," a remarkably suitable name.

More than once Hawaiian delegates to International Conventions have proved their love for Christian Endeavor by bringing gifts for the Headquarters Building. This time a Honolulu pastor, Rev. William K. Poai, brought $30 from his society, the Kalihi and Moanalua society. This is an average of about twenty-five cents a member, but the pastor is not satisfied. He thinks the Hawaiians should do still more.

In ·New Mexico there are only forty-seven societies, and thirty-five delegates were all that could attend the recent State convention. New Mexico is a country of long distances. Some of the delegates travelled sixty or seventy miles away from the railroad to attend. They came riding on horseback and in wagons.

There are eight fundamental elements that are being emphasized in young people's work to-day, says Rev. A. L. Phillips, D.D., superintendent of the Sunday-school and young people's department of the Southern Presbyterian Church. They are the study of the Bible, the promotion of prayer, Christian culture, missionary interest, stewardship, extension work, personal evangelism, and social service.

Christian Endeavor has the opportunity of its life in Canada, says Rev. S. A. Martin, field secretary for Manitoba. During the last three years Canada has been developing at the rate of one town a day. These towns need Christian Endeavor societies.

California pays the salaries of two field secretaries, has a budget of $5,000 a year, and never has trouble in raising the money.

While the Endeavorers were at Hotel El Tovar, at the Grand Cañon, the Brazilian ambassador, Dr. Lauro Muller, and suite were also there.

Not a few Chinese have added to the Quiet-Hour covenant a clause promising to establish family worship in their homes. Think what that means in a land like China.

One Scottish missionary in Manchuria said, "I left the home land before Christian Endeavor was introduced, and I don't know how it works there; but I want to say that the Chinese take to it as a fish takes to water."

The field workers did a graceful thing in procuring a book of greeting, getting the workers to sign it, and forwarding it to Editorial Secretary Amos R. Wells.

The daughter of the train-conductor who took care of the New England Endeavorers is an Endeavorer, and sent a greeting to the party through her father. A postal card carrying the signatures of Dr. Clark, the United Society's officers, and others was sent to her.

The Efficiency literature is being translated into Chinese, says Mrs. Edgar E. Strother, and some Chinese Endeavorers are already Christian Endeavor Experts. More are preparing for examination.

In the Floating Christian Endeavor booth at Los Angeles one of the decorations was a flag which had been used as a sail to save some shipwrecked seamen off the coast of Japan, and some embroidered silk banners from the old Christian Endeavor societies on the Charleston and Chicago. Besides flags and banners were curios such as a blue-jacket register from a church in New York City, shells, emblems, and pictures of Floating societies and individual workers in this field.

"Chicago, 1915," is to be the slogan of the next two years. Winnipeg and Toronto both wanted the Convention for that year, and wanted it badly, and for a time it seemed as if one of these cities would be the place of meeting; but Chicago prevailed.   For many years now we have been holding Conventions upon the rim of things—Atlantic City, St. Paul, Baltimore; and many felt that the time had come to hold a big Convention in a central city, accessible alike to East and West. Chicago seemed to be the proper point, and Chicago was chosen.
    1915 is to be the year of the Panama Exposition in San Francisco, and doubtless on that account there will be a vast amount of travel through Chicago. Canada's claim for the

meeting, however, is a strong one; and, if the Dominion comes again with a request for 1917, the result will hardly be in doubt.

Publication-Manager Shartle presented each of the pages at the Hotel Alexandria, and the young ladies who assisted at the United Society literature and supply booth, with a Christian Endeavor seal pin.

One of the New England delegates was so delighted with the California climate and the city of Los Angeles that he secured a position in Los Angeles and decided to become a future citizen and booster.

The official flag of the Los Angeles convention was a beauty. Hundreds of these flags were bought by delegates and friends as souvenirs.

For all-around efficient service in handling a large convention, our hats are off to Los Angeles.

On Monday, July 7, two of the Endeavorers from the New England delegation stopping at El Tovar descended on foot to the bottom of the Grand Cañon, where the temperature was well over a hundred. They were Dr. Clark's youngest son, Sydney A. Clark, and Mr. Frank A. Ekstrom, both Dartmouth College men. They started from the hotel a few minutes before the muleback party, which leaves daily at 7:45. The Bright Angel trail which they took was ankle-deep in dust, sometimes reddish in color and sometimes brown or gray; and the heat soon became terrific. But they kept on without resting, and finally reached the Colorado River a good hour in advance of the mules. They took a dip in the edge of the swirling river, and then started back up the seven-mile trail.

The ascent was a continual strenuous pull, up and up, always plodding through the thick dust. What breeze there was seemed more like the blast of a furnace than anything else. At the half-way house they filled a bottle with water to help them in the long pull which was yet to come, but before they had been fifteen minutes on the upper trail the terrific sun had made the water in the bottle actually hot.

At three o'clock in the afternoon, two hours before the muleback party was due to return, the two young men reached the hotel, apparently in good condition. The people at the top who had assured the young men in the morning that they could not possibly make the trip on foot in the broiling July weather, and had prepared to send a doctor and some mules to rescue them, opened their eyes in amazement when they saw them in good health and spirits, trying to pretend that they were not even tired. It was said by one of the guides that no one had accomplished the feat for at least a month, and that all who had tried it had to give up and send for assistance. The temperature at the bottom of the cañon was exactly 104 in the shade.

FLOATING CHRISTIAN ENDEAVOR BOOTH.

Auditorium.

A large display of rare curios was that in the booth of the "World's Floating Christian Endeavor Union."

A large American flag was draped overhead, one used by shipwrecked sailors who used it as a sail to reach the port of Nagaski, Japan, and who gave it to Mr. Makins there.

From San Diego came a large banner with the lettering and "anchor-C. E." design all made in navy cap ribbons, a great attraction. A fine embroidered banner brought by Miss Jones among many other articles and pictures, sent by the Floating Society of Christian Endeavor on the old U. S. S. Charleston, in 1895,—a picture of the ship in very delicate work. A banner from the old "Concord" Floating Society of Christian Endeavor, also sent in 1895, an "Increase and Betterment" banner awarded at Baltimore, '05, for over 33 per-cent increase.

From Liverpool, England, again came their respective banner that had hung in the same group of banners at Boston, '95, Washington, '96, and San Francisco, '97.

Many photographs were displayed from different ports, illustrative of their port, and some representative members, groups from many Floating societies ashore and afloat,—"Olympia," "Charleston," "Vermont,"—well remembered for their faithful membership.

A glass case held many smaller curios,—a navy ditty-box, a cube of "salt-water soap," dishes and other articles that are familar to the men of the navy and their friends.

A series of pictures represented the Christian Endeavor Home for Seamen, Nagasaki, Japan.

A large flag made on the U. S. S. Chicago and used in the San Diego "Rest" showed the scorching when the old "Rest" was burned.

From this booth various typical printed matter was given away. A sheet arranged by Miss A. P. Jones showed what some Floating Christian Endeavorers who had come ashore and "made good" were doing in the service of Christ. The local ports each had some distinctive literature,—song-sheets, reports, showing the importance of the work in different parts of the world.

INDEX

INDEX.

TOPICS OF ADDRESSES

www.ingramcontent.com/pod-product-compliance
Lightning Source LLC
Chambersburg PA
CBHW030107070426

42448CB00036B/321